BALANCING STATE INTERVENTION

BALANCING STATE INTERVENTION

The Limits of Transatlantic Markets

Edited by Roger Benjamin, C. Richard Neu, and
Denise D. Quigley

A RAND Book
St. Martin's Press
New York

337.73
B171

BALANCING STATE INTERVENTION
© 1995 by The RAND Corporation

H

ISBN 0–312–12401–5

RAND Research is available on a wide variety of topics. To receive more information on RAND publications, contact RAND Distribution Services, 1700 Main Street, Santa Monica, CA 90407-2138, (310) 451-7002, Fax: (310) 451-6971, Internet: order@rand.org.

Library of Congress Cataloging-in-Publication Data

Balancing state intervention : the limits of transatlantic markets /
  edited by Roger Benjamin, C. Richard Neu, and Denise Quigley.
      p.   cm.
  Includes bibliographical references and index.
  ISBN 0–312–12401–5
    1. United States—Foreign economic relations—European Union
countries.   2. European Union countries—Foreign economic relations-
-United States   3. United States—Economic policy—1993-
4. European Union countries—Economic policy.   5. Trade regulation-
-United States.   6. Trade regulation—European Union countries.
I. Benjamin, Roger W.   II. Neu, C. R. (Carl Richard), 1949-
III. Quigley, Denise.
HF1456.5.E8B34 1995
337.73—dc20
                                                    94–23389
                                                       CIP

First Edition: August 1995
10 9 8 7 6 5 4 3 2 1

CONTENTS

PART II: The Purposes of Public Action

PART III: Social Structures and the Demand for Public Sector Intervention

LIST OF FIGURES AND TABLES

Figures

Tables

FOO

PREFACE

In recent decades international trade and investment have contributed strongly to the prosperity of the developed world and, despite the poverty in much of the third world, have helped to lift a number of newly industrializing countries to developed levels of economic performance. Tariff reductions in successive rounds of the General Agreement on Tariffs and Trade (GATT) negotiations, revolutionary developments in transportation and communications, and the rise of the multinational corporations with their own internal markets for goods and services across national frontiers have ensured that growth in world trade and investment have persistently outstripped growth in output. The collapse of communism in 1989–1991 and continuing advances in telecommunications, transport, and finance all suggest that the internationalization of the world economy will continue.

The increasingly open national markets that have fostered and that in turn have been fostered by this rapid internationalization of the world economy rest upon bases of political support that appear to have grown over time. Almost everywhere, "protectionists" have lost ground to "free traders." Nonetheless, there are questions hanging over the future of the international regime for trade and investment, and there is no guarantee that further liberalization of this regime will be as rapid or as pervasive as it has been in recent decades. Debates about fair versus free trade, discussions of competitiveness and its various meanings, and charges and countercharges regarding social dumping, ecological dumping, and even cultural dumping suggest that the relationship between international trade and investment and their domestic effects—political, social, and cultural as well as economic—is being intensely debated in many countries.

As the fiscal, administrative, and physical barriers to international exchange have been dismantled through GATT rounds and advances in technology, whether and on what terms trade and investment take place are increasingly seen as determined by system factors: Japan's persistent trade surpluses are linked to the high propensity of the Japanese people to save; American preeminence in aerospace, biotechnology, and microelectronics is attributed to a complex system of federally supported laboratories, universities, and procurement mechanisms that is not open to outsiders; developing country success in many industries is attributed to poor working conditions, weak trade unions, and low environmental standards.

These and many other success factors—savings rates, national support for universities and laboratories, as well as labor and environmental standards—have not been the focus of traditional trade negotiations, nor are such issues easily discussed within GATT and other fora. Nonetheless, as was seen in the bilateral U.S.–Japan Structural Impediments Initiative and in the mandates given to the new World Trade Organization, there is a growing tendency to bring such system factors into the arena of bilateral and multilateral trade negotiations.

This process of broadening the international trade agenda raises many questions. Given that nearly all countries are committed in principle to free trade, when is it permissible for governments to interfere in trade to pursue other goals such as national security, cultural autonomy, and quality of life? Should governments be allowed to prop up or restrict foreign ownership of certain industries for reasons of national prestige and security, or should ordinary rules governing investment apply? Are movies and television shows commodities to be traded like any other, or are they part of a national culture and thus outside the realm of trade? Are store opening hours, the use of credit cards, and local zoning regulations as they apply to retail stores a legitimate subject of international trade negotiations? And when does public support for ostensibly noncommercial activities in research, worker training and retraining, regional development, and so forth constitute an unacceptable distortion of commercial activities across national borders?

There are no hard and fast answers to these questions, many of which touch upon key questions of the relationship between markets and society. But these questions are sure to persist and to affect bilateral and multilateral economic relations for the foreseeable future. If internationalization is leading to a gradual diminution in the differences between regions and countries, the contentious role of system factors is likely to diminish over time. But if such differences persist or even increase, then the members of the international community will need to find ways to balance participation in the international economic order with the protection of domestic social, political, cultural, and economic values in ways that are not disruptive of that order.

This book is an attempt to look at some of these questions as they relate to economic relations between the United States and the European Union. The United States and the EU are the two largest actors in the world economy, and their responses to these questions will set the tone for the future of the international economic system. The United States and the EU also share many values and historical experiences. If they are not able to resolve or contain their differences regarding the relationships between markets and society, then one can expect even greater difficulty and divergences of view with other regions of the world which, as Samuel Huntington has argued, are becoming increasingly conscious of themselves as "civilizations" whose values need not necessarily be those of the Atlantic world.

The book is the result of a project undertaken by the RAND European-American Center for Policy Analysis (EAC). The EAC is located in Delft, the Netherlands, and was established by RAND in 1992, in part to further exchange between European and American researchers and policymakers as well as to conduct joint research on policy issues affecting both sides of the Atlantic. This project involved the participation of scholars and policy-makers from the United States and many European countries, and as such reflects the broad international participation that is central to the EAC's mission.

The project would not have been possible without the generous support of many individuals and organizations. EAC/RAND gratefully acknowledges the financial assistance of the Commission of the European Communities (Directorate-General for External Relations), the main project sponsor, and of the Government of the Netherlands, which provided startup funding to the European-American Center for Policy Analysis. We also thank our host institution in the Netherlands, the Delft University of Technology, and in particular the Faculty of Systems Engineering and Policy Analysis.

Of the many individuals who contributed to the success of the conference and the book, a special word of thanks goes to John Richardson of the European Commission, with whom I first discussed the project in May 1991, and who first highlighted "markets and society" as a crucial issue in the U.S.–EU relations, and Eckart Guth of the Commission who saw the project through to completion. We wish to thank all of the participants in the conference that took place in Delft in June 1993. Special thanks go to Professor Jacques Vandamme, chairman of the Transeuropean Policy Studies Association, and to Hans Labohm of the Netherlands Institute of International Relations, both of whom were instrumental in enlisting conference participants and whose many valuable interventions are reflected albeit indirectly, in the chapters that follow.

Finally, I would like to thank my secretary, Loes Romeijn, for organizing the conference with her usual efficiency, and the book's editors, Dick Neu, Denise D. Quigley, and especially Roger Benjamin, for their efforts in seeing the book through to completion. The editors would also like to thank Roseanna Klingelhofer, Roger Benjamin's secretary, who worked to make this a cohesive text.

John van Oudenaren
Director of RAND European-American Center

I

Historical and Cultural Background:

Forces and Circumstances that Have Shaped European and American Attitudes toward the Role of Markets

1

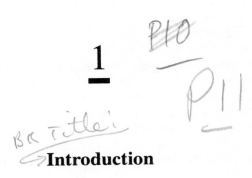

Introduction

Roger Benjamin, Denise D. Quigley, and C. R. Neu

GENERAL DISCUSSION

All advanced countries recognize the benefits of allowing economic decisions to be driven principally by competitive market forces. Nonetheless, few would argue that simply allowing market forces free rein would in all circumstances result in outcomes that are socially acceptable or desirable. There is widespread consensus about the circumstances that might justify interventions in the workings of markets: When market forces fail to provide minimum acceptable levels of essential goods and services; when collective provision of goods and services will be more efficient than private provision; when market fluctuations will impose large costs or place unacceptable burdens on particular groups; or when market-driven behavior will result in significant "externalities"—costs or benefits that accrue to parties other than those making decisions. Most leaders in advanced countries also recognize that there is also a "social/political dimension" to economic behavior and decision-making that is not always well served by the unhindered operation of competitive market forces. Despite this general agreement, all advanced industrialized countries have adopted policies to restrict or redirect market forces in an effort to achieve particular social ends.

Moreover, there is considerable variation among countries in terms of how much they intervene in the market and about the specific circumstances deemed to require or justify some form of intervention. For example, across nations, transportation, health care, and education are provided both publicly, privately, or through a public/private mix. Nations also differ in their attitudes toward monopolies, in their provisions for compensating the victims of misfortune or negligence, and in their approach to meeting the needs of the elderly. As a result, there is considerable variation from one country to another in the extent to which market forces are allowed free rein and in the specific circumstances in which some form of intervention is required or justified.

There is, of course, no reason why policies, practices, and attitudes about the workings of markets should be the same in all countries. The underlying differences in policies, which affect the role of markets and contribute to their differing roles, clearly represent and highlight the more fundamental social and cultural differences between countries. However, such differences in attitudes about the appropriate role of market forces can complicate trade relations among nations and the international system as a whole. For example, competition from abroad may lead to pressures to eliminate policies that raise business costs and allow market forces greater freedom. Alternatively, desires to maintain particular social policies and practices may bring calls to limit foreign competition, which if heeded, could result in trade disputes.

While such differences exist between all countries, they are particularly important and striking between Europe and the United States because of the dominant global role of their economies. There are basic differences in the U.S. and European approaches to state and market. Even by the crudest measures, the public sector's role is much greater in Europe than in the United States. Europeans have comprehensive modern welfare states, while the United States tends toward policy measures outside the realm of government intervention, such as market-oriented policies and a large nonprofit sector. Additionally, these differences have had and continue to have consequences in the way in which the U.S. and European governments approach problems, interact with each other, and seek to construct a Western (European/American) order. Most important, these divergent approaches to the relationship of the state and market are becoming more consequential in Atlantic relations at the same time that differences between the Atlantic partners are declining.

The last 50 years of American global engagement and hegemony altered and muted the differences between the American and European approaches to the market. Global engagement also profoundly altered American political development by strengthening the state, economic management, and social equity and welfare. During the Cold War and the period of external focus on the American system, compromises between the different American and European styles were made and approaches melded. The result was "embedded liberalism," a watering-down of multilateral agreements, and the removal of the great internal conflicts between the types of capitalism within the West. Thus, the forces of convergence overpowered the forces of fragmentation and division within the Western capitalist world.

Despite the past high degree of convergence and integration within the West, there are current pressures and circumstances disrupting transatlantic relations and requiring a new look at the relations between state and market: the changing international system; the gradual erosion of state control over industrial change, public action, and political authority; the changed relationship between the United States and Europe; and the changes in U.S. and European economic, political, technological, social, structural, and demographic circumstances, which are affecting how Europe and the United States must interact in the future.[1] More important, the state of the international system sets the constraints for the individual countries, and the divergent European and American approaches to market and government intervention dominate how domestic changes and pressures are handled.

A Changing International System

The move from a hegemonic bipolar international system to a multipolar system has reduced the ability of the international system to handle differences among nations because states and markets are influenced by the state of the international system: weak or strong, hegemonic or multipolar.

When the international system is strong, nation-states and markets adjust to it and converge, meaning that the international system can accommodate persistent and deep-rooted differences in nation-states and markets. The pressures are relatively milder on slow-growing sectors and the costs of providing international public goods are more than proportionally borne by the hegemonic country. This has been the environment over the past 50 years. Currently, however, the bipolar international system has disintegrated and a new international system needs to be established. The differences among nation-states and markets have lead to large ex-ante differences in the preference for the design of the international system itself. Countries, states, and markets with slower growing industries are affected more severely by the pressures of change in the international system. Moreover in a multipolar international system, the conditions for providing international public goods are more stringent and more difficult to obtain. As a result the international system is less and less able to accommodate differences in nation-states and markets.

The definition and establishment of a new global regime and a strong international system, rather than the convergence of the relationship between state and markets toward a common goal, may be required to promote a deeper and sounder integration between Europe and the United States. Therefore, within the current international system it is in the interest of Europe and the United States to establish global cooperation and to work together toward the next phase of European integration.

The Gradual Erosion of State Control over Industrial Change, Public Action, and Political Authority

Decay and disorder at the core of American industrial society continues to impinge on relations with Europe. The intensification of interdependence through foreign investment has resulted in the gradual erosion of state control over industrial change, meaning that the fate of American and European economies are increasingly out of the hands of government leaders.

The role of the state today is also more limited. The evidence is in the number of differences between the United States and Europe in their approach to public action and their organization of social activity. These differences exist because market outcomes tend to organize social activity, in addition to regulating private provisions and state production, and because the purposes of public action range from providing public goods to redistributing income and wealth. Even when considering these differences, public policies in today's environment for both Europeans and Americans tend to be intermediate goods. Thus, the role of the state on both sides of the Atlantic is currently quite limited in the economic sphere to providing a basic institutional framework and to compensate for market failures, especially in terms of emphasizing human capital formation and research and development efforts.

Moreover, there is no governing body overseeing the world market economy. The sharing of state authority with others and an asymmetric distribution of power in the political system have led to an increasing level of impotence in responding to markets and implementing policy. The result is the absence of an effective political authority to rule over today's powerfully integrated world market economy.

Previous debates about state intervention, appropriate policy responses, and political authority over markets need to be reopened in a wider format that introduces nonstate sources of authority over both society and the economy. The question of political authority and markets needs to be addressed in a new and different way—not on a state-by-state basis, but on a global one—with emphasis on the relation of authority to society and the economy. A new transnational framework for analysis is needed that views political economy in terms of international societys needs and markets.

The Changed Relationship between the United States and Europe

The relationship between the United States and Europe has changed significantly. With the completion of the single European market, relations between the United States and Europe are increasingly taking on the character of bilateral dealings between equals, rather than multilateral relations with one party frequently in the dominant position. And with the decline of the common military threat, U.S.-European relations are increasingly centered on economic matters.

Differences over trade and investment that once may have been swept under the rug in the interests of maintaining a strong alliance may in the future become major irritants. For example, even though the Uruguay Round of GATT negotiations was successfully concluded at the end of 1993, a host of trade-related points of friction remain between Europe, represented by the European Union countries, and the United States. As the degree of economic interdependence grows between the two blocs on either side of the Atlantic, the points of potential conflict deepen in areas such as agricultural subsidies and tariffs, subsidies for steel among other manufacturing industries, high-tech industries such as aerospace, and services ranging from banking to air transportation. The conflicts arise partly because the Americans prefer less market intervention and the Europeans tend to want more. Different European and American views over the scope allowed to market forces may also be the seeds of disputes over what constitutes "fair" policies governing international trade and investment. Furthermore, both Europe and America face growing economic challenges from Japan and the newly industrializing countries of the Pacific Basin. Here, both sides must seek a transatlantic balance on how the state should relate to the market to enhance the benefits of increasing international economic interdependence and to avoid the worst case scenario of a negative spiral of trade-related conflicts.

Additional Domestic Pressures

Changes in relations between the United States and Europe are further complicated by changes in domestic U.S. and European economic, political, and demographic circumstances. On both sides of the Atlantic strong pressures for change in the social aspects of the market economy are increasing. In the United States, continuing immigration is producing an increasingly diverse, multilingual, and younger population. Further integration of the U.S., Canadian, and Mexican economies is likely, which will bring a new set of demands for relief from cost-imposing policies and a new set of demands for protection from the consequences of expanding competition. In Europe, the completion of the single market has put in motion strong forces for the convergence of previously divergent national views on the role of the market. European populations are aging and immigration is increasing, indicating that the need for assimilation and changes in the social security and welfare systems will increase. Moreover, the current convergence pressures and demands will increase to a larger degree if the European Union is expanded to include the economically and politically reforming societies of Eastern Europe.

These issues represent the social, demographic, political, and economic conflicts that will dominate the public agendas of Brussels and Washington. Current economic, technological, demographic, social, and structural pressures have spurred debates on the role of government involvement in markets and societies. Moreover, both sides of the Atlantic are questioning the advantages and disadvantages of their economic and social systems. Sustaining the current modern European welfare state may not be feasible without major changes and substantial reductions in expenditures on income maintenance transfers and subsidies. The United States is also assessing its social welfare and health care systems. In addition, debates are developing about the convergence or divergence of European and American policies and economies and how this affects their relations and interaction in an increasingly interdependent world.

During the 1980s, the market-related policy direction on both sides of the Atlantic has converged because the European Union countries developed relations and polices of a more market-oriented nature. Therefore, policies between the United States and Europe may become even more similar as global economic pressures increase and lead to less government control over the changes in the economy and over the success of public policies. This move toward similar market-oriented policies will continue to pressure European relations within markets, societies, and governments to intervene less in the market, particularly in terms of public-sector intervention. In addition, as demographic, technological, budgetary, and global economic pressures mount, the American government may increasingly contract with private-sector and nonprofit agents to fulfill its missions. It is likely that the U.S. government will further structure private markets so as to reduce the need for direct government action. However, American and European citizens will probably pressure their governments to take action against perceived imbalances and advantages because of differences between Europe and the United States. For example, encouraged by Boeing, Washington is aggressively challenging European subsidies for Airbus. Encouraged by major U.S. airlines, Washington is questioning subsidies to state-owned European airlines. Pressured by the French film industry, the Uruguay Round negotiators were unable to settle the conflict over French subsidies. The list goes on.

OBJECTIVE

By helping to understand these differing views and debates, this book intends to help policymakers anticipate and perhaps avoid potential points of friction. In the chapters that follow distinguished European and American scholars discuss the social and cultural circumstances that create different roles for market forces in Europe and America. The volume illuminates the current and future problems about the appropriate role of market forces and economic competition among advanced industrial societies, outlines the main concerns in this regard for European and American governments within the international environment, and provides a future agenda for political and economic leaders in Europe and the United States.

ORGANIZATION OF THIS BOOK

To deepen the understanding of the general discussion described earlier, the chapters of the book were organized into four parts. Throughout this work, the authors focus on differing transatlantic perspectives about the need for, and the nature of, public-sector interventions and on potential difficulties that may arise in American-European relations because of these different views. In particular, part I sets the stage for the volume and reviews the historical and cultural circumstances that have led to divergent American and European approaches to the state, the market, and international interaction.

Part II discusses the primary purposes of public sector interventions into market forces, emphasizing the need for change in providing collective goods in an environment where power in the political system is distributed asymmetrically and where government leaders have less and less control over industrial change and less political authority over the integrated world economy.

Part III centers on how the different demographic, ideological, economic, and sociological makeup of Europe and America may contribute to different attitudes about the relative roles of the market and the public sector. Moreover, it discusses the future demands on public-sector intervention, regulation, assimilation, and immigration policy in terms of the future global environment.

Part IV analyzes how American and European attitudes about the market may change in the future. In particular, the American response to current demographic, technological, budgetary, and global economic pressures on the future roles of markets and governments is assessed according to the distinctive American attitudes and perspectives of the role of states and markets.

CHAPTER THEMES

During the postwar period, the United States primarily defined the structure of transatlantic relations. Present transatlantic relations are determined in terms of economic interdependence, foreign policy, and security issues, however the solid basis for the transatlantic relationship are economic ties.

To determine the prospects for the future transatlantic relationship, Paul Vandoren in Chapter 2 assesses current changes and the present transatlantic relations. He finds that there are new opportunities for closer transatlantic cooperation, that the European Union should contribute to the reshaping of the transatlantic relations into a balanced partnership, and that despite the current importance of U.S.-EU relations for transatlantic relations, the U.S.-EU relationship should be assessed from an even wider perspective: as a relationship between the European and the North American continents.

In terms of a wider perspective, the European Union and the United States are at a comparable stage of economic and social development and face some common structural constraints and temporary problems. Thus, there is room for wider U.S.-EU collaboration and cooperation. In particular, because of new approaches adopted by President Clinton with respect to various problems of joint concern to the European Union and the United States, new areas for cooperation include environmental problems, the social aspects linked to labor and the displacement of labor outside the European Union and the United States to "cheap labor" countries, as well as higher education. However, even in the present U.S.-EU relationship, communication and coordination also needs to be bolstered. Even though the vast majority of U.S.-EU bilateral trade flows are trouble free, there is an urgent need for dialogue and coordination to avoid incompatible responses to the deterioration of global economic prospects. In terms of foreign policy and security issues, the current changes in the world's security environment directly impact the architecture and functioning of the United Nations, NATO, CSCE, and WEU and make it necessary that both partners deepen their cooperation and define many actions. Moreover, the United States should consult and coordinate more with the European Union rather than dealing with the individual governments of the major member states. In short, the European Union and the United States, in adjusting to their new environments, including many global changes, still require strong ties of communication and collaboration across the Atlantic.

Professor Padoan in Chapter 3 examines the relationship between the state and the market within the evolving international system as well as U.S.-European relations within a conceptual framework based on the political economy of international regimes. The basic premise is that the state and market in each country is influenced by the state of the international system: weak or strong, hegemonic or multipolar. If the international system is strong, then nation-states and markets adjust to it and converge, meaning the international system can accommodate persistent and deep-rooted differences in nation-states and markets. On the other hand, when the international system is weakening or when a new international system must be established, the differences among nation-states and markets lead to large ex-ante differences in the preference for the design of the international system itself. Therefore, as a result the international system is less and less flexible to the differences in nation-states and markets.

The definition of a new global regime and a strong international system, rather than the convergence of the relationship between state and markets toward a common goal, is what is necessary to promote a deeper and more sound integration between Europe and the United States. Therefore, within the current international system it is in the interest of Europe and the United States to establish global cooperation and to work together toward the next phase of European integration.

By reviewing current thought on the longstanding differences in the traditions and structure of capitalism and their effect on the political and economic order in the West, G. John Ikenberry in Chapter 4 finds that the current positions do not address the important dynamics that arise from the interplay between the developmental logic of advanced capitalism and the autonomous political logic of the state and society. This apparent absence of analysis and the fact that these forces help shape American and European orientations toward government involvement in the market and the evolution of Atlantic relations motivated his chapter.

There are basic differences in American and European approaches to the state and market. Additionally, these differences have had and continue to have consequences for the way in which American and European governments approach problems, interact with each other, and seek to construct the larger Western order. Furthermore, with the end of the Cold War and declining American hegemony, these divergent approaches to state and market are becoming consequential in Atlantic relations at the same time differences are declining. Therefore, the next phase in the continuous and permanent revolution of industrial capitalism will consist of conflict, convergence, and interdependence.

Many debates have existed over time about the role of state intervention, the definition of appropriate policy responses, and the establishment of political authority within markets so as to provide the bare minimum of collective goods necessary for the successful survival of the world market economy. Chapter 5 by Professor Susan Strange is foremost a plea for these debates to be reopened in a wider format that introduces non-state sources of authority in society and economy.

The sharing of state authority with others and an asymmetric distribution of power in the political system has led to an increasing level of incompetence in responding to the changing markets and subsequently in implementing policy. Moreover, the gaps in the political system have left no effective political authority over the current integrated world economy. In response, the question of political authority and markets needs to be addressed in a new and different way—not on a state-by-state basis, but on a global one. A new transnational framework for analysis is needed that views the international political economy as one society integrated with world markets.

Building this framework requires answering two questions. One is how to arrange for the provision of those collective goods found by experience to be necessary in the long run for the functioning of a stable efficient market economy—defense of the realm with a collective security system; the provision of stable money; legal protection for buyers and sellers to invest in capital, trade, and production; a state-financed welfare system, and countercyclical intervention. The other question is how to substitute on a global scale the social cohesion and consensus achieved by the modern state through a redistribution of wealth by rules and resource transfers for the benefit of those left underprivileged and defenseless by the operations of the market.

Dr. Robert T. Kudrle's chapter 6 examines the uses of market outcomes as a means of organizing social activity as opposed to regulated private provision and state production. It focuses on the differences and similarities between the United States and Europe by examining whether the purpose of public action is to provide public goods, to redistribute income and wealth, or to do something else. The approach to policy determination used is closely related to public choice theory and the new institutional economics. Four factors—ideological consonance, impact transparency, the distribution of apparent costs and benefits, and the institutional setting—are assessed to determine the purpose of public action in factor markets (land, capital, and labor), and markets for goods and services, primarily in terms of privatization, cultural industries, competition policy, and the emerging problem of investment-related trade measures.

Examining public policies and their purposes within the framework of these four factors indicates that public policies can be considered intermediate public goods. Furthermore, in most policy areas dealing with the relation of government to markets, the policy direction on both sides of the Atlantic has converged. This partial conversion is a result of the European Union countries developing relations and polices of a more market-oriented nature. Kudrle's modified public choice model also predicts a limited reversal to previous practices. The role

of the state, as illuminated by this framework, in the economic sphere
is currently quite limited to providing a basic institutional framework
and compensating for market failures, especially in terms of emphasizing human capital formation and research and development efforts.
The sustainability of the welfare state is currently in debate. Victor
Halberstadt, Hans Van de Kar, and Kees Goudswaard in Chapter 7
contribute to this discussion by examining the past and probable
development of relevant categories of public expenditure and by ana-
lyzing the possible policy reactions to demographic and social structure
changes within three scenarios: Global shift, Balanced growth, and
European renaissance. They use the Netherlands as an example of a
European welfare state in transition.

Public sector expenditure was reduced in the Netherlands in the
1980s, but few fundamental reductions have occurred in government
activities. Moreover, all three scenarios indicate a necessity for fundamental changes in the welfare state and substantial reductions in
expenditures on income maintenance transfers and subsidies. Government intervention in merit goods sectors, however, is not expected to
decline. Most important, the future relationship between markets and
societies in Western Europe will be characterized by more free market
orientation, but not necessarily less coordination.

Christian Stoffaës's Chapter 8 presents an instructive case study.
Over the past few years the pursuit of the single European market has
required large industrial and commercial public services to change in
accordance with the liberal ideas of free trade and competition. As a
result of these changes, the European Union is in the process of spec-
ifying founding principles for its future regulation of public services.
Only by providing these guidelines will they dissipate the climate of
uncertainty and legal insecurity that has been felt over the past few
years in the individual nation states and in the single European market.

The "American model" is a useful reference for the single European
market as the European Union searches for guiding principles. The
American model is useful not because it is the ideal structure, but
rather because the American model encourages modesty and pragmatism. The American model is not ideal for Europe because its technical
and economic performance of public services, particularly in terms of
tariffs, service quality, redistributed equity, and so on, are not always
of the same standard as the models for public trusts in Europe. However, the American experience provides insight for the Europeans on
how liberalism devises and manages public services.

In the United States the evolution of regulation is very different than
in Europe. Regulation of network industries in the United States began

with the activity of private firms and the operation of the free market. Regulation was not based on the authority of the central state and public intervention as it was in Europe. "Public service" in the United States was built on the ideas of competitive markets and not in opposition to them.

In many European countries, industrial and commercial public service was most often built on the "kingly" state of public authority. Recently the philosophy of social law has been added to the "kingly" tradition of network management. Thus, in the spirit of "social law," public service now consists of both an essential place for the arbitration of macrosocial conflicts, as with employers, management, workers, executives, and regions with different levels of development, as well as a privileged way of promoting social equality between both prosperous and impoverished regions, and social classes with different income levels.

The very different historical evolution of American and European public service provides insight on how the European Union should view deregulation and its future regulation of public services. First of all in the United States it is more accurate to speak of regulatory reform rather than deregulation. Additionally, the American model highlights that the European Union needs to establish founding principles that specify a future orientation for network regulation directives, resolve conflicts of interpretation embedded in the array of varying and contradictory national texts, assist judges in Luxembourg, and provide a framework of institutional stability.

The existing literature's nonchalance about elucidating the causes of the "Great Assimilation" motivates the writing of Thomas Ferguson's chapter 9. He argues that the Great Assimilation was the unintended product of another, more fundamental historical process: the mass mobilization of immigrants and their children alongside many "older stock" workers into unions and the Democratic Party during the New Deal.

Ferguson's chapter contains three clearly defined sections before concluding with current lessons and policy prescriptions for Europeans. First, the Great Assimilation was not brought about by World War II or by the prosperity of the 1950s and 1960s, but rather by the critical changes in popular culture and official policies that took place in the 1930s—the slowest growing decade in the twentieth-century American experience. Second, up to the very eve of the New Deal, the melting pot is better characterized as a boiling pot, in which any number of ethnic groups, races, and minorities battled one another while struggling with the dominant WASP upper classes and their use of "creative federalism" to limit the right to vote. Third, during the New Deal, a novel power bloc of capital-intensive industries, investment banks, and internationally oriented commercial banks was able to accommodate millions of mobilized workers amidst world depression and bring about an assimilated American society. Thus what actually melted the pot was a series of concrete political movements that succeeded in bringing millions of previously scorned and largely powerless citizens into at least the antechambers of power.

The lessons for Europe are threefold. First, talking about and achieving multiculturalism and (pluralistic) assimilation are vastly different. Second, the American "Great Assimilation" was not a product of promoting small business, ethnic chambers of commerce, and what not, but was assisted more through ensuring the right to vote for all citizens. Third, the somber reality is that history can also go backward.

Chapters 10 and 11 look to the future. The first, by American Dr. Robert D. Reishauer, argues that Americans' aversion to strong central government, their glorification of the individual, their pragmatic and nonideological approach to public policy, and the existence of a strong and diverse nonprofit sector have circumscribed the role of government and left much to markets, the private sector, and individuals. These four aspects of American experience and attitude toward the role of market forces, as opposed to public sector forces, result in Americans implementing complex mechanisms that encourage private agents to change their behavior in ways to help to achieve public purposes, instead of direct government involvement.

As demographic, technological, budgetary, and global economic pressures mount, the American government will in general increasingly contract with private-sector and nonprofit agents to fulfill its missions and will further structure private markets so as to reduce its need to take direct action. Robert Reischauer details the probable American government response to each of these pressures in the near future in Chapter 10. In addition to the government's response to these pressures, the American public will pressure the government to take action against the perceived imbalances for Americans due to the extensive role of governments elsewhere in Europe and Asia.

A second look into the future, in Chapter 11, presents the European view. Dr. Peeters argues that socialism has inexorably given way to capitalism, meaning that in the future socioeconomic rivalry will exist between the various forms of capitalism. To understand where conflicts could lie, the similarities and differences should be made explicit.

In both Europe and the United States there are common trends occurring. Less government and more market in economic decision-making is dictated by the growing complexities of societies and heavily influenced by the changing perception and shift in the underlying theoretical justification for government intervention in economic activity. There is general agreement today that the efficiency of markets has been underestimated and that the power of governments to correct market failures has been overestimated. In Europe in particular there has been a shift from discretionary and interventionist government action in the economy toward rules and government behavior that conform to market principles.

Moreover, fine-tuning aggregate demand has lost much of its appeal as the basis for sound macroeconomic policies. Emphasis has shifted toward structural adjustment, supply-oriented policies, and demand-management policies that stress stability and predictability. This is true for both monetary and budgetary policies. In Europe in particular, the White Paper on Growth, Employment, and Competitiveness from the Commission of the European Communities has focused on three main areas of necessary structural measures that emphasize market flexibility instead of interventionist rigidities. For a more detailed assessment Peeters highlights the ongoing reappraisal of the role of governments and markets in the European economies in three specific examples: the single market project, the common agricultural policy, and the steel industry.

Even though there are many similarities between Europe and the United States, it is recognized that markets underestimate what is at stake in the long term, affect different social categories unequally, and spontaneously promote concentration, which results in inequality between regions. Awareness of these insufficiencies in the marketplace has led European countries to develop collective solidarity mechanisms in varying degrees. The essence of collective solidarity mechanisms is not questioned in Europe. In short, economic and social cohesion still remain essential pillars of the European variant of the capitalist model.

ENDNOTES

1. The following discussions are in part the conclusions from various chapters and their authors.

2

A European Union Perspective on the Prospects for the Transatlantic Relationship

Paul Vandoren

POLITICAL AND ECONOMIC CHANGES IN EUROPE AND THE UNITED STATES

Political events outside the European Union have overriding importance over the internal aspects of the European Union, meaning that important political changes on the other side of the Atlantic are of utmost importance to the European Union. In essence, U.S.-EU relations, already an important part of broader transatlantic relations, need to be assessed from an even wider perspective: as relations between the European and the North American continents.

Continental Europe

After several decades of relative stability during the Cold War period, an era of instability has emerged simultaneously with the collapse of the Berlin Wall, the disintegration of the Iron Curtain, the disappearance of several states (East Germany, the Soviet Union, Yugoslavia, and Czechoslovakia), and the emergence of no less than 21 new states. Above all, these changes have led to the collapse of an entire political and economic system that, during the post–World War II period, codetermined world politics and characterized strong East-West antagonism. The changes have also led to the resurgence of ethnic conflicts, a new flood of migration, and the reemergence of the racist movement. Moreover because of current worldwide interdependence, these changes affect all players of the political scene in Western, Central, and Eastern Europe as well as in the United States.

The European Union

In the European Union a movement toward widening and deepening is in progress.

European agreements were negotiated with Poland, Hungary, the Czech Republic, Slovakia, Bulgaria, and Romania as a result of the progress and developments east of the European Union. The European Union is also negotiating a partnership and cooperation agreement with Russia and will probably do so with the members of the Commonwealth of Independent States. These agreements are destined to provide ways and means for increased market access to the European Union, but pursuing enlargement is not an easy task during a time of economic recession in the European Union. These agreements, however, are important political signals.

In the near future, the European Union and most of the former members of the European Free Trade Association (such as Austria, Finland, Iceland, Norway, Sweden, and possibly Liechtenstein), will put the "European Economic Area" into practice. Participation in the EEA will serve as a transition toward full membership for most of these countries. The negotiations for enlargement with Austria, Finland, Norway, and Sweden are well underway. As a result, the European Union will have 16 member states in the near future. The possibility of accession has also been offered to countries with negotiated Europe agreements provided that a number of basic principles (such as respect for democracy and human rights, existence of a market economy, and so on) are implemented. Turkey, Malta, and Cyprus have applied for membership.

The European Union has established the world's largest internal market and is developing a common foreign and security policy and an economic and monetary union. These developments have created future concerns for the European Union's partners, in particular, the United States. In the beginning, the United States was very worried about a single market turning into a protectionist bloc. Now, U.S. business circles are generally convinced of the overall liberalizing effects of the union and the resulting new business opportunities. Economic and monetary union is also of great importance to the United States because of the size of the European economy and the European Union's external trade. But there is no doubt that the international monetary situation, in particular the role of the U.S. dollar, will be affected. The ratification of the Maastricht Treaty, furthermore, requires the implementation of common foreign and security policy and therefore means that the European Union will become a more powerful interlocutor to the United States in foreign policy and security matters. Admittedly, for historical reasons and because of divergent interests among member states, there are limits to how the European Union can challenge U.S. foreign policy. But if the European Union is to develop an increasingly independent foreign policy during the coming years, it is likely to be in direct confrontation with the United States unless a solid U.S.-EU political dialogue prevails.

These developments offer many opportunities but they also can be perceived as threats. The United States should consult and coordinate more with the European Union rather than dealing with the individual governments of the major member states. In the future, the European Union will be the more powerful actor in transatlantic and international relations.

The United States

Political economic changes in the United States appear to have been less dramatic than in Europe. However, many observers are of the opinion that American society has fundamentally changed over recent decades. Many changes have taken place within American society. The United States has become less European and less Europe-oriented. Political leaders no longer come from the Northeast. New business poles have developed and there is a clear shift to the South and the West. Many business people in the western part of the United States are looking primarily toward the Pacific Rim for partnership, even though American business lost part of its competitiveness to Southeast Asia. These trends will have an impact on long-term U.S.-EU relations.

A similar regional phenomenon, although more restricted in its scope than the trend toward regional integration in Europe, is the North American Free Trade Agreement, which created a free trade area between the United States, Canada, and Mexico. The European Union welcomes this development as long as it is consistent with GATT.

President Clinton, elected on the basis of change and renewal, along with his new U.S. administration are looking at foreign policy in close conjunction with economic policy. Moreover, the range and complexity of domestic problems (crime, drugs, health care, and education) have increased and are forcing the new administration to pay more attention to the domestic agenda. But it remains to be seen to what extent the president can translate this call for change into reality.

Common Problems in Europe and the United States

The European Union and the United States are in a comparable stage of economic and social development and face some common structural constraints and temporary problems.

Both economies are increasingly service economies with a relative decline in the size of the manufacturing sector. Labor costs are relatively high, so both countries also face similar competitive pressures from low-wage countries. The populations of both regions expect high living standards. Unemployment has reached unacceptable heights in both Europe and America, although the economic situation is better in the United States than in the European Union. Budget deficits are rising so high that drastic cuts in public expenditures are unavoidable. The social security and health care systems are nearly bankrupt. There are also microeconomic problems such as overcapacity in some key industrial sectors, such as automobiles, steel, and shipbuilding.

On both sides of the Atlantic, there is a significant mistrust by the population in political leaders. The political crisis in Italy and the "Ross Perot phenomenon" in the United States are similarly illustrative of the discontent with the traditional political establishment. Europeans and Americans want better choices for leaders than are offered by current political party systems. Leaders with a vision and a plan of action are lacking. Government inaction and stagnation must be overcome by both the Europeans as well as the Americans. Furthermore, the European Union encountered great difficulties when ratifying the Maastricht Treaty. The treaty was presented to a population, which did not grasp what was at stake, in the midst of an economic crisis.

These fundamental economic and political problems on both sides of the Atlantic require an urgent and possibly radical solution. However, the needed radical political solutions are seldom being chosen.

FACTORS DETERMINING PRESENT
TRANSATLANTIC RELATIONS

Economic Interdependence

The solid basis for the transatlantic relationship are economic ties. The European Union and the United States are each other's largest single trading partner. U.S. exports to the European Union amounted to more than $100 billion in 1992, or nearly one quarter of total U.S. exports, making the European Union the largest export market for the United States. European Union exports to the United States amounted to about $96 billion in 1992 or 20 percent of total U.S. imports. In addition, cumulative U.S. direct investment in the European Union was close to $200 billion in 1992, almost half of total U.S. direct investment abroad, making the European Union the most important foreign investment market for U.S. companies. European Union investment in the United States ($232 billion) amounted to more than half of total foreign investment in the U.S. market, making the European Union the largest foreign investor in the United States.

The importance of economic and trade relations will increase with the further enlargement of the European Union. Economic interdependence will increase. Fortunately, the vast majority of U.S.-EU bilateral trade flows are trouble free.

Foreign Policy and Security Issues

With the disappearance of the bipolar world, new challenges to the world's security have emerged. The European Union and its member states, together with the United States, are bound to remain in the forefront of regional crisis management, especially within the framework of the UN. They will also contribute to stability and constructive change in Central and Eastern Europe, the former Soviet Union, and Yugoslavia. Both partners continue to share a common interest in the management of other political issues: China, the Middle East, Somalia, and the promotion of democracy and human rights in the world. Moreover, there is an obvious need for the two largest donors of development aid to organize more effective cooperation with the developing countries.

The current changes in the world's security environment directly impact the architecture and functioning of the UN, NATO, CSCE, and

WEU and make it necessary that both partners deepen their cooperation and define the following concrete actions:

- To organize and improve cooperative security mechanisms, con-
  flict prevention and resolution;
- To build the two-pillar Atlantic Alliance;
- To organize the division of responsibilities between NATO and
  WEU;
- To maintain the U.S. military presence in Europe, despite the
  temptation to "cash in" a perceived peace dividend prematurely.

OPPORTUNITIES FOR CLOSER
TRANSATLANTIC COOPERATION

In the Economic Field

In view of the delicate state of the world economy, the European Union
and the United States, together with Japan, have the common responsibility and the economic strength to stimulate world trade, to revital-
ize global economic growth, including employment, and to reduce
exchange-rate instability. Therefore, there is an urgent need for dialogue and coordination to avoid incompatible responses to the deterioration of global economic prospects.

The European Union and the United States must keep their bilateral
disputes under control, because the delicate balance between the
United States and the European Union may inadvertently dissolve and
lead to the disappearance of the mutual trust that has been built up
between the new U.S. administration and its major partner.

Foreign Policy and Security Area

Whether the European Union and the United States want it or not, they
must deal with the conflicts in the former Yugoslavia and Russia. In
former Yugoslavia, the European Union and its member states have
not been successful in managing a settlement between the warring parties. The dimension of the situation was seriously underestimated when
it emerged. It is only after the European countries failed in their attempts to negotiate a settlement that the United States started taking a
direct interest. President Clinton first reviewed the policy of his pre-
decessor and arrived at a position that was not in line with that of his

European allies. This led to extensive consultation between the United States and the European Union to bridge the diverging positions. Even now, there remain important differences of view in terms of the ways and means of containing the conflict within its present limits.

In Russia, both the European Union and the United States have opted to support economic and political reform. The Commission and the U.S. President have been in very close contact and have created a framework for granting assistance. The success of this policy, however, is not guaranteed given that the internal position of the Russian President remains uncertain. Not providing aid doesn't seem viable.

New Areas for Cooperation

Because of the new approach adopted by President Clinton with respect to various issues, which are of joint concern to the European Union and the United States, there is room for wider U.S.-EU cooperation.

The first step could be in terms of solving environmental problems. The environment is now a major concern for the new U.S. administration. Moreover, during the Rio conference, there were major divergences regarding the environment between the United States and most other countries, including the European Union. The European Union and the United States should take the lead in the international environmental fora, especially now that the United States has signed the biodiversity treaty and both the European Union and the U.S. administration are in favor of an energy tax.

Social aspects linked to labor and the displacement of labor outside the European Union and the United States to "cheap labor" countries is another important concern to both President Delors and President Clinton. There is no need to wait to tackle issues, such as the relationship between trade and environment, competition, investment, and social aspects.

Population growth is another issue that will be of increasing concern to all of us over the years to come. The European Union and the United States did cooperate to achieve a strategy toward effective control of population growth with the developing countries. The International Conference on Population and Development in Cairo in September 1994 was able to produce a broad-ranging strategy to guide humanity's effort to curb population growth over the next 10 to 20 years.

The European Union and the United States have agreed to boost their cooperation in higher education. They agreed to launch a new initiative that will add a European dimension to cooperation and exchanges between universities in the United States and the European Union. As of the academic year 1993-94, there is support for up to 30 consortia or partnerships of EU and U.S. higher education institutions to cooperate in the design of collaborative teaching programs, course credit transfer measures, and visiting fellowships for teaching staff. Cooperation in the field of vocational and continuing education should be developed further.

FRAMEWORK FOR THE TRANSATLANTIC RELATIONSHIP

During the postwar period, the United States primarily defined the structure of transatlantic relations. Now the European Union should contribute to the reshaping of the transatlantic relations into a balanced partnership. For example, the European Union should explain to the U.S. political leaders and public the rationale for its policy approach in areas of common interest and concern.

Presently, the architecture of EU-U.S. relations is built upon the "Transatlantic Declaration," which was adopted by the European Union, its member states, and the United States, in November 1990. In this declaration, the parties reaffirmed their determination to strengthen their partnership in order to achieve a number of common goals: democracy, peace and international security, and market economy. To this end the principle of reciprocal information and consultation on important matters of common interest has been laid down. An institutional framework for such consultations has been set up, but in practice, consultations have taken place at different levels on a more-or-less regular basis.

Besides the Transatlantic Declaration, there exists a wide range of agreements and administrative arrangements covering a number of very different subjects, such as agriculture, securities markets, competition matters, and so on. However, both the European Union and the United States at the present time consider the Transatlantic Declaration an adequate and sufficient framework for their bilateral cooperation. Future coordination could be improved with a more effective and flexible approach, but on the European Union's side, the time does not seem ripe for a far-reaching type of institutional framework. The Maastricht Treaty needs to be fully implemented first. Meanwhile, a strong and integrated Europe should translate into a real partnership between the European Union and the United States.

3

The International System and the Diversity of States and Markets

Pier Carlo Padoan

This chapter looks at the relationship between the state and the market within the context of the evolving international system. The conceptual framework, which is based on international political economy, is applied to U.S.-European relations. The argument is that what is necessary to promote a deeper and sounder integration between Europe and the United States is the definition of a new global regime rather than the convergence of the relationship between the state and the market toward a common model. If the international regime is strong it can accommodate, as recent historical experience shows, persistent and deep-rooted differences in national relationships between the state and the market. This task is presently complicated, however, by the current phase of European integration, and the institutional pressures from the creation of a single market, monetary unification, and enlargement.

THE STATE AND THE MARKET:
A CONCEPTUAL FRAMEWORK

The starting point assumes the following: the state and the market cannot live without the other in advanced industrialized countries. The state is broadly considered to include public institutions as well as the government. The market is understood as the network of interrelations among private and independent agents engaged in profit (firms) and utility (household) seeking activities. A "pure" marketplace, a totally decentralized system where only fully independent agents interact, is bound to generate market "failures" and produce suboptimal outcomes.[1] The state must provide public goods and coordinating mechanisms, such as institutions, to overcome these failures (Stiglitz 1991).[2] Even the most liberal thinkers agree that the market requires a system of property rights to operate efficiently.[3]

The state needs the market because to sustain itself the state requires a system for the production of wealth, and the market, in this respect, is the most efficient system available. The state must extract resources from the market to survive and possibly grow. Simultaneously, the state monitors the operation of the market to extract political consensus.[4]

Assuming that the state and the market inevitably interact, or in other words that politics and economics are inseparable, the important issue to consider is to what degree, in which forms, and through which ways, their relationship exists and how this relationship evolves.

This, of course, is a very complex issue, in which the temptation is to assume that the core issue lies within the realm of political economy. Thus, a more precise and narrow definition is necessary.

This framework assumes that the relationship between the state and the market is determined by how economic and political actors, such as the government, the central bank, the bureaucracy, business and financial communities, and trade unions interact when determining the performance of the economy, and when implementing policies, agreements, and both formal and informal regulations. Within this framework, policy outcomes and the performance of the system reveal different preferences, power relations among actors, and the efficiency of institutions in providing conflict resolutions and in coping with collective action problems. Therefore, changes in the state and market, as defined earlier, lead to changes in policy outcomes and in the performance of the economy.

The main point of this approach is that the state and market in each country is influenced largely by the condition of the international system, understood as the set of rules and institutions that govern the interaction among international actors including, but not limited to, nation-states.[5]

The international system (IS), by being able to establish regimes, provides some of the coordinating mechanisms necessary for the market to operate. This capability, therefore, partly relieves national policymakers from the task of providing coordinating mechanisms.[6]

Conversely, nation-states can extract benefits from a larger, more integrated, and more dynamic international market, in terms of higher growth and/or in terms of political consensus,[7] rather than relying solely on domestic sources for growth.

Unfortunately the international system, thought of as a formalized international relationship between states and markets, is much more unstable than national states and markets. International systems are established, evolve, decline, and collapse much more rapidly than states and markets. Their relatively rapid evolution heavily influences the behavior of state and markets and their mutual relationship. Their rapid evolution occurs because no supranational government exists. Therefore, the establishment of international regimes requires at least some degree of cooperation among national governments (Kindleberger 1986).

A "strong" international system, defined as a well-designed and efficiently functioning set of rules and norms by which national governments operate, provides some of the public goods for national states and markets. A liberal and strong trade regime and a stable international macroeconomic regime together generate higher growth, ease pressures for protection within nations, and eventually, decrease the amount of government intervention necessary to sustain national states and markets. On the contrary, a weak trade regime and/or a collapsing macroeconomic regime generate an increasing demand for government intervention at the national level. At the same time, more public assistance would be required to obtain political support for the incumbent government (Guerrieri and Padoan 1988).

Because the literature on the relationship between international regimes and domestic politics is large and rapidly expanding,[8] this chapter will not develop this point in more depth. However, figure 3.1 summarizes the possible cases of policy performance for the two main international economic regimes: trade and macroeconomics.

The state of international regimes, weak or strong, influences the behavior of national states and markets as well as their mutual relationships. This chapter suggests the following: When the IS is strong, national states and markets adjust to it and converge, at least partially, to a common model. In other words, when the international system is strong, differences among national states and markets become less relevant for international relations. The differences become more relevant, however, in two cases: 1) when the IS is weakening and its ability to provide public goods declines accordingly;[9] and 2) when a new IS must be established and differences among national states and markets

Figure 3.1

International Regimes and States of the System

		Regime	
		Trade	Macroeconomics
State	Strong	Liberal	Expansionary
	Weak	Protectionistic	Restrictive

lead to large ex-ante differences in the preferences for the design of the IS itself.

States and markets and IS exhibit a reciprocal influence. Even though the evolution of the IS influences the evolution of a national state and market, the latter eventually determines the extent to which the IS survives and later collapses.[10] In other words, during its expansion phase the IS leads to a convergence of the national state and market, but during its declining phase the IS is less and less able to accommodate differences in the national state and market. Thus, the relations between the IS and the national state and market in the two cases mentioned earlier are most relevant in the current historical phase.

Finally, the relationship between the IS and the national state and market varies with the type of IS itself. An IS can be either hegemonic or multipolar.[11] In a hegemonic IS, the costs of providing international public goods are more than proportionally borne by the hegemonic country and, as a consequence, the pressures for adjustment of the state and market in smaller countries are proportionally lower, and the risks of free riding (as in a behavior that exploits the IS rather than contributing to its support) are higher.

In a multipolar IS, as described in more detail later, the conditions for providing international public goods are more stringent and more difficult to obtain because the pressures on national states and markets are stronger and the interplay of national differences is larger. The multipolar IS is relevant for the current situation in international relations in general and in U.S.-European relationships in particular.

THE GLOBAL SYSTEM TODAY: REGIONALISM AND DOMESTIC POLITICS

The global system is now in what can be called a post hegemonic world (Gilpin 1987), as in no single country can provide unilaterally the public goods required for the operation of the system itself. It is often argued that one possible configuration of the global system for the foreseeable future is "regionalism." This should, however, be understood not so much as the result of the concentration of trade and investment activities around major integrated regions (Europe, North America, Asia) but rather as a policy option pursued by the industrialized world in response to the failure of the post hegemonic world to provide international public goods.

Regionalism may be "conflict-oriented" or "cooperative." In the first case, regional agreements provide collective goods for countries in the respective regions and exclude nonmembers from consuming collective goods (for example, a discriminatory trade agreement). In such a case, the state and market of member states are relieved from the pressure of adjustment from the outside of the region. One obvious example is the (perhaps abstract) possibility that the European Community would follow a protectionistic policy vis-à-vis the rest of the world in order to maximize the benefits of their large market—the Single Market Program—to the advantage of European-based firms (Katseli 1988).

Cooperative regionalism, on the contrary, could be understood as the formation of regional agreements as a precondition for cooperation at a global level.

Comprehending the reasons behind cooperative regionalism is crucial in understanding the relationship between international regimes and national states and markets. To develop this point consider the following conceptual aspects: 1) the conditions for cooperation without hegemony, as in within a multipolar world, and 2) the interaction between domestic, regional, and international policy determination.

The theory of international cooperation without hegemony offers a list of conditions to reach agreements on supplying international public goods:[12] 1) the number of actors involved must be small; 2) the time horizon for actors must be long; and 3) actors must be prepared to change their policy preferences. Condition one allows for the possibility of dealing with free riding and is verified with a tripolar context. Condition two allows for repeated interaction among players, which is both necessary and unavoidable in an increasingly interdependent world. Condition three is the most relevant for this chapter because itrequires national states and markets to adjust to the international environment to reach agreements. During this adjustment the interaction among different levels of politics is more relevant.

Robert Putnam (1988) has suggested that during the formation of an international regime agreement is required at two levels: 1) between national governments (level I politics), and 2) between each national government and domestic interest groups (level II politics). In terms of this terminology, level II politics requires the adjustment of national states and markets to the international environment. In addition, level I agreements must be designed so as to be consistent with the specific level II agreements in each of the participating countries. Therefore, agreements at both level II politics and level I politics must be consistent.

The interaction between level I and level II politics in determining the success of international cooperation is a complex one and its implications are currently being explored in the literature.[13] The complexity of the interaction between different levels of politics consists of one characteristic of international negotiations that is sometimes forgotten, but which may be quite relevant during periods of rapid institutional change, such as the present one. Negotiations between and within nations can hardly be represented by "pure" cooperation or "pure" defection. In an ongoing negotiation process, as well as during the life of an agreement, both elements of cooperation and defection are present, although their relative weight varies over time (Sebenius 1992).

In terms of the approach of this chapter, cooperative attitudes prevail when the regime is strong, while the propensity to defect prevails when the regime is declining. A strong regime provides benefits for all actors involved so that there are widespread incentives to cooperate for the support of the regime itself. A declining regime provides a lower amount of global benefits and members will tend to look at relative, rather than absolute, gains in determining their behavior. In the first case of a strong regime, international cooperation is likely to be sustained over time, while in the second case of a declining regime, it is much less likely.[14] Moreover, redistributive considerations are stronger if level II politics prevail over level I politics and international negotiations are very dependent on domestic pressures. For example, in this case the ability of national states and markets to set the pace of international negotiations becomes more relevant. In the opposite case, absolute gains considerations are stronger.

The tendency toward global regionalism adds a third level to politics: regional politics, defined as a common regional policy, which operates between domestic and international politics.

To answer the question whether regionalism will assume benign or malign characteristics requires an examination of the role of regional (level III) politics as an intermediary between level I and level II politics. This also requires a closer look at the necessary conditions to consolidate regional agreements, as in, the conditions when level II politics "melt" into level III (regional) politics. Once level II politics are consolidated into level III politics, international (level I) politics interact only with regional (level III) rather than with domestic (level II) politics.

De Melo, Pangaraya, and Rodrik (1992) develop this point analytically within a framework that bears several similarities to the approach described here. Their framework considers regional integration as both an economic and a political process that is the outcome of a relationship between national governments and domestic pressure groups (level II politics in Putnam's terminology).[15] They show that the formation of supranational institutions, in other words regional agreements, has a positive effect on the economic efficiency of national economies. The positive effect is a result of the reduced impact of domestic pressure groups on the policy stance of the supranational institution in relation to their impact on single national governments. Without the integration of national governments, they would provide "excessive" intervention, in terms of the economically optimal amount of intervention, because of the strong influence of domestic pressure groups (the so-called preference dilution effect). However, if large differences among national preferences on the degree of government's intervention exist, the incentive to integrate may be insufficient (the "preference asymmetry effect"). To operate supranational institutions (the "institutional design effect") efficiently, they must be designed to minimize the influence of countries whose domestic pressure groups demand a high amount of government intervention.

In terms of the framework outlined in this chapter, the preference dilution effect relates to the increased roles of national states and markets when international regimes are absent. The preference asymmetry effect relates to the role of differences in national states and markets in favoring or hindering international regime formation. The institutional design effect emphasizes that regional politics requires the formation of some supranational institution, and thus also supranational state and market relations, to avoid the risk of being captured by a special interest action. With these simple concepts in mind, this chapter turns to the issue of state and market and U.S.-European relations.

STATE AND MARKETS AND THE U.S.-EUROPEAN RELATIONSHIP

To consider U.S.-European relations the framework sketched in the previous paragraphs must be further broken down in the following ways: a) when only two international regimes interact, as in (1) the "Atlantic regime"—the set of relations involving the United States and Europe—or (2) the "European regime" centered on the European Community (EC); and b) when the European regime is based on nation states whose national state and market in some cases differ quite significantly.

Elements a and b are interconnected and affect the evolution of national states and markets. Examining the period of hegemonic stability until the collapse of the Bretton Woods system, the "long decade of U.S. Hegemony" to use Keohane's (1984) expression, and the subsequent period provides simple insight into the interactions between elements a and b.

The two international regimes, the "Atlantic" regime and the "European" regime, have interacted positively. They have reinforced each other, and have generated a "strong" international system only during the period of persuasive U.S. hegemony. U.S. hegemony has favored the formation and strengthening of the European regime, centered around the European Community, by creating conditions for the reconstruction of Europe and by accepting partial discrimination, especially in trade relations to foster European integration. In other words, the United States has acted as an hegemon. It willingly bore a disproportionate cost to supply the international public good within the international regime.[16]

The establishment of the Atlantic regime provides Western European countries the opportunity to exploit new development opportunities on an export-led basis. Trade expansion, increased openness, and macroeconomic stability were the international public goods that proved to be the key to their success. The process of providing these international public goods also generated an increasing integration and an adjustment to a new division of labor for European economies that had previously operated on a quite different basis, sometimes under autarky, before the war. The adjustment costs involved in this process, however, were overcome with relative ease because of the stable and expanding international environment.

One of the peculiar features of this process was the combination of a common export-led orientation and the presence of relevant differences in national states and markets. The latter did not represent a serious obstacle to international integration as long as the former element maintained a dynamic of its own. In other words, the expansion of the international system had to relieve the national governments from their task of sustaining employment and growth while, at the same time, providing resources and consensus for the national governments.[17] In short, the sound operation of the international system largely fulfilled the Keynesian concern for full employment. Thus, it was in the interest of the single nation-states that such an international system operate successfully.

This model provides one important distinction between two sectors in each national economy: one sector is exposed to international competition and one sector, which includes the public sector, is "protected" from such competition. This distinction highlights the fact that even though participation in international regimes benefits states as a whole, only one part of the economy bears the burden of international competition. This fact is quite important when competitive pressures from the international economy are more stringent, for example, when the international regime weakens. The "exposed sector" benefits more from the coordination effects provided by the international system and the "sheltered sector" benefits from the resources in terms of political consensus generated by the system. In other words, as long as the international regime is strong, both sectors benefit.

Even though this distinction may be relatively unimportant for the United States, it is of great importance for Europe. Differences in both exposed and sheltered sectors among the European countries produced different outcomes in terms of their capacity to extract resources from the international system. Countries, such as Germany, the United Kingdom, or France, whose exposed sector includes fast-growing industrial sectors, such as sectors producing goods facing a rapidly growing world demand, benefit more from a given rate of expansion of world markets than countries such as Italy, Greece, and Spain, whose exposed sector includes slow-growing sectors. The increased benefits for the exposed sector spill over into the sheltered sector in two ways. Faster-growing sectors normally provide more employment, and thus more consensus resources for the national government, and at the same time they rely less on the national government for support.

A strong international system allows for a generalized distribution of benefits while exerting a relatively milder pressure on slower growing sectors. Conversely, a weak international system affects the states and markets of countries with slower-growing industries more severely.

The Formation of a European Regime

During the period of strengthening U.S. hegemony, the different national states and markets did not obstruct the formation and consolidation of a European regime. The European regime at its inception was basically a trade regime. The European Community was substantially a custom union with a few supranational powers in specific issues, such as the common tariff and the Common Agricultural Policy. It evolved both by strengthening the trade regime (the Single Market Program) and by expanding its role into other areas, most notably into the macroeconomic regime (the European Monetary System).

From the point of view of a state and market, European integration required a more radical process than the edification of the Bretton Woods system, not only because it exerted deeper adjustment pressures on European state and market (a fact that proved to be crucial in later developments) but also because it generated a totally new state and market structure. The new state and market structure was a supranational one associated with the definition and enforcement of Community regulations as opposed to national regulations. It also required a transfer of resources, such as the Community budget.

Within this framework, it is only natural that the Community evolved in steps through successive enlargements (widening) and transfers of powers (deepening). When the European Community was formed, a few of the European states, notably the United Kingdom and the Nordic countries, were not in favor of relevant transfers of sovereignty to supranational institutions. Others, however, such as the southern European states, were not yet in the position to withstand the adjustment pressures on their state and market.

In summary, the formation of a European regime differed from the formation of the Atlantic regime in one major element. The Atlantic hegemonic regime, as long as it operated successfully, produced relatively little pressure on existing national states and markets, because as discussed earlier, it provided some of the public goods necessary for sound interaction between the state and the market at national levels. Level I and level II politics proved to be mutually consistent under hegemony. The European regime, on the contrary, required the gradual implementation of new supranational relations.

Level III politics, which were substantially absent in the Atlantic regime, generated brand-new problems in the European regime. The new European institutions could have provided some of the public goods that an international regime offers to nation-states, however, to reach this goal, much stronger pressure on European states was necessary.

The continuous "deepening versus widening" dilemma in the evolution of the European Community reflects this same issue. Widening allows member states to retain much of their national sovereignty with little pressure on national state and market. Thus, level II politics is not put under severe pressure. Deepening requires the strengthening of supranational institutions with the goal of forming a strong European regime and a sound provision of (regional) public goods, but only at the cost of increasing pressures on national state and market. Consequently, the problems associated with level II politics mentioned earlier (see De Melo, Pangaraya, and Rodrik 1992) came to the fore. The history of EC integration can, in several cases, be interpreted in terms of such a dilemma.

The Interaction between the Two Regimes

The interaction between the "Atlantic" and "European" regimes in the post–World War period is clarified when the collapse of the international macroeconomic regime, as in the fixed exchange rate system set up at Bretton Woods, is reconsidered.[18]

At the end of the 1960s the relative weakening of the gold standard, which eventually collapsed in 1971, could have been rectified by sharing the responsibilities of managing macroeconomic policies and the exchange rate system. The international public goods of monetary and macro stability, for example, could have been provided within a multipolar framework since the hegemon was not willing or able to do so anymore (Guerrieri and Padoan 1986). A new multilateral management of the system, however, required a dramatic shift in attitude in the major European countries. This shift included stronger support for international effective demand and/or coordinated currency realignments consistent with the new economic conditions. Even though such actions would have relieved some on the pressure on the United States, it would have also imposed adjustment pressures on the major European economies and on their states and markets.

Failure to reach an agreement transformed the international system from a provider of public goods to a generator of negative shocks. At the beginning of the 1970s the collapse of the international monetary regime and the oil shock forced industrialized countries to implement individual responses. This eventually led to stagflation that accentuated the negative consequences of the absence of international ex-ante coordination.

Diffuse unemployment and recession, in the presence of rising inflation, both weakened the ability of markets to produce resources and increased the demands for state support at the national levels. Gaps between national performance—reflected in growing inflation differentials—increased, thus highlighting differences in national states and markets.

The crisis within the Atlantic regime, paradoxically strengthened the European regime, which was pressed by the necessity to react to the negative externalities—particularly monetary instability and recession—generated by the crisis. Europe had to react by regionally providing some of the public goods previously supplied by the international system. The reasons to pursue level III politics increased in response to the growing inconsistencies between level I and level II politics.

Some, and initially only partial, success was obtained in the monetary arena. In the early 1970s a regional monetary regime started to emerge in the forms of a European "snake" and later as the European Monetary System. Attempts to support growth at a global level, through the so-called locomotive strategy, however, eventually failed.[19]

The evolution of the European macro-monetary regime is a clear example of the role national states and markets have in influencing the formation of international agreements.[20] Its success can be explained by the presence of one regional leader. Germany was able to provide some international public goods, notably monetary stability, and to force other European states and markets to adjust to her leadership. This mechanism is sometimes described as "imported discipline" from Germany. For example, other European countries have tried to adjust their inflation rates to the nominal anchor provided by German monetary policy, through the constraint imposed by the exchange rate mechanism. National states and markets were adjusted accordingly in both quantitative and qualitative terms. Quantitatively, the exchange rate stability was inconsistent with an increasing role of the state and thus required fiscal discipline. Qualitatively, inflationary convergence required new and more disciplined industrial relations. In turn, the establishment of regional monetary stability in Europe provided some shelter from monetary disturbances generated by the unstable behavior of the dollar in international markets. Level III politics acquired strength as a result of the weakening of level I politics.

Even though the goal of monetary stability seemed to be obtained by the end of the 1980s, strains on national states and markets eventually grew stronger. Inflation-prone countries such as Italy and the United Kingdom—also incurred real appreciation (see table 3.1). As a result, the continual growth of the nontradable sectors, a generalized phenomenon in Europe (see table 3.2)[21] decreased the ability of national economies to provide resources because of declining competitiveness and decreased the ability of national governments to provide support for expansion.

In contrast to the Atlantic regime, the European regime, centered around the European Monetary System, has not provided the other essential macroeconomic public good: growth. The relative success of the European monetary regime in the past decade was accompanied by growth provided, however, internationally by the Atlantic regime. U.S. policies implemented during the Reagan administration generated both rising demand through fiscal expansion and dollar appreciation through monetary tightening. These policies thus boosted European exports and growth. It is therefore not surprising that the crisis within

Table 3.1
Real effective exchange rates, intra-EC trade, 1985–1991
(yearly averages, 1980 = 100)

	1985	1986	1987	1988	1989	1990	1991
France	98.7	102.4	101.6	101.0	99.8	100.8	99.6
Germany	98.0	103.9	106.5	105.3	103.4	103.7	103.6
United Kingdom	103.9	96.7	95.1	103.7	102.6	100.0	106.5
Italy	104.9	104.5	104.8	102.2	105.3	106.8	107.6
Spain	101.8	97.5	94.5	97.9	103.1	103.8	104.0

Source: Bank of Italy.

Table 3.2
**Percentage share of "nontradable" production (services
and government expenditure) in total value added**

	1980	1989
Italy	59.0	61.1
France	60.0	64.3
Germany	53.4	56.8
United Kingdom	57.4	65.1

Source: Bank of Italy.

the European regime in the early 1990s is associated with the lack of growth and a diffuse recession.

THE CRISIS WITHIN THE EUROPEAN REGIME

The support from the Atlantic regime provided only partial relief. Thus, at the beginning of the current decade EC countries decided to proceed toward monetary unification. The Maastricht Treaty recognizes that monetary stability, the most relevant public good, should be produced at the European level. Strengthening a European supranational state and market, while simultaneously reducing the role of national states and markets and forcing their convergence to a common model by imposing fiscal discipline, will achieve monetary stability.[22] Moreover this process is also crucial for achieving another fundamental public good: a fully integrated market (Commission of the European Communities, "One Market, One Money," European Economy).

The collapse of the Exchange Rate Agreements (ERMs) in Europe between September 1992, when Italy and the United Kingdom left the ERM, and July 1993, when the fixed exchange rate mechanism was replaced by a de facto flexible system, may or may not be the final blow to monetary unification. The collapse could push the goal of stable prosperity promised by the Single Market quite far into the future.

In terms of the framework outlined here, the large drawback of the European regime is described as follows: Facing a major shock, such as German unification, the European regime proved unable to resist still quite large differences between national states and markets. National states and markets serve national goals, such as adjustments to shocks, rather than supranational ones, such as monetary unification. Despite the major shock the European Monetary Union suffered, the Single Market project is still under way. Formally complete on January 1, 1993, it still needs to be achieved in substance since several differences in regulation still separate national markets.[23]

The Single Market represents an interesting case of international regime formation. Its full implementation requires both "negative" and "positive" integration. "Negative" integration is the suppression of remaining barriers to the movements of goods and factors. "Positive integration" is the establishment of common rules and standards. In both cases international (regional) public goods are provided through appropriate collective action. Therefore, supranational states and markets must replace national ones.

Collective action of this sort is not easy to obtain because the formation of a true common market is bound to distribute costs and benefits asymmetrically across member states. An implicit sign of the relevance of this issue is the EC Commission's identification of the "sensitive sectors" in European industry (Commission of the European Communities 1990 "Social Europe," European Economy, Special Issue). "Sensitive sectors" are most affected by the completion of the Single Market. Empirical analysis concerning the distribution, evolution, and weight of sensitive sectors across Europe (Smith and Wanke 1991; Padoan and Pericoli 1993) shows how the single European economies react differently to the Single Market. Implicitly, it also shows the spillover of adjustment pressures onto national states and markets in Europe.

The formation of a trade regime in Europe requires at least some of these pressures to be coped with at a supranational level. Consensus for further industrial deepening requires some redistributive mechanism, and hence intra-EC cooperation. This mechanism must provide support for the countries and regions adversely affected by the formation of the new regime. Community structural funds are an example of such mechanisms. Their dimension and scope, however, are too limited in this case (Marques Mendez 1990). The Single Market requires new forms of supranational management to achieve its integration goals, such as a new supranational state and market with some form of fiscal federalism. Level III politics must fully absorb level I politics and their differences within an appropriate institutional design.

However this is not the end of the story. Europe is now facing the consequences of a third and possibly more devastating institutional shock than EMU and the Single Market—the opening up of Eastern

Europe. These shocks are all consequences of the dramatic changes in the postwar international system, primarily the collapse of the East-West confrontation.[24] Tremendous pressures are building within the European regime.

THE EUROPEAN COMMUNITY FACING THREE INSTITUTIONAL SHOCKS

The three institutional shocks facing Europe, in addition to the process of both widening and deepening, produce cumulative asymmetric consequences for the EC member states. Costs are concentrated on weaker (southern) members of the European Community and benefits on richer (northern) EC members. Thus the straightening of the European regime requires some further supranational coordination mechanism and also further modification of state and market relations in Europe. The "New Economic Geography" analyzes the effects of integration processes and bares light on the necessity for further supranational coordination and modification of states and markets in Europe.[25] In particular, the role of international investment in generating concentration of production in integrated areas is insightful.

Let's say there are two countries, both members of the EC, North (N), which has a larger domestic market than South (S). Given the overall dimension of the EC market and the assumption of increasing returns, one of the main assumptions of the Single Market Program is if each country exploited only its domestic market, country N, for the sheer reason of size, would produce at a lower cost than country S. The cost differential in the absence of barriers to factor mobility make production location profitable in country N for firms operating at the European level. However a barrier (T), which offsets the cost differential, maintains a location incentive in country S. The Single Market can be thought of as the elimination of the barrier necessary for offsetting such a cost differential (Krugman 1992).

For example, let's say that country S credibly entered an exchange agreement. In such a case (see, for example, Branson 1990, Krugman 1990), the currency of the "weak" country (S) experiences a nominal and subsequently real appreciation signaling the successful choice of joining a currency agreement to "import discipline." This shifts the cost curve of country S upwards as costs, expressed in North's currency, increase. Then the cost differential rises to the disadvantage of country S.

During enlargement the assumption is made that an increase in market size only benefits country N. This is not an unrealistic assumption, even though it is an extreme one, given the available empirical evidence (see, for example, Collins and Rodrik 1991, Padoan and Pericoli 1993). The increase in market size generates a further enlargement of North's market and a further decrease in its average costs. Clearly the only way the South could resist this combined pressure is to massively restructure. This shifts country S's cost curve down, narrowing the cost gap. South could also introduce some form of "horizontal industrial policy" aimed at improving locational advantages. Without these measures, the "southern" members of the Community, assuming they are committed to the Single Market program and to (some form of) monetary integration, would oppose the rapid accession of the Eastern European economies to the European Community. Alternatively, as seen during the currency crisis that started in the fall of 1992, the fixed exchange rate regime in Europe would be under severe stress and could collapse.

Available evidence on international investment decisions since the launching of the Single Market program (see table 3.3) do not contradict the idea that central locations (for example, the northern economies) have been favored by market decisions and that there is a definite risk of increasing differences between the "South" and the "North" in the European Community.

Table 3.3
Foreign direct investment in the European Community as a percentage of total EC foreign direct investment: country breakdown by destination and origin

Investments from Abroad									
	N	S	P	Gr	Ir	I	G	F	UK	B
1988	9.1	12.9	1.7	1.0	0.2	12.4	2.1	15.6	33.6	9.6
1989	11.1	11.1	2.3	1.0	0.1	3.3	8.8	13.6	9.3	9.3
1990	9.0	15.9	2.4	1.9	0.1	7.3	1.6	14.6	38.5	8.1

Investments Abroad									
	N	S	P	Gr	Ir	I	G	F	UK	B
1988	8.3	1.5	0.1	0.0	0.0	6.7	14.0	17.9	45.9	14.3
1989	15.3	1.5	0.1	0.0	0.0	2.1	14.7	20.1	36.9	7.1
1990	10.9	2.7	0.1	0.0	0.0	6.5	20.7	31.9	19.6	6.2

Source: IMF.

Therefore, if the European regime is to proceed successfully, new forms of support at the European supranational level must be implemented. For example, consequences from the reaction of market forces to the formation of a European regime must be met with new policy attitudes in Europe. Without an appropriate institutional design at level III politics, level II politics will again dominate the scene. The pressures of adjustment would require an increased role of national support policies, which only widens the gaps in national states and markets. The appropriate institutional design is necessary not just to support further progress in Europe but also to make Europe's role within the definition of a new and healthy international system a positive one.

PROSPECTS FOR GLOBAL COOPERATION AND FACTORS OF CONVERGENCE

In theory, conditions for the formation of international regimes do exist in a multipolar, posthegemonic world. In the current historical phase they can also be achieved. Moderate optimism is warranted, however, since international relations can seldom be characterized by pure cooperation or pure conflict. Both elements coexist with their relative weight varying over time.

This framework has indicated at some length that a strong European regime is necessary to achieve global cooperation. A strong European regime requires that level II politics must be melted into level III (regional) politics to decrease the impact of national states and markets on international relations. This is the preference dilution effect. Level II politics tend to be the relevant level of decision-making when level I politics weaken and international regimes are weak. This task is particularly hard in Europe given the existing differences in the state and market of the current members of the European Community (the "core" of the European regime) and the negative impact of the three institutional shocks.

The very nature of the widening and deepening process adds a new dimension to the issue of converging states and markets because it increases the spectrum of national preferences reflected in national state and market differences. This is the preference asymmetry effect. However, this is not only the consequence of an increasing number of potential members of the European regime because of enlargement, but it is also the consequence of cumulative asymmetric shock, which changes the distribution of costs and benefits among existing members of the European Community for participating in the European regime. Consequently, a new European regime must be designed and implemented to overcome these problems and to establish the conditions for more fruitful global interaction. Level I politics requires the successful accomplishment of level III politics.

In terms of forming an international regime, many things differ on the two sides of the Atlantic. The only major regional agreement in America, the North American Free Trade Agreement (NAFTA), deals with trade relations and does not involve forms of supranationalism, although it requires some adjustment by national states and markets. Above all, NAFTA relies on the presence of a regional hegemon, the United States, as the provider of (local) public goods. On the contrary, a positive development in European regionalism requires some form of supranational institution. A true regional hegemon is lacking. Moreover, the deep-rooted differences among European nations could easily lead to a decreased level of cooperation worldwide. The existing regional (level III) politics in Europe would be captured by national, and often purely sectoral, interests. The dispute over agriculture within the GATT clearly shows this. In a stronger and more robust supranational European regime, however, specific interests and national states and markets designed to serve these interests would have less impact on regional politics. In short, benign regionalism worldwide requires that regional politics shift as rapidly as possible from the role of a pure intermediary between domestic and international politics to one of active policy aimed at constructing a global order.

Factors of convergence between blocs exist and may increase the propensity to cooperate as opposed to the propensity to defect. These factors are linked to the forces of integration within the global marketplace.

The most powerful forces of integration are represented by the activities of multinational firms (MNEs). These activities not only increase the degree of economic interdependence but may also lead to (partial) convergence in government polices and thereby contribute to narrowing gaps among national states and markets.

Economic convergence has increased in importance because MNEs are the most powerful vehicles of innovation diffusion. In a world in which technological progress is the key determinant of growth and competitiveness, the diffusion of knowledge is the crucial factor for disseminating the benefits of growth.[26] Knowledge can be considered as a public good par excellence as long as its diffusion is truly general.[27]

MNEs however may be a powerful factor in "political" convergence. As Froot and Yoffie (1991) have shown, MNE activities decrease the incentives of national governments to supply protection for their economies. In a world of highly mobile capital, MNE activities are the typical response to protectionistic barriers. They are erected to protect nations or regions. As the amount of foreign investment in protected areas increases, the rents from protection increasingly accrue to foreigners, for example, to the owners of foreign capital in the region rather than to domestic residents. Hence protectionist governments receive a decreasing share of political support in exchange for their intervention. Thus, their benefit from this form of political exchange decreases. In a world of countries or regions, each pursuing a policy of protection, international mobility of long-term capital tends to weaken the power of such policies and, indirectly, decreases the relevance of differences in national or regional states and markets.

This is true as long as this process is symmetrical, meaning if capital mobility is a two-way activity. When capital flows only in one direction, the government of the region or country where the foreign capital does not penetrate maintains the political benefits of protection. Only when investment flows in both directions do global market forces represent a powerful vehicle of economic integration and of state and market convergence.

If capital integration is not symmetrical, the region where foreign investment does not penetrate looses part of its (potential) benefit from innovation diffusion and the respective growth. Thus in a world with high mobility of long-term capital, new policy incentives emerge, such as incentives to attract foreign MNE activities. One of the possible adverse consequences of widening and deepening in Europe is the creation of locational incentives for international investment that benefit some parts of Europe at the expense of others. Less-favored regions, the South in our example, should respond by implementing policies, such as horizontal industrial policies, which increase the attractiveness of locating foreign MNEs in their region.[28] This is a new European, and not only European, response that leads to changes in national state and market behavior and in their interaction with international regimes.

As Rauscher (1993) shows, lobbying activity, for example, by trade unions interested in creating new employment opportunities, does not necessarily generate a need for more protection. The opposite may even be true since the lobbyists will be pressuring the government for more rather than less openness.

A new form of competition—competition for location sites—will emerge that requires some form of regulation. Regulation is needed because location advantages may be created by the investment of regional development funds, which may be excessive ex-post facto. Moreover, the competition will be "competition among rules," since regulations affecting locational incentives, such as environmental and labor market regulations, already exist. The attempt to attract foreign investment might create incentives towards a "deterioration" of rules, or of rule enforcement. Both of these decrease the private costs of investment at the detriment of social costs, a problem faced by both NAFTA and Europe.

In summary, increasing long-term capital mobility represents a powerful element of convergence since it creates incentives in level II (domestic) politics to pursue more open and less protection-oriented (or more "market" oriented) policies. These policies tend to favor cooperative level III (regional) policies and, even more important, cooperative level I (intraregional) policies. By definition, MNE operations are global and MNEs by themselves, to an increasingly lesser degree, are considered tied to a specific country or region.[29] This international nature reinforces the need, however, to establish level I and level III regimes that facilitate the operation of market forces at a global level. After all, it is a basic premise of this chapter that to operate efficiently a market needs some form of public intervention.

SUMMARY AND CONCLUSIONS

One of the questions asked here is whether one should encourage convergence in the relations between the state and the market in industrialized countries to strengthen the relationship between the United States and Europe. There is an important relationship between the state and the market and the evolution of the international system. When the international system is strong, meaning its ability to provide international public goods and coordination mechanisms to the global market is strong, national governments are partially relieved from these tasks and the individual national economies are in a better position to provide resources to the national governments. Furthermore, differences in national states and markets do not represent a serious obstacle to the evolution of international relations. Hence, instead of convergence in national states and markets, a strong international system is needed.

These differences in national states and markets do become relevant, however, if the international regimes weaken, because then their capacity to provide international public goods is greatly diminished. Therefore, national governments must replace the international regime, partially at least. In this case, as seen today, domestic political considerations tend to prevail over international political concerns. Therefore, national governments are more easily subject to pressures from special interests, and the propensity to cooperate internationally tends to increase.

Important factors of convergence, both economic and indirectly political, are generated by global market forces and in particular by the action of multinational enterprises. Long-term investment, however, exacerbates in some cases, rather than decreases, the differences in national economic performance and as a result calls for diversified state intervention. So, to reap the full benefits of global market forces international regimes must be properly designed.

The current state of U.S.-European relations is further complicated by the emergence of a new dimension of regional politics. Regional politics, which in the case of Europe also involves the attempt to create some form of supranational state and market relationship, may, in principle, support or hinder global cooperation. In the current situation, and for many years to come, Europe will face the consequences of three institutional shocks: the Single Market, Monetary Unification, and the pressure from the former Eastern bloc and Soviet States to join the European Community. How Europe copes with these huge pressures from widening and deepening will influence how Europe participates in constructing a new global system. If sectoral interests prevail in establishing narrowly defined national interests, then international and regional politics will fall prey to nationalistic attitudes. Therefore, it is a common interest to both Europe and the United States to have a successful completion of the next phase in the process of European integration. International cooperation efforts should be directed toward this goal.

ENDNOTES

1. One example are the so called coordination failures as in, cases in which rational individual behavior leads to aggregate suboptimal outcomes. An early investigation of this issue is provided by Akerlof, 1970.

2. We will define institutions as rules and norms governing social interactions, both in domestic and in international relations.
3. An extreme liberalistic view would probably suggest that the market itself would indigenously generate the institutions without any need for the state to intervene.
4. One obvious example is the political business cycle and the electoral manipulation of the economy.
5. It is a definition close to Krasner's, 1983, definition of international regimes.
6. An exchange rate agreement, such as the European Monetary System is an obvious example of a macroeconomic regime. A regional agreement such as NAFTA provides an example of a trade regime.
7. This generates the so-called international political business cycle. For a discussion of this and related points see Guerrieri and Padoan, 1986, and Padoan, 1986.
8. See Ikenberry's chapter in this volume for a survey.
9. One example is the case in which exchange rate instability increases and national responses, in the absence of ex-ante coordination, lead to interest rate wars and generalized deflationary pressures.
10. Consider the role of strengthening European nations and of a weakening United States in determining the collapse of the Bretton Woods system.
11. For a discussion of these differences see, for example, Guerrieri and Padoan, P. C., eds., 1989.
12. See the articles in Oye, 1985, in particular the paper by Axelrod and Kehoane, and Guerrieri and Padoan, 1989.
13. See, for example, Guerrieri and Padoan, P. C., 1988, Mayer 1992, and, in a different theoretical framework, Grossman and Helpman 1992.
14. Snidal, 1991, offers a formal treatment of this point. He shows how international negotiations shift from "positive-sum games" (absolute gains guide individual behavior) to "zero-sum games" (relative gains guide individual behavior) according to the overall performance of the system.
15. For further discussion of their framework refer to "The Regionalism: A Country Perspective," CEPR Discussion Paper No. 715, 1992 by De Melo, J., Panaganiza, A. and Rodich, D. Brada and Mendez, 1993, offer empirical evidence that successful integration processes require the fulfillment of both economic and political conditions.
16. Security reasons have also played a major role in the process of regime formation.
17. Again, security reasons played a crucial role. The commitment to the Atlantic community as a protection against the Communist threat was a fundamental element for the political support of several European governments.

18. See Guerrieri and Padoan, P. C., 1986, and references therein.
19. The attempts to organize a joint management of the global regime were particularly concentrated in the G5 and later G7 summits. Putnam and Bayne, 1984, offer a fascinating account of this still ongoing experiment.
20. For an account of the European Monetary System experience, see Tsoukalis and De Cecco in Guerrieri and Padoan, 1989, and for a more recent assessment, Gros and Thygesen, 1992.
21. For an analysis of the relationship between tradable and nontradable sectors and exchange rate policies, see Frieden, 1991.
22. The Maastricht conditions require, inter alia, that public debts and deficits should not be larger than 60 percent and 3 percent of GNP, respectively.
23. The most notable examples still include the lack of fiscal harmonization and a European industrial policy.
24. Enlargement of Eastern Europe is one of the components of the new wave of the widening process, the other being the association of the European Free Trade Agreement countries to the European Community.
25. See, for example, Krugman, 1991, and Bertola, 1993. I have developed this point more fully in Padoan, 1994.
26. A recent formal assessment is provided by Grossman and Helpman 1991.
27. Innovative activity illustrates one of the typical cases of market failure. If knowledge were a pure public good returns from innovation would not be privately appropriable, hence individual firms would have no incentives in investment in research and development and the provision of the public good would be suboptimal. An appropriate institutional structure designed to preserve property rights is then necessary to create incentives to innovate.
28. One example in Europe of a successful policy of this kind is Spain, see Vinals et al., 1990.
29. It is an open question what is meant by, for example, "European firms" when talking about firms operating in Europe, a large number of which have their homebase in America or Asia.

REFERENCES

Akerlof, G. "The Market for "Lemons": Quality Uncertainty and the Market Mechanism." *Quarterly Journal of Economics,* vol. 84, no. 3 (1970): 488–500.

Axelrod, R., and Keohane, R. "Achieving Cooperation Under Anarchy: Strategies and Institutions." in Oye, K., ed. *Cooperation Under Anarchy.* Princeton: Princeton University Press, 1986.

Bertola, G. "Models of Regional Integration and Localized Growth." *CEPR Discussion Paper,* no. 651 (1992).

Bliss, C., and Braga De Macedo, J., eds. *Unity with Diversity in the European Economy.* Cambridge: Cambridge University Press, 1990.

Brada, J., and Mendez, J. "Political and Economic Factors in Regional Economic Integration." *Kyklos,* vol. 46 (1993): 183–201.

Collins, S., and Rodrik, D. *Eastern Europe and the Soviet Union in the World Economy.* Institute for International Economics, no. 32, Washington, D.C. (1991).

Commission of the European Communities. "One Market, One Money." *European Economy* (1990a).

Commission of the European Communities. "Social Europe." *European Economy,* special issue (1990b).

De Melo, J., Panagariya, A., and Rodrik, D. "The New Regionalism: A Country Perspective." *CEPR Discussion Paper,* no. 715 (1992).

Frieden, J. A. "Invested Interests, The Politics of National Economic Policies in a World of Global Finance." *International Organization,* 42 (Autumn 1991): 425–51.

Froot, K., and Yoffie, D. "Strategic Trade Policies in a Tripolar World." *The International Spectator,* no. 3 (1991).

Gilpin, R. *The Political Economy of International Relations.* Princeton: Princeton University Press, 1987.

Gros, D., and Thygesen, N. *From the European Monetary System to European Monetary Union.* Oxford: Oxford University Press, 1992.

Grossman, E. *Innovation and Growth in the Global Economy.* Cambridge, MA: MIT Press, 1991.

Grossman, G., and Helpman, E. "Trade Wars and Trade Talks." *NBER Working Paper,* no. 4280 (1992).

Guerrieri, P., and Padoan, P. C. "Neomercantilism and International Economic Stability." *International Organization,* 40, (1986): 29–42.

Guerrieri P., and Padoan P. C., eds. *The Political Economy of International Cooperation.* London and Sydney: Croom Helm in cooperation with Methuen, Londra, 1988.

———. *The Political Economy of European Integration: States, Markets and Institutions.* New York: Harvester Wheatsheaf, 1989.

Katseli, L. "The Political Economy of European Integration: From Euro-Sclerosis to Euro-Corporatism." Centre for Economic Policy Research Discussion Paper, no. 317 (October 1989).

Keohane, R. *After Hegemony.* Princeton: Princeton University Press, 1984.

Kindleberger, C. P. "International Public Goods Without International Government." *American Economic Review,* 76 (1986): 113.

Krasner, S., ed. *International Regimes.* Ithaca: Cornell University Press, 1983.

Krugman, O. *Geography and Trade.* Cambridge, MA: MIT Press, Harvard, 1992.

Krugman, P. *Integration, Specialization and Regional Growth: Notes on 1992, Emu and Stabilization.* Mimeograph (1991).

Marques, M. A. J. "Economic Cohesion in Europe: The Impact of the Delors Plan." *Journal of Common Market Studies,* no. 1 (September 1990): 19–36.

Mayer, F. "Managing Domestic Differences in International Negotiations: The Strategic Use of Internal Side-Payments." *International Organization,* 46 (Autumn 1992): 793–818.

Oye, K., ed. *Cooperation Under Anarchy.* Princeton: Princeton University Press, 1986.

Padoan, P. C. *The Political Economy of International Financial Instability.* London and Sidney: Croom Helm, 1986.

———. "The Changing European Political Economy," in Stubbs, R., and Underhill, G., eds. *Political Economy and Changing Global Order.* New York: St. Martin Press, 1994.

Putnam, R. "Diplomacy and Domestic Politics: The Logic of Two-Level Games." *International Organization,* vol. 42, no. 3 (Summer 1988): 427–60.

Putnam, R., and Bayne, N. *Hanging Together, The Seven Power Summits.* London: Heinemann, 1984.

Rauscher, M. "Provision of Public Inputs and the Effect of Successful Lobbying in Open Economies." *CEPR Discussion Paper,* no. 807 (1993): 1–18.

Sebenius, J. "Challenging Conventional Explanations of International Cooperation: Negotiation Analysis and the Case of Epistemic Communities." *International Organization,* 46, no. 1 (Winter 1992): 323–65.

Smith, D., and Wanke, J. *Completing the Single European Market: An Analysis of the Impact on the Member States.* Paper presented at the Annual Meeting of the American Political Science Association, Washington, D.C., August 1991.

Snidal, D. "Relative Gains and the Pattern of International Cooperation." *American Political Science Review.* (September 1991): 738–43

Stiglitz, J. "The Invisible Hand and Modern Welfare Economics." *NBER Working Paper,* no. 3641 (1991).

Vinals, Jose, et al., "Spain and the EC Cum 1992 Shock." *Centre for Economic Policy Research Discussion Paper,* no. 388 (March 1990).

4

Capitalist Conflict? State and Market in America and Western Europe

G. John Ikenberry

INTRODUCTION

The United States and Western Europe confront each other and the emerging world order with different traditions and institutions of state and market. But what is the nature and consequences of these differences? Are there differences in style and policy fashion that evolve and adapt with the times, or are the differences anchored deeper in divergent political cultures, socioeconomic structures, and capitalist organization? The answer has consequences for Atlantic relations. The more fundamental the differences, many analysts would argue, the greater the prospects for conflict and disarray in Atlantic relations. This issue is particularly troubling today because the various circumstances that have masked and overridden these differences—such as the postwar Soviet threat and American hegemony—have disappeared or declined in recent years. Will long standing differences in American and European traditions and structures of capitalism, left obscured during the last half century, finally resurface to threaten political and economic order in the West?

To ask these questions is to revisit old and enduring issues about the nature of advanced capitalism and the trajectory of modern industrial societies. Prophets of capitalist rivalry and division have made pronouncements at every historical turn since the early nineteenth century. Following Marx, Lenin argued that the falling rate of profit, periodic crises of surplus production, and competition over markets and territory in the periphery were fueling division and, eventually, war between capitalist states.[1] Capitalism contained the seeds of its own destruction. Schumpeter argued that precapitalist social formations persisted into the modern capitalist era, and were the source of irrational and destructive political conflicts.[2] The landed and military castes in Japan and the Junkers in Prussia were only the most visible and reactionary forms of militarism and aristocracy to destabilize capitalist society. Building on Schumpeter, Arno Mayer has argued that throughout Europe in the years before World War I, the bourgeoisie was everywhere outflanked by the established nobility and the elites of the ancient regime. The war itself, according to Mayer, had its origins in the reaction of these traditional power-holders to the rising bourgeoisie.[3] In the Schumpeterian view, it was the weakness and incompleteness of capitalism, not its internal contradictions, that were ravaging the Western world.[4]

In more recent years, scholars have advanced different claims about fragmentation and conflict within modern capitalism. One argument is simply that there are distinctive types or models of capitalist organization within the West that have deep roots in political culture and economic history and that inevitably clash. The most systematic claims about different types of capitalism have focused on comparisons between Japan and the United States, but European differences are also noted. Chalmers Johnson argues that Japan has pioneered a fundamentally distinct type of capitalism—what he calls the "developmental" state—that contrasts with the American "regulatory" state.[5] The differences are manifest in the basic logic and organization of state, society, and market. Other writers, such as Robert Gilpin, take this argument a step further and suggest that these differences are reinforcing a long-term movement toward regionalism and conflict among the leading capitalist states.[6]

A very different picture of the relations between capitalist states is provided by other thinkers. Since the early eighteenth century, theorists have argued that the coming of commercial, industrial, or late-industrial society would result in more civilized, liberal, and pacific relations within and between capitalist states. Early liberal theorists argued that the expansion of market relations and trade had a progressive impact on society—stimulating democratic and cosmopolitan tendencies and reinforcing peaceful international relations.[7] Theorists of industrial society in the 1950s and 1960s, such as Ralf Dahrendorf, Clark Kerr, and Raymond Aron, argued that industrialism as such—

whether capitalist or socialist—had a logic that was producing common types of political institutions and economic hierarchies in all the major industrial states.[8] The organizational and technological imperatives of industrialism were generating convergence among all the leading states.[9] Raymond Aron took this argument to its natural conclusion, arguing that in a real sense the world was becoming a single world industrial society.[10]

It is remarkable how utterly diverse these views are of the logic and trajectory of relations among the leading Western capitalist states—ranging from the inevitability of war to the gradual convergence of industrial societies into a single whole. These extreme positions, however, miss important dynamics that arise from the interplay between the developmental logic of advanced capitalism and the autonomous political logic of state and society. Both these forces are at work in shaping American and European orientations toward government involvement in the market and the evolution of Atlantic relations.

This chapter contains three arguments. First, there are basic differences in American and European approaches to state and market—rooted in different historical traditions and different phases and sequences of political and economic development. Second, these differences have had and continue to have consequences for the way in which American and European governments approach problems, interact with each other, and seek to construct the larger Western order. Third, with the end of the Cold War and declining American hegemony, these divergent approaches to state and market are becoming more consequential in Atlantic relations, but this is happening just as these differences are declining. The West may not be moving toward a single industrial society, but the forces of convergence are overpowering the forces of fragmentation and division within the Western capitalist world.

In what follows, the nature and logic of state-market patterns in Europe and the United States are explored, although the focus is mostly on the American case and how American hegemony and global engagement altered and muted these differences. In particular, the impact of these differences on foreign economic policy, Atlantic relations, and the process of convergence are examined.

MODELS OF STATE AND MARKET

In the mid-1960s, Andrew Shonfield presented his classic survey of modern capitalism, arguing that in the years since the Great Depression all the major Western states had transformed their economies into a new type of capitalism. They all had become modern and government-managed capitalist systems that looked very different from what they had been in the nineteenth century. Despite this common transformation, however, Shonfield found striking differences in the way the major Western states organized their economies—reflecting "profoundly different styles of managing the problems of contemporary capitalism."[11] Shonfield and others since the 1960s have sought ways to describe and explain the nature of these differences.

Although each country in the West has its own distinctive traditions and institutions, observers searching for generalities about state-market organization have tended to identify three basic types: a market-oriented model, most fully seen in the United States; a state oriented model, seen in France; and a corporatist model, seen in Japan and Germany. Each model seeks to identify where the center of gravity of economic decision-making lies among the various governmental and societal groups, whether business, labor, banks, parliament, or the executive establishment.[12]

In an influential attempt to develop basic models of state-market relations in the late 1970s, Peter Katzenstein focused on differences in the centralization of power within the realms of state and society. In Katzenstein's view, France had a "strong" state and a "weak" society—political power was highly concentrated within the presidency and the executive ministers. Likewise, the United States had a "weak" state and a "strong" society—political power was diffused in a system of social pluralism.[13] These basic differences in the institutions and relations of state and society, in turn, gave shape to differences in networks of policymaking and the types of policy instruments available to the state for conducting foreign economic policy. In France, policymaking is seen as highly centralized within the state, with the bureaucracy commanding great power and able to use a full range of specific policy instruments to pursue state-led economic goals. In the United States, policymaking is seen as highly decentralized with a dispersal of authority across Congress and the executive establishment, and with executive officials equipped with few policy instruments.[14]

Others have built upon this basic framework. John Zysman has looked primarily at differences in the ability of Western governments to use financial instruments to conduct industrial and growth policies. According to Zysman, there are three basic types of financial systems within the advanced industrial world—each producing a different type of politics of industrial adjustment. One type is a "capital-based" financial system, as seen in the United States, which reinforces an arm's length relationship between government and business. A second type is a "credit-based" financial system, as seen in Japan and France, where government-administered pricing and allocation of credit facilitate government involvement in industrial affairs. Finally, there is a "credit-based" system dominated by financial institutions whose market power gives them influence in industry and produces a negotiated style of capitalism. Germany is an example of this type of system. In each model, the nature of the financial system is different, which in turn produces differences in the role of the state in industrial adjustment as well as wider differences in the politics of economic change.[15]

More recently, Jeffrey Hart has examined American, Japanese, and Western European capacities to encourage industrial competitiveness through research and development, restructuring, and other sorts of industrial policies in the auto, steel, and semiconductor sectors. According to Hart, variations in state-society relations are the key to understanding the difference in success at encouraging industrial competitiveness. These variations in state-society relations fit the overall pattern. France is dominated by the state with low business influence, and the United States is dominated by business with a weak state. Germany and Japan are mixed cases: Germany has a strong business-labor corporatist system with the state playing a more subsidiary role, and Japan has a strong state-business system with labor playing a weak role.[16] In Hart's view, the mixed systems of Germany and Japan are particularly well organized to adapt to changing economic realities and diffusing new technologies and innovations. The United States—with a fragmented state, weak labor, and a highly influential, if somewhat fragmented, business sector is less well organized to pursue industry-specific policies or to build coalitions to pursue competitiveness policies.[17]

When these scholars refer to the distinctive "society-led," "business-dominated," or "regulatory" character of American state-market relations, they are attempting to isolate the general tendencies and biases of American institutions and traditions. Although the models differ in various ways, they agree upon the basic character of American state-market relations: very little of industrial and economic change is state-led; there tends to be an "arm's length" relationship between government and business; the government has little capacity for programmatic or strategic planning; and the government has mostly broad and diffuse policy tools with which to shape industrial and economic change.[18] It is useful to look more closely at the logic of this American model.

AMERICAN PATTERNS OF STATE AND MARKET

In explaining the distinctive characteristics of the American system, many scholars have looked to the sequences and patterns of economic and political development. Building on the work of Alexander Gershenkron, Karl Polanyi, and others, economic historians and political scientists have probed the interplay between processes of industrial change and political development. The result has been the elaboration of a logic of economic and political change that sheds light on the distinctive American system.

The American "Weak" State

The relative weakness of the American state is rooted in the absence of preindustrial bureaucratic structures. From a comparative perspective, the most powerful state bureaucracies are to be found in those advanced industrial nations where monarchical state-building preceded the emergence of representative institutions.[19] Bureaucratic organization became one of the accessories of state-making in continental Europe. The building of states involved the territorial struggles of kings, the incorporation of existing political structures, the extraction of resources from a local population. State-makers first had to raise taxes and deploy military forces, precisely the activities facilitated by bureaucratic staffs. Those political leaders in early modern Europe who developed specialized staffs and bureaucracies gained an "organizational advantage" over their rivals, and so national bureaucracy—relatively autonomous and powerful—attended the successful emergence of the first nation-states.[20]

American national political institutions, by contrast, were established without a strong or centralized state bureaucracy. The absence of an aggrandizing state-maker and hostile external powers goes far to explain the modesty of the organizational center of the American state, which has remained "underdeveloped" because of the persistent prominence of other political mechanisms, such as political parties and the judiciary. As one author notes, "When the new nation was established in 1789, there was a very weak bureaucracy. And because of the decentralized federal system, political parties were essentially locally oriented. Indeed, throughout the nineteenth century, most of the federal bureaucracy was dominated by a locally oriented party system, thus reducing the ability of the central government to penetrate the society."[21]

A system of courts and parties, Stephen Skowronek argues, provided a powerful bulwark for political order in nineteenth-century America. In the last decades of the century a highly competitive national party system set constraints on administrative development. Electoral struggle was the dominant mechanism for the dispensation of political goods and power. Politicians divided the spoils of office, and public policy fed the imperatives of state and local patronage systems. "The creation of more centralized, stable, and functionally specific institutional connections between state and society was impeded," as Skowronek notes, "by the tenacity of this highly mobilized, highly competitive, and locally oriented party democracy."[22] While political parties were emerging in European countries to challenge national administration, American reformers were seeking institutional alternatives to party dominance. State-building in its American setting moved along a unique trajectory.[23]

Much of the history of political reform around the turn of the century involved an effort to forge new bases for government authority. In its early phase, between 1877 and 1900, this reform struggle involved an unsuccessful attempt to establish a national administrative apparatus. Later, between 1900 and 1920, coalitions of reformers were able to break into national office and establish some forms of administrative power. These institutional breakthroughs, established within a rapidly growing and increasingly complex industrial order, brought bureaucratic administration into the political system. But the political strategies for reconstituting national political authority shifted with each presidential administration, and as a result bureaucratic administration remained disbursed and fragmented.[24] The most important new form of administrative authority was the regulatory commission. This institutional creation provided a new center for public authority, but it did so at the expense of centralized bureaucratic capacities.[25]

The postwar growth of the executive establishment saw a continued layering and specialization of the federal bureaucracy.[26] The dispersed, shifting, and fragmentary character of the American state mirrored the pluralism of the larger society. As Shonfield has argued, whereas in other Western nations, "the general trend is to use the aggregation of public power in order to create a coherent force whose significance will be greater than the sum of its individual parts," in the United States, a "curious disorder" resided at the "heart of the American administrative process."[27] Such a pattern of state organization can be found in government-business relations as well.

Government-Business Relations

The distinctive political development of the nineteenth century gave shape to an American state in which a centralized and weighty bureaucratic core was striking by its absence. That sequence of political development, when juxtaposed with the phases of economic development, provides a powerful explanation for patterns of state involvement in the economy. Early industrializers did not face an established, competitive world industrial order, nor were the first industrial sectors, such as textiles, as capital-intensive as the later sectors. Accordingly, private entrepreneurs did not have the same reliance on government for investment needs. As new industries emerged, moreover, already accumulated capital kept investment resources and industrial decision-making beyond the realm of state control.

Those nations that industrialized relatively late ("backward development") faced larger and more complex problems of economic development.[28] The types of industries that backward nations needed to encourage, such as steel, required large-scale and intensive industrial, banking, and state organizations. Large investment and export promotion served to bring the government into a close relationship with industry, and industry's economic dependence on government brought political dependence with it. In late-industrializing Germany, for instance, relations between banks and industry were close. The investment needs of German industrialists, requiring rapid and massive capital expenditures, differed substantially from those of Britain.[29]

Late industrializers tend to have more concentrated financial and industrial institutions, and the state is likely to be more directly involved in industrial development. State dominance does not simply reflect the level of economic backwardness, however, for complex historical antecedents conditioned the state's involvement. For example, the Russian state, without large-scale banking institutions, sought rather unsuccessfully to use direct government intervention in order to force industrialization. German state involvement, on the other hand, was directed at infrastructural investment and the maintenance of political stability.[30]

It was not simply the demands of national economic welfare or efficiency that led the state directly into the economy of late-industrializing countries. A geopolitical logic made national defense important to European state involvement in economy. As one analyst notes, "only the perception of external threat from the prior presence of already industrialized countries prompted considerably enhanced State involvement with industrialization, and explains the rapidity of progress."[31] Geopolitical pressures created incentives for the state to speed up industrialization and encourage industries of strategic importance to the national economy. This geopolitical logic and the unique capital and technological needs of late-arriving industries gave the state an added presence in the economy.

In the United States the early growth and maturity of big business and the strikingly late growth of national public administrative institutions were, as Alfred Chandler argues, crucial for the distinctive American relationship between government and business.[32] Unlike continental Europe, where a state bureaucratic apparatus appeared before large-scale industrialization, in the American business sector growth preceded national institutions. In the crucial early period of industrial development the federal government remained outside the emerging institutional realms of economy and society.

Also of importance to American business-government relations, according to Chandler, was the substantive character of economic growth. External trade was of early importance to European industry, which reinforced collaborative relations with the state by creating incentives to seek government assistance in securing overseas markets. Furthermore, the emerging large firms in Europe tended to be in heavy industry, such as chemicals, metals, and machine tools, and did not have smaller entrepreneurial rivals. In the United States, however, the demands for government involvement were quite different. With large domestic markets and intense conflicts between large business and small merchants and wholesalers, the state played a peacekeeping rather than a promotional role.

Internal conflicts in American business and the limited organizational capacities of the state made antitrust and regulatory tools the state's dominant means of intervening in the turn-of-the-century national economy. Regulatory institutions grew in reaction to rapid growth of large business, first the railroads and later industrial manufacturers, and in a context shaped by contention over vertical integration and intra-business hostilities. Between 1887 and 1914 an institutional framework was established through the Interstate

Commerce Act, the Sherman Anti-Trust Act, and the Federal Trade Commission Act. As Chandler argues, "when the large governmental bureaucracies did come in this country, the basic role of government toward business had already been defined; and that definition developed largely as a response to an influential segment of business community to the rise of modern big business. A comparable response did not occur abroad."[33] After World War I regulation expanded to include consumer goods: automobiles, appliances, packaged foods. The evolution of regulatory control followed a stream of Supreme Court decisions that delineated the proper sphere of regulatory action in setting standards and rates, in market conditions, and in antitrust.[34]

The regulatory approach was particularly compelling in the United States and it came to define the American style of state and market. In a rapidly expanding economy with large internal markets, the government was not confronted directly with a need to cartelize basic industry for the purpose of international competition. Rather, its central task was the incorporation of public interest goals into conflicts among business and between business and society. Strong collaborative relationships between business and government were not necessary. Just as importantly, the slowly evolving federal and state-level political institutions limited the opportunities for government intervention. The regulatory system created new realms of public authority, based on experts and commission staffs, but the relation remained at arm's length, delimited by the courts, and substantially beyond direct congressional and bureaucratic reach.[35] When the institutional structures defining business and government relationships were formed, American government was left with primarily reactive, peacekeeping responsibilities.

THE IMPACT OF AMERICAN GLOBAL ENGAGEMENT

The American rise of global activism during World War II and the Cold War had a dual impact on its distinctive institutions of state and market. On the one hand, the overwhelming hegemonic position of the United States provided opportunities to build a postwar economic order that was more-or-less congenial with its domestic state-market institutions. The United States could make the world safe for a "weak" state and a liberal market economy. On the other hand, the demands of global engagement provided opportunities for American government to expand its capacities for managing a modern capitalist economy and society. In both of these ways, 50 years of American global activism helped "solve" American dilemmas arising from limited government and the primacy of market society, and thereby obscuring the underlying U.S.-European differences in state-market relations.

Externalizing the American System

When State Department officials contemplated the shape of the postwar economic order they envisaged a liberal system built around free trade and limited government. These ideas had been championed by Secretary Cordell Hull since the early 1930s, and within the State Department multilateralism and free trade had become an article of faith. Hull and his colleagues believed that the bilateralism and economic blocs of the 1930s, practiced not only by Germany and Japan but also Britain, were a root cause of the instability of the period and the onset of war.[36] In their initial thinking, these officials desired a "one world" economic order that was multilateral and open—a global economy that was in many ways an extension of the American domestic liberal market economy.[37]

European wartime and postwar governments never fully bought into this conception. Conservative groups and party factions within Britain and elsewhere in Europe remained wedded to imperial and regional postwar economic arrangements. Labor Party officials were concerned about protecting postwar full employment and the emerging welfare state, and they saw American ideas of liberal multilateralism as a threat to European governments pursuing an activist socioeconomic agenda. The result was an odd coalition of the left and the right, which rejected liberal multilateralism in favor of the continuation of the Commonwealth and economic regionalism. As Alfred Eckes noted: "In Britain an unlikely coalition of socialists and conservative imperialists favored this alternative—the socialists to achieve full employment and domestic reform, the imperialists to preserve traditional ties with the Commonwealth."[38] This clash of views reflected deeper differences in overall outlook and orientation of American and European officials as they approached the postwar economic order.

The conflict in American and European thinking was revealed very early during the war when State Department and British officials discussed postwar economic arrangements, which were mandated by the Anglo-American Lend-Lease agreement. John Maynard Keynes, representing the British government, arrived in Washington in the summer of 1941. The Americans were intent on ensuring that the British imperial preference system and bilateral trading agreements of the 1930s were eliminated, and they maintained that the British must agree to eliminate trade barriers and preferential duties. Keynes resisted such agreements, arguing that to maintain economies in balance after the war would require trade restrictions and exchange controls. But, more generally, the British delegation found the American position troubling as it "saddled upon the future an ironclad formula from the Nineteenth Century"—the rigid and mechanical devices of the gold standard and unrestricted trade.[39] In return, the State Department was unsettled by Keynes's seeming unwillingness to commit the British to an open postwar world economy.

Although the State Department and British officials deadlocked on postwar trade arrangements, there were glimmerings of a compromise over the postwar monetary order. While in Washington, Keynes met with Treasury officials who were more taken by Keynesian "new thinking" than free trade. Upon returning to London, Keynes came to the view that perhaps an agreement could be reached on a monetary system that would be expansionary and could keep the trading system open but safeguard against depression.[40] In the following years, the center of gravity of Anglo-American talks shifted from trade to monetary arrangements, and both sides engaged in intensive planning and drafting of proposals, which culminated in agreements at the 1944 Bretton Woods conference. General agreement over the postwar economic order was achieved: it would be more or less open and multilateral, but the monetary order would promote expansionary adjustments to imbalances and the trade system would allow safeguards and abridgments to open trade.[41]

Differences in American and European views on postwar economic order and the virtues of liberal multilateralism persisted into peacetime, despite the agreement at Bretton Woods. These divergent views reflected differences in American and European postwar economic and geopolitical circumstances as well as differences in views about free trade, the emerging welfare state, and the end of empire.[42] American efforts to overcome these differences became a complex process involving the use of coercion, inducements, and compromise.

Three factors were particularly important in securing a loose agreement on the general contours on the postwar economic order. One involved the reworking of the ideas themselves. The United States gradually accepted exemptions and abridgments in trade and financial arrangements, which together allowed a larger measure of national economic autonomy and a stronger role for the state in pursuing full employment and social welfare. These compromises between multilateralism in international economic relations on the one hand and state intervention in the domestic economy and society on the other constituted what John Ruggie has termed "embedded liberalism."[43] The British and other Western Europeans moved slowly to multilateralism, and the United States came to accept the primacy of the welfare state in the organization of the international economy.

Another process that served to yield a loose consensus on postwar economic order was more directly associated with domestic politics in Britain, France, and Italy. The resistance to American liberal ideas after World War II came from both the left and right within Western Europe. Right-wing parties sought to protect the fragments of empire and preserve their status as great powers, a status that liberal multilateralism would necessarily undermine. Left-wing parties feared the erosion of national autonomy and the effects of multilateralism on independent economic planning.[44] Both groups were vocal in seeking to protect and extend programs of full employment and social welfare. European movement toward a loose, liberal multilateral system involved the gradual decline of these positions. On the right, the ravages of war utterly weakened the capacity of Britain and France to maintain the cloakings of colonial empire. Likewise, the watering-down of the liberal multilateral agreements—modifications that served to protect the obligations of the welfare state—served to undercut the impact of the left.[45]

Finally, American occupation and reform efforts in Germany (and Japan) established agreement among the West on a loose system of liberal multilateralism. The U.S. occupation of Germany had a profound impact on German postwar institutions and political values at home and abroad.[46] Efforts to purge old elites and build new democratic institutions had uneven success. The occupation forces found it easier to promote demilitarization and democratization of Germany than to promote the restructuring and decartelization of the German economy. The most enduring economic reforms carried out during the Allied occupation were those of currency reform and trade liberalization. As Henry Wallich argues, "American authorities in Washington and Paris had decided to make Germany into a test or showcase of liberalization."[47] Through these efforts (as well as through less direct programs of political reeducation and cultural exchange) the United

States helped encourage the growth of German political and economic institutions in a direction that was generally congenial with America's larger postwar designs.

Overall, the United States was able to use its commanding position after World War II to significantly structure its external environment in a way that "fit" with its domestic political economy.[48] But the manner in which this was accomplished is a bit surprising: the overt use of American power was less important than the gradual modification and abridgment of the original American postwar designs. It became a mixed system with a lot of room for activist governments and liberal policies.[49] Through the complex process of arriving at an agreement, the free trade and laissez-faire ideas of the State Department became less important than the New Deal thinking that existed elsewhere within the executive branch and the larger political system. But the overall achievement was the same: lowering the barriers to global economic openness, making compromises where necessary. As Charles Maier argues, "The central conflict defining international political economy from World War I until about 1950 was not that between American and Soviet alternatives, between capitalism and communism. . . . Viewed over the whole half century, the American international economic effort of the era of stabilization centered on overcoming British, Japanese, and especially German alternatives to a pluralist, market-economy liberalism."[50] Some of the American and European differences were papered over, but the great internal conflicts between types of capitalism within the West were removed from the postwar system.

Strengthening the State through Global Engagement

The United States did not simply "externalize" its domestic system during its era of hegemony, it also altered its domestic order in response to World War II and the Cold War. Specifically, 50 years of American global engagement became an important impetus for building a stronger state and managing the industrial economy. External involvement helped the United States to "solve"—or at least mitigate—the underlying weaknesses and vulnerabilities of its unique structures of state and market.[51] With the end of the Cold War these domestic advances are put in question.

In the 1930s, the United States had in many respects confronted an "impasse" in its political development. The Roosevelt administration

struggled with the problems of economic collapse and social reform—
doing so within the constraints imposed by a fragmented and limited
government. By the mid-1930s, when the first New Deal had run its
course, the future of American politics involved continued economic
stagnation, rising class antagonisms, and institutional disarray. Despite
the magnitude of the problems and the breadth of the awareness that
change was necessary, the decentralized American political system impeded the mobilization of sufficient political power to restructure core
American sociopolitical and economic institutions.[52] The basic source
of this pre-World War II impasse was rooted in the political institutions
themselves—which were designed to impede central government activity and fragment public purpose—and the nineteenth-century market
economy that eschewed government economic management.

Throughout American history—and in other countries as well—war
has been a catalyst for mobilizing support for far-reaching socioeconomic reform and building a more centralized and capable state.[53] Beginning with rearmament in anticipation of World War II, intensifying
with the war itself, and continuing through the Cold War, American
political development was profoundly altered by global engagement.
These impacts can be seen in various areas: strengthening of the state,
economic management, and social equity and welfare.

World War II and the Cold War profoundly altered the institutional
balance in favor of the center. The demands of war greatly enhanced
the power and prestige of the central or federal government at the
expense of the states. Within the national government, the power of
the executive grew at the expense of the judicial and legislative
branches of government. These wars transformed the president from
being a chief administrative officer in a federal and balanced system
into a paramount leader—or what Arthur Schlesinger called the "imperial presidency."[54] As leader of the free world and sole commander-
in-chief of nuclear forces with global reach, the American presidency
gained an almost monarchical aura.[55] Often this concentration of power
could be brought to bear for domestic agendas as well as national
security—particularly if they could be linked to national security goals,
however tenuous the actual links.

Continuous global engagement also generated requirements for centralized economic management. In the conditions of total war, it was
politically possible for the federal government to effectively manage
labor and capital in the pursuit of maximum economic output. After
World War II, much of the structure of controls was dismantled, but
the techniques of Keynesian macroeconomic management and a

commitment to federal responsibility for full employment were maintained.[56] During the longer Cold War struggle, direct federal involvement concentrated on key technological sectors. In the cases of the atomic energy and aeronautics and space programs, the federal government called whole industries into existence and dramatically forcefed the pace of innovation. During the 1950s, the expansion of the federal highway transportation system and the science and education system were justified as national defense measures.

The Cold War's impact on equity, class, and social welfare was equally significant, if less direct. The expansion of the defense budget and related manpower requirements led to programs and instructions that advanced social equity and the mobility of citizens. Veteran's benefits, particularly the G.I. Bill, opened the door to the middle class for millions of Americans. The post-Sputnik commitment to improve education was a further boost to further broadened social opportunity. Moreover, the pace of racial integration within the military quickened the pace of racial integration within society at large.

The peculiar character of the Soviet Union and communism as antagonists during the Cold War heightened American sensitivity to social and class issues. Unlike the Japanese and German threats, the Communist challenge contained an ideological commitment to build a "worker's paradise" as well as a great power military threat. In this highly charged international environment, the performance of American capitalism in meeting social goals such as full employment, health care, and adequate housing took on expanded significance.[57] The willingness of political and economic elites to make concessions to better the condition of workers and marginal persons was increased by the existence of the Communist movement. At the same time, the fact that the United States was threatened by a Communist state served to delegitimize radical programs and comprehensive agendas for change. Thus, the Communist challenge tended to help American capitalism overcome many of its flaws and instabilities so manifest in the 1930s.

The global struggles of the last 50 years provided the opportunity and necessity for the United States to modernize its economy and polity—rooted as they were in eighteenth and nineteenth-century traditions of limited government and market capitalism. It remains an open question whether, with the end of these struggles, the United States will loose the ability to centralize governmental power and mobilize political purpose.[58] But during the last five decades, the external pressures of world politics helped narrow the differences in American and European systems that along with American hegemonic activities helped to contain divisions within the capitalist West.

THE IMPACT OF DIVERGENT STATE AND
MARKET TRADITIONS

Differences in American and European states and markets—and the change in these differences over time—are most interesting when they impact on Atlantic relations and world politics. Such impacts are difficult to establish because cooperation and discord in Atlantic relations have a multitude of sources, only some of which originate in the deep structures of state and market. But differences in these structures do influence the policy orientation and governmental capabilities in the United States and Europe, which influence Atlantic and international relations.

In some respects, the differences in political economic traditions have only influenced the ways in which governments in the United States and Europe handled the common problems of the industrial age and the global economy. The United States lagged behind most European states in the provision of the social "safety net" of labor laws, unemployment insurance, retirement income, and welfare provisions. Such programs were introduced in European countries earlier and more comprehensively, some scholars argue, because they were championed by state bureaucracies and labor parties, which were agents of change not fully present in the United States.[59] But the United States did develop alternative mechanisms for the provision of social assistance, beginning with the Civil War pension program. According to one account, the United States was not a welfare state "laggard," but rather found ways within the prevailing political order to pioneer social welfare provision.[60] The political structure of the United States did have an impact on the timing and shape of the social safety net, but in its own way the United States joined the ranks of the advanced industrial world as a modern welfare state.

Likewise, the American government has not had the tradition and capacities to pursue specific industrial policies, but it has nonetheless found functional substitutes in military research and development and other types of defense-related spending programs. Even a "weak" state apparently can find avenues and vehicles of action that advance the goals embraced by its incumbents.

Differences in policy orientation, nonetheless, are evident—differences that can lead to conflicting foreign economic policies. As noted earlier, the Western industrial states differ in the institutions and tools available to conduct economic and industrial policy. In his mid-1970s comparative study, Katzenstein distinguished between the Anglo-American commitment to the principles of a liberal multilateralism and the continental European commitment to export-led growth and the protection of national industries.[61] The American liberal tradition and its arm's-length relationship between government and business are reflected in American political structures, but they are also reflected in its postwar liberal economic policy bias. France's extensive government ownership of firms within traditional industrial sectors and use of export promotion as a means to defend and modernize leading industries are aspects of a continental European orientation—although direct government involvement has declined in recent years in France and elsewhere.

These differences in state structures, capacities, and policy orientations were seen in the politics of economic adjustment during the 1970s energy crisis. The United States did not have the readily available capacities to respond internally to the great oil price upheavals and supply problems of the period. This internal "weakness" of the state was seen both in its inability to deregulate oil prices—and thereby expose American consumers to the full costs of oil prices—and in the limitations it found in using government powers to encourage alternative energy supplies. The result was that the United States tried instead to "solve" its adjustment problems through international actions. Initially, this took the form of an effort to rollback OPEC price increases in late 1973, but eventually the international efforts of the American government were focused on the formation of a consuming country alliance aimed at lowering consumption and sharing supplies in emergencies. The International Energy Agency was the institutional result of this energy diplomacy. In effect, American administrations during the 1970s pursued "international" rather than "domestic" adjustments to the oil crisis—finding the state's external capacities greater than its internal capacities.[62]

France and the other European states had different capacities and assets, and their responses differed. France relied on its domestic energy strengths—state-owned or affiliated oil firms were able to maneuver and protect sources of supply and the French government was able to expand its already ambitious atomic energy program.[63] As a recent study concludes, "French political institutions facilitated an interventionist energy strategy."[64] There were strong links between government elites and the oil sector, which had long been an area of state involvement. The government was also leading a big French push in nuclear energy generation. As a result, French policy moved in a different direction than American policy. They had different incentives to cooperate and different capacities to implement agreements.

This pattern is also found in the trade area. As part of a more general postwar American effort to construct a Western world economy that was congenial with American institutions, the United States attempted to get other capitalist states to buy into the American approach to trade liberalization—centered on GATT-sponsored multilateral tariff reductions. These efforts were largely successful. As William Wallace argues, "the United States in the postwar international economy *did* successfully persuade its trading partners to become 'more like us': most impressively in Western Europe through the Marshall Plan, the conditions it laid down and the advisers it sponsored."[65] This unrivaled American commitment to GATT trade liberalization was based partly on its "fit" with its own view of the limited role of the state in the domestic and world economies: that governments should set and enforce the rules while letting markets and prices determine the pattern of trade.[66] But it was also due to the dramatic American economic gains that were possible through trade liberalization.

During the economic crises and malaise of the 1970s and 1980s, American and European governments have all responded with a mixture of selected protectionism, export promotion, and multilateral agreement. Divergent state structures had some impact, but their impact was not overpowering.[67] The Atlantic trade conflicts, at least in part, are caused by the similarity of government involvement in trade policy—responding to threatened industries in the manifold ways that domestic trade institutions make possible.

The absence in the United States of the capacities to pursue industrial policies has had an impact on American trade policy options. When the United States is confronted with foreign trade competition in politically sensitive areas, it is more capable of responding by erecting trade barriers than engaging in government-led competitiveness policies. Lacking more positive trade adjustment mechanisms, trade policy is used as a substitute for industrial policy—mostly taking the form of tariffs and other types of trade barriers. Likewise, some observers have argued that the United States needs to develop a capacity for conducting more systematic and coherent industrial policy so as to be in a position to bargain with European and other trade partners in lowering government involvement on both sides.[68]

Overall, it is easy to identify differences between the United States and Western Europe in the role of the state in the economy and in the capabilities of the state to influence or direct industrial change. It is more difficult to trace the implications of these differences to Atlantic discord or cooperation. There is some evidence that the "weakness" of the American state—manifest as limits and constraints on its interventionist capacities—has provided incentives for it to accomplish its economic goals by attempting to get other states to adjust their policies. In some sense, all states attempt to do this.[69] But the commanding position of the United States since 1945 has provided unusual opportunities to negotiate the terms of economic change abroad rather than at home.

CONCLUSION: CONFLICT, CONVERGENCE, AND INTERDEPENDENCE

The United States and Europe have traveled a common historical path in building modern industrial societies. But they have done so in distinctive ways. Unique political histories and cultures combined with different patterns and sequences of political and economic development to produce remarkably different institutions and traditions of state and market. It remains an unsettled question whether the common trajectory of industrial change and the lapping tides of capitalism are significantly eroding national differences—or whether those national differences are as deeply rooted as capitalism itself.

There are forces operating in both directions, but a stronger argument can be made for the gradual convergence of types of industrial capitalism. The forces resisting convergence are several. One is simply the ongoing play of the competitive state system, which reinforces nationalism and distinctive ideologies of state and market. Of course, even if there is convergence in styles and institutions, such competitive forces might still produce conflict in Atlantic relations.[70] The other aspect concerns the changing position of the United States. The argument was made earlier that World War II and the Cold War were international struggles that forced and enabled the United States to develop more centralized and capable political institutions. With the radical decline in American global engagement it is possible that centrifugal tendencies will reemerge and serve to destabilize Atlantic relations. The weakness of the American system—its difficulty in summoning political purpose—will return and promote disarray. In this view, it is not the convergence of industrial societies that will mark the coming era, but it will be decay and disorder at the core of American industrial society that will impinge on relations within the West.

But other factors and trends point overwhelmingly to continued convergence and integration within the West. Perhaps the most powerful force is the relentless globalization of industrial production and finance. Direct foreign investment has continued to rise dramatically across the Atlantic and elsewhere in the capitalist world. The most dramatic increases of American investment flows into Europe have come since 1985, with the launching of the European single market. In the late 1980s, U.S. foreign investment in Europe eclipsed American investment in the rest of the regions of the world.[71] In return, European investment in the United States has also grown. Britain alone accounts for approximately a quarter of all direct foreign investment in the United States, with the Netherlands, Germany, and France also major investors.[72]

One result of this intensification of interdependence through foreign investment is the gradual erosion of state control over industrial change. In this sense, both American and European leaders are increasingly finding themselves in a similar predicament: the fate of their economies are increasingly out of their hands.[73] Another result is that it is harder for states to invoke nationalistic sentiment and national economic interests to discriminate against foreign economic interests. The internationalization of the American and European economies creates a larger constituency in support of economic openness. Not only do the costs of closure rise in these circumstances, but the political support for doing so is more problematic.

A second factor is the ongoing integration of Europe. European integration is eroding the most statist forms of economic organization on the continent. As Europe has moved to a single market, the role of state ownership and subsidy of industry are under increased economic and political pressure. One sign of this development is the European Commission's proposal for a coherent and uniform approach to industrial policy—the so-called Bangemann report. The report rejects the old choice between "liberalism" and "interventionism" in favor of a view that approves government involvement primarily in the "precompetitive" stages of industrial adaptation, encouraging research and technological innovation.[74] This community-wide intellectual rethinking is unfolding in parallel with economic pressures that naturally arise when industries with state-sanctioned monopolies or subsidies find themselves competing within a larger regional or global marketplace—the state's protective role becomes more difficult.[75]

A third factor that is promoting convergence is more difficult to discern, but it involves the rise in what might be called intersocietal "learning" or "lesson-drawing."[76] Although difficult to measure, there has been a noticeable increase in the use of comparison of national experiences and borrowing of ideas across the advanced industrial world. Some of it appears in political discourse. In recent elections, American presidential candidates have referred much more frequently to the successes and failures of Japan and Western European countries in making arguments about policy change in the United States. This has been most dramatic in the area of health care reform, where the industrial world is seen by many American politicians as one great laboratory of social experimentation. The intensification of comparison-drawing can also be seen in the areas of labor, retraining, education, and privatization. The proliferation of think tanks and policy institutes on both sides of the Atlantic also encourages cross-border lesson-drawing and policy-borrowing. The activities of such organizations as the OECD and the IMF also promote comparison and policy-borrowing.

The rise of Atlantic interdependence—particularly direct foreign investment—is also triggering closer attention to differences in taxation, antitrust laws, and other forms of national treatment. Disputes at this level do reveal quite different approaches to economic management and business law.[77] But these are precisely the types of controversies and antagonisms that arise when economic zones come closer into contact—precisely what the twelve states of the European Community are experiencing as they take halting steps toward greater integration.

Finally, in the battle of the "deep" theories of Western capitalism, those that anticipate greater convergence and commonality in the problems and institutions of state and market can claim some victory. Certainly those that see greater divergence and break down—such as Schumpeter—are having some difficulty in explaining the overall trajectory of postwar Western industrial capitalism. During this period, the most radical and divergent types of industrial capitalism—such as emerged in Nazi Germany and Imperial Japan in the 1930s—have disappeared. Some argue that these radical nonliberal varieties of capitalism might have survived into the late-twentieth century and pioneered a very different trajectory of capitalist history if not for their decisive defeat in World War II.[78] But, in reality, it was not war that spelled the end of nonliberal advanced capitalism as much as the relentless transformation of industrial society itself. It is the permanent revolution of industrial capitalism—the great universal demiurge of our time—that is the final arbiter of this century's politics and history.

ρ 53 Commentary: The Perspective from Germany

Ernst-Otto Czempiel

Since I admire the analyses and share the basic findings of G. John Ikenberry's chapter, "Capitalist Conflict? State and Market in America and Western Europe," my comments will be nothing more than a variation of compliments. I share the author's conviction that the economies of Western Europe and the United States have converged considerably and that they will continue to do so.

The dynamic behind these processes of convergence and partial integration is cross investment. Cross investments between Western Europe and the United States also distinguish the U.S.–Western European relationship from the American position towards the Pacific. Although this may change, since 30 percent of American investments now are made in the Pacific Basin, it will take years before the investments reach the degree they are in Western Europe. The American-European relationship is, and will be, a very particular one. Both sides are economically intertwined; this most certainly influences their respective foreign policy behavior.

As the successful conclusion of the Uruguay Round of GATT, the acceptance by the Clinton administration of the Maastricht Treaty, and the accelerating process of European integration demonstrate, the convergence between Western Europe and the United States is a process that can no longer be explained by the external pressures of the conflict with the Soviet Union. However, it is certainly very early to draw a final conclusion in this regard. Four years of experience after the end of the Cold War do not have sufficient historical weight. It is possible that under the current pressures of economic recession, economic competition between Europe and the United States could increase to the degree that the Atlantic Community might be endangered. In the past, common defense against the common enemy had a beneficial impact on political cooperation, because for the sake of common defense the Europeans accepted the hegemony of the United States and the Americans tolerated a very unequal distribution of the burden. Thus more time is needed before final conclusions are drawn about the effects of economic convergence on political cooperation in the Atlantic context.

Ikenberry is correct that the economic systems and the markets of the United States and Western Europe have converged. It is true that geopolitical pressures have strengthened the arm of the state in industrialization, in particular, and in the market in general. However, this convergence was the outcome of two different, if not inverse, processes. In the United States the political system gained power vis-à-vis the economy, whereas in Western Europe the political system lost power. First of all, the European states in trying to free themselves from the autocratic regimes of monarchs, and facing all throughout the nineteenth century the permanent danger of their security, kept a strong state. There were differences in degree, of course, ranging from Germany down to Great Britain, but compared to the United States, the political systems throughout Europe were much stronger than in the United States. Secondly, being founded as an outright alternative to the "European systems" and with no external threat against its security, the American society could afford a weak federal government. Moreover, to keep the federal government weak and to watch out against any tendencies for the political system to gain power are the most important traits of the political culture in the United States.

These processes began to change in 1945, because for the first time in its history the United States was exposed to an external threat and was challenged geopolitically by the Soviet Union first in Europe and after the mid-1970s all over the world. The United States, therefore, is for the first time in history in the same position that the European states experienced and have grown accustomed to. Interestingly enough, the United States reacted in the same way as the Europeans had in the nineteenth century. Slowly, but definitely, the power of the political system rose whereas the autonomy and the liberties of the society shrunk. The Imperial Presidency, Watergate, and the Iran-contra affair are the most remarkable stepping-stones of this process.

While in the United States the strong state emanated and remains in power, in Western Europe a reverse process has taken place. The societies after 1945 experienced a dramatic push toward democratization and democratic control of the government. Enhanced by the processes of industrialization and rapid economic growth the political emphasis shifted more and more toward the societies. Of course, there was the necessity of defense against the threat from the Soviet Union and the Warsaw Pact, but the burden of defense was shouldered by the United States, the benevolent hegemon. The Europeans had to arm and to pay but they did not have to care. Although the Federal Republic for so many years had been a front state, it afforded to have a societal revolution at the end of the 1960s and the beginning of the 1970s that strengthened democracy and weakened the political system. With some nuances the same is true for most of the other Western European states.

When the Cold War came to an end, the convergence of the United States and Western Europe was achieved by the strengthening of the political system in the United States and by the weakening of the political system in Western Europe. Therefore, if the political structures in Western Europe and in the United States have converged, it is only at this given moment of historical time, because they met each other on their way to different destinations. The United States is heading toward global supremacy and leadership that certainly demands new sacrifices from American society. As a candidate, Bill Clinton promised to abandon the power play of foreign policy and to fulfill the societal demands for more well-being and economic development. However, one year into his presidency he began to emphasize the global leadership of the United States and the military strength it takes to exercise this leadership. The Europeans, by contrast, have concluded the Treaty of Maastricht by establishing a common foreign and security policy. But as their failure vis-à-vis Bosnia bears out, the European governments are not capable of mustering the societal support for a coherent and strong foreign policy. The European political process is weakened and unified.

I agree completely with John Ikenberry's statement that the five decades of the Cold War "helped narrow the differences in American and European systems." However, this narrowing will only remain for a certain period of time after which the United States and Western Europe will again continue in their different directions.

This outcome is, of course, not deterministic. Within the American society there are very strong democratic forces who have only waited for the end of the Cold War to call for the return to traditional American democratic values. However, with the power of geopolitical challenges and the existence of a strong and effective military-political structure that the United States has established over the last forty years, the possibility exists that this structure will not dissolve but will re-create international conditions to justify its existence.

The political development of European societies is also not determined. In Brussels the nucleus of the strong state is already active. British conservative criticism has a point here. Frankly the European Union is nondemocratic, authoritarian, and bureaucratic. If this process is not halted, and if, perhaps, the new division of labor between the United States and the European members of NATO leads to a strong and semi-independent military establishment within the European Union, then the historical movements of Western Europe and the United States might fall in line. But it is impossible to predict that this new synchronization of structural developments in the United States and in the European Union will result in a new dimension of convergence and enhanced cooperation.

Determining whether there is some convergence between the United States and Western Europe or not should include an analysis of the structure of markets and the capability of governments to intervene. But finding evidence of economic convergence, the identity, or similarity of markets and economic subsystems offers no guarantee for ongoing political cooperation. The reason is not that theories submitting a covariation of liberal economies and political cooperation are wrong. They are correct. But they overlook that the structure of economic subsystems is only one factor influencing the foreign policy of states and the resulting patterns of international relations.

The same argument is true within ongoing discussions about the relationship between democratic structures of government and peace. This relationship also is clearly established. Empirical findings show that democracies until now never have fought each other. This adds historical value to the theoretical assumption that democratic structures of government and liberal capitalist structures of the economy are strong incentives for nonviolent conflict solutions in the international system. This influence is valid but not sufficient. As I have discussed elsewhere there are six causes of violence in the international system, with the system of rule (Herrschafts system) and the structure of the economy constituting only two of those factors.

With regard to markets and society, it is even more important to note that neither in the United States nor in Western Europe do we have fully developed democratic systems of government or fully developed markets. Democracy and economic liberalism are still incomplete. Both are influenced, if not dominated, by particular and powerful interest groups. Economic competition between Western Europe and the United States gives ample evidence to the assumption that markets are still imperfect. Many branches of businesses, which are internationally noncompetitive, seek shelter and protection from their respective governments. Furthermore, for almost a decade the GATT Treaty had been hampered by a small number of powerful French and German agro-businesses. In early 1994, the American government intervened internationally in favor of the American aviation industry. We have seen European governments subsidize the steel industry. The list goes on.

In short, while it is true that the economic systems in the United States and in Western Europe have converged, we should not remain content with this degree of knowledge. In the second half of the nineteenth century the European societies had more or less the same structural features and this did not keep them from fighting each other. Of course, the situation at the end of the twentieth century is different from that of 100 years earlier, for the degree of democratization and capitalist liberalism is much higher now than it was between France and Germany after 1871. Historical examples and theoretical insights, however, recommend adding a political framework to the convergence of economic and societal systems. This framework would not only guard against unwelcome developments getting out of hand and producing unnecessary clashes of interests, but it could encourage channels of cooperation, which automatically strengthen convergence and interdependence.

The Atlantic Community would be very well served by a "Supervisory Board of Atlantic Interdependence" divided up into several boards supervising trade, monetary matters, political cooperation, and other issues. Certainly, Atlantic interdependence is not strong enough to permit, nor to demand, integrated institutions. However, even though the Atlantic Community is, and will remain, different from the European Union, the processes of convergence and interdependence need a framework reflecting both the American and European structures, while at the same time strengthening them.

It is precisely because I do share the optimism of G. John Ikenberry with regard to the American-European convergence and the commonality of interests that I argue strongly in favor of institutions, or regimes that cultivate and nurse cooperation as a functional outcome of convergence. It is anachronistic that the only institutionalized link between the United States and Western Europe is a military alliance dominated by political systems. The political systems are, as G. John Ikenberry pointed out several times, not converged but different. The element of convergence lies within the societies and their economic subsystems. Their cooperation should be facilitated and enhanced; they should serve as a watchdog against governmental interference favoring particular interests and groups.

Societal cooperation could be a strong element in harmonizing and synchronizing the development of political structures on both sides of the Atlantic. The interests of the societies are more or less similar. The differences stem from the political systems, which are moving in different directions. The American system is evidently heading toward political supremacy and necessary social change. The cooperation between the Atlantic societies could make it easier for the United States to avoid the pitfalls of the "Primat der Aussenpolitik." What the Europeans—above all the Germans—have learned from the United States after 1945, they could now give back as societal advice to strengthen the liberal tradition in the United States. Political convergence could then be added to the convergence of the market and stable cooperation would be the secured outcome.

ENDNOTES

1. Lenin, V. I., *Imperialism: The Highest Stage of Capitalism* (New York: International Publishers, 1939), originally published in 1916.
2. Schumpeter, J. A., "The Sociology of Imperialisms," in Sweezy, P., ed., *Imperialism and Social Classes* (New York: Kelley, 1951), originally published in 1917. Twenty years later, Schumpeter made a very different—but equally pessimistic—argument about the dynamics and fate of capitalism. See Schumpeter, *Capitalism, Socialism and Democracy* (New York: Harper & Row, 1942).
3. Mayer, A., *The Persistence of the Ancient Regime* (New York: Pantheon Books, 1981).
4. See Hirschman, A. O., "Rival Views of Market Society," in *Rival Views of Market Society* (New York: Viking, 1986).
5. Johnson, C., *MITI and the Japanese Miracle: The Growth of Industrial Policy, 1925–1975* (Stanford: Stanford University Press, 1982). See also Johnson, "Japan: Their Behavior, Our Policy," *The National Interest* (Fall 1989): 17–27.
6. Gilpin, R., *The Political Economy of International Relations* (Princeton: Princeton University Press, 1987).
7. See Hall, J. A., *Liberalism* (London: Paladin, 1988).
8. Dahrendorf, R., *Class and Class Conflict in Industrial Societies* (Stanford: Stanford University Press, 1959); Kerr, C., et al., *Industrialism and Industrial Man* (Cambridge, MA: Harvard University Press, 1960); and Kerr C., *The Future of Industrial Societies: Convergence or Continuing Diversity* (Cambridge, MA: Harvard University Press, 1983).
9. Zbigniew Brzezinski and Samuel Huntington argued that because of the convergent trajectories of advanced industrial states, even the United

States and the Soviet Union would come to resemble each other. See *Political Power: USA/USSR* (New York: Viking Press, 1964).

10. Aron, R., *The Industrial Society* (New York: Simon and Schuster, 1968), esp. pp. 97–105.

11. Shonfield, A., *Modern Capitalism: The Changing Balance of Public and Private Power* (London: Oxford University Press, 1965), p. 123.

12. On this general comparative institutional approach, see Peter Hall, *Governing the Economy: The Politics of State Intervention in Britain and France* (New York: Oxford University Press, 1986), Chapter One.

13. The original framework was presented in Katzenstein, P. J., "International Relations and Domestic Structures: Foreign Economic Policies of Advanced Industrial States," *International Organization,* vol. 30, no. 1 (Winter 1976): 1–46. For a more developed version of the argument, see Katzenstein, P.J., ed., *Between Power and Plenty: Foreign Economic Policies of Advanced Industrial States* (Madison: University of Wisconsin Press, 1978).

14. See Katzenstein, P. J., "Conclusion: Domestic Structures and Strategies of Foreign Economic Policy," in Katzenstein, ed., *Between Power and Plenty.*

15. Zysman, J., *Governments, Markets, and Growth: Financial Systems and the Politics of Industrial Change* (Ithaca: Cornell University Press, 1983), p. 18.

16. Hart, J., *Rival Capitalists: International Competitiveness in the United States, Japan, and Western Europe* (Ithaca: Cornell University Press, 1992).

17. Hart, J., *Rival Capitalists,* Chapter Six.

18. See Vogel, D., "Why American Businessmen Distrust Their State," *British Journal of Political Science,* vol. 8 (1978): 45–78; and McCraw, T. K., "Business and Government: The Origins of the Adversary Relationship," *California Management Review,* vol. 26, no. 2 (Winter 1984): 33–52.

19. See Moore, B., Jr., *Social Origins of Dictatorship and Democracy: Lord and Peasant in the Making of the Modern World* (Boston: Beacon, 1966); Bendix, R., *Kings and People: Power and the Mandate to Rule* (Berkeley: University of California Press, 1978); Hans Rosenberg, *Bureaucracy, Aristocracy and Autocracy: The Prussian Experience, 1660–1815* (Boston: Beacon, 1958); and Mann, M., *The Sources of Social Power: The Rise of Classes and Nation-States, 1760–1914,* vol. II (New York: Cambridge University Press, 1993).

20. This argument is made by Charles Tilly, *Coercion, Capital, and European States, AD 990–1990* (Cambridge: Basil Blackwell, 1990). See also his

"Reflections on the History of European State-Making," in Tilly, *The Formation of National States in Western Europe* (Princeton: Princeton University Press, 1975), p. 30.

21. Hollingsworth, R., "The United States," in Grew, R., ed., *Crisis of Political Development in Europe and the United States* (Princeton: Princeton University Press, 1978), p. 165.

22. Skowronek, S., *Building a New American State: The Expansion of National Administrative Capacities, 1877–1920* (New York: Cambridge University Press, 1982), pp. 39–40.

23. This argument is made is the area of socioeconomic and welfare policy in Skocpol, T., *Protecting Soldiers and Mothers: The Political Origins of Social Policy in the United States* (Cambridge, MA: Harvard University Press, 1993). See also Skocpol, T., and Ikenberry, G. J., "The Political Formation of the American Welfare State in Comparative and Historical Perspective," *Comparative Social Research*, vol. 6 (Greenwich, CT: JAI Press, 1983).

24. See Skowronek, *Building a New American State*, pp. 165–76.

25. See Katznelson, I., and Prewitt, K., "Constitutionalism, Class, and the Limits of Choice in U.S. Foreign Policy," in Fagen, R., ed., *Capitalism and the State in U.S.-Latin American Relations* (Stanford: Stanford University Press, 1979).

26. Heclo, H., "Issue Networks and the Executive Establishment," in King, A., ed., *The New American Political System* (Washington, D.C.: American Enterprise Institute, 1978): 87–124.

27. Shonfield, *Modern Capitalism*, pp. 318–19.

28. Gerschenkron, A., "Economic Backwardness in Historical Perspective," in Gerschenkron, A. ed., *Economic Backwardness in Historical Perspective: A Book of Essays* (Cambridge, MA: Harvard University Press, 1962), pp. 5–30.

29. Gerschenkron, A., "Economic Backwardness in Historical Perspective," p. 14. The argument has been developed by Kurth, J. R., "The Political Consequences of the Product Cycle: Industrial History and Political Outcomes," *International Organization 33* (Winter 1979): 1–34, and Kurth, J. R., "Industrial Change and Political Change: A European Perspective," in Collier, D., ed., *The New Authoritarianism in Latin America* (Princeton: Princeton University Press, 1979).

30. Gerschenkron, A., "Economic Backwardness," pp. 16–21. Also see Gourevitch, P., "The Second Image Reversed," *International Organization*, vol 32, no. 4 (Autumn 1978): 881–992.

31. Sen, G., *The Military Origins of Industrialization and International Trade Rivalry* (New York: St. Martin's Press, 1984), p. 79.

32. Chandler, A. D., Jr., "Government versus Business: An American Phenomenon," in Dunlop, John T., ed., *Business and Public Policy* (Cambridge: Harvard University Press, 1980); also Chandler, A. D., *The Visible Hand: The Managerial Revolution in American Business* (Cambridge, MA: Harvard University Press, 1978); and Chandler, A. D., "The Coming of Big Business," in Woodward, C. V., ed., *The Comparative Approach to American History* (New York: Basic Books, 1968), pp. 220–35.

33. Chandler, A. D., "Government vs. Business," pp. 4–5, 10–11.

34. See Keller, M., "The Pluralist State: American Economic Regulation in Comparative Perspective, 1900–1930," in McCraw, T. K., ed., *Regulation in Perspective* (Cambridge, MA: Harvard University Press, 1981), pp. 74–94.

35. As one analyst notes: "While most other states in capitalist societies increased their role and power as industrialization proceeded, the authority of the American state declined and its size remained relatively small. When seen in comparative terms, it simply had a less necessary role to play." Vogel, D., "Why Businessmen Distrust Their State," *British Journal of Political Science*, 57.

36. Pollard, R. A., *Economic Security and the Origins of the Cold War, 1945–1950* (New York: Columbia University Press, 1985), pp. 11–12.

37. The sequence of American proposals and compromises are outlined in G. J., Ikenberry, "Rethinking the Origins of American Hegemony," *Political Science Quarterly*, 104 (Fall 1989): pp. 375–400. On the initial "one world" conception of American postwar thinking, see Gaddis, J. L., "Spheres of Influence: The United States and Europe, 1945–1949," in J. L. Gaddis, *The Long Peace: Inquiries into the History of the Cold War* (New York: Oxford University Press, 1987), pp. 48–71.

38. Eckes, A. E., Jr., A Search for Solvency: Bretton Woods and the International Monetary System, 1941–1971 (Austin: University of Texas Press, 1975), pp. 64–65.

39. "Memorandum of Conversation by the Assistant Secretary of State (Acheson)," 28 July 1941, in Perkins, E. R., ed., *Foreign Relations of the United States, 1941*, vol 3, (Washington, D.C.: Government Printing Office, 1959), p. 11. These exchanges are discussed in Ikenberry, G. J., "A World Economy Restored: Expert Consensus and the Anglo-American Postwar Settlement," *International Organization*, 46, 1 (Winter 1992): 312–15.

40. Eckes, A. E., Jr., *A Search for Solvency*, p. 65.

41. See Gardner, R., *Sterling-Dollar Diplomacy: Anglo-American Collaboration in the Reconstruction of Multilateral Trade* (Oxford: Clarendon Press, 1956).

42. See Watt, D., "Perceptions of the United States in Europe, 1945–1983," in Freedman, L., ed., *The Troubled Alliance: Atlantic Relations in the 1980s* (New York: St. Martin's Press, 1983), pp. 29–30. On European and American differences concerning regionalism and blocs, see Calleo, D. P., and Rowland, B. M., *America and the World Economy: Atlantic Dreams and National Realities* (Bloomington: Indiana University Press, 1973).

43. Ruggie, J. G., "International Regimes, Transactions, and Change: Embedded Liberalism in the Postwar Economic Order," *International Organization,* vol. 36, no. 2 (Spring 1982): 379–416. See also Ruggie, J. G., "Embedded Liberalism Revisited: Institutions and Progress in International Economic Relations," in Adler, E., and Crawford, B., eds., *Progress in Postwar International Relations* (New York: Columbia University Press, 1991): 130–221.

44. See Gardner, *Sterling-Dollar Diplomacy,* pp. 31–35.

45. This argument is developed in Ikenberry, G. J., and Kupchan, C., "Socialization and Hegemonic Power," *International Organization,* 44, 3 (Summer 1990): 300–303.

46. See Montgomery, J. D., *Forced to be Free: The Artificial Revolution in Germany and Japan* (Chicago: University of Chicago Press, 1957).

47. Wallich, H. C., *Mainsprings of the German Revival* (New Haven: Yale University Press, 1955), p. 372.

48. This argument is made in Krasner, S., "United States Commercial and Monetary Policy: Unravelling the Paradox of External Strength and Internal Weakness," in Katzenstein, P. J., ed., *Between Power and Plenty,* pp. 51–87; and also Schurmann, F., *The Logic of World Power: An Inquiry into the Origins, Currents, and Contradictions of World Politics* (New York: Pantheon Books, 1974).

49. See Strange, S., "The Persistent Myth of Lost Hegemony," *International Organization,* vol 41, no. 4 (Autumn 1987): 551–574.

50. Maier, C., "The Two Postwar Eras and the Conditions for Stability in Twentieth-Century Western Europe," in Maier, C., ed., *In Search of Stability: Explorations in Historical Political Economy* (New York: Cambridge University Press, 1987), p. 183.

51. This argument is developed at length in Deudney D., and Ikenberry, G. J., "After the Long War," *Foreign Policy* (Spring 1994): 21–36.

52. See Karl, B. D., *The Uneasy State: The United States from 1915 to 1945* (Chicago: University of Chicago Press, 1983); and Skowronek, *Building a New American State.*

53. On this general phenomenon, see Tilly, C., *Coercion, Capital, and European States*; Shaw, M., ed., *War, State, and Society* (New York: St. Mar-

tin's Press, 1984); McNeill, W. H., *The Pursuit of Power* (Chicago: University of Chicago Press, 1982); and Stein, A., *The Nation at War* (Baltimore: Johns Hopkins Press, 1978).

54. Schlesinger, A. M., Jr., *The Imperial Presidency* (Boston: Houghton Mifflin, 1973).

55. This phenomenon has not been inadequately studied. Some work has been done on the rise of the American "national security state" and the "nuclear presidency." See Yergin, D., *Shattered Peace: The Origins of the Cold War and the National Security State* (Boston: Houghton Mifflin, 1977); and Michael Mandelbaum, *The Nuclear Revolution: International Politics Before and After Hiroshima* (New York: Cambridge University Press, 1981).

56. Salant, W. S., "The Spread of Keynesian Doctrines and Practice in the United States," in Hall, P. A., ed., *The Political Power of Economic Ideas: Keynesianism Across Nations* (Princeton: Princeton University Press, 1989); and Stein, H., *The Fiscal Revolution in America* (Chicago: University of Chicago Press, 1969).

57. In the 1960 presidential debates, candidate John F. Kennedy made this argument explicitly.

58. See the speculations in Deudney, D., and Ikenberry, G. J., "After the Long War."

59. See Heclo, H., *Modern Social Politics in Britain and Sweden* (New Haven: Yale University Press, 1974).

60. See Skocpol, T., *Protecting Soldiers and Mothers.*

61. Katzenstein, P. J., "Conclusion: Domestic Structures and Strategies of Foreign Economic Policy," in Katzenstein, P. J., ed., *Between Power and Plenty,* pp. 297–301.

62. This is the argument in Ikenberry, G. J., *Reasons of State: Oil Politics and the Capacities of American Government* (Ithaca: Cornell University Press, 1988).

63. See Feigenbaum, H., *The Politics of Public Enterprise: Oil and the French State* (Princeton: Princeton University Press, 1985).

64. Feigenbaum, H., Samuels, R., and Weaver, R. K., "Innovation, Coordination, and Implementation in Energy Policy," in R. Kent Weaver and Bert A. Rockman, eds., *Do Institutions Matter?* (Washington, D.C.: The Brookings Institution, 1993), p. 75.

65. Wallace, W., "The USA and Europe in the 1990s: A Changing America in a Transformed World Order," Report for Commission of the European Communities, January 1993, p. 30.

66. See Goldstein, J., "Ideas, Institutions, and American Trade Policy," *International Organization,* 42 (Winter 1988): 179–218.

67. This is the argument made by Milner, H., "Maintaining International Commitments to Trade Policy," in Weaver R. K., and Rockman, B. A., ed., *Do Institutions Matter?*.

68. See Zysman J., and Cohen, S. S., "Double or Nothing: Open Trade and Competitive Industry," *Foreign Affairs,* 61 (Summer 1983): 1113–1139. This is an implicit argument in Tyson, L., *Whose Bashing Whom? Trade Conflict in High-Technology* (Washington, D.C.: Institute for International Economics, 1993).

69. See Ikenberry, G. J., "The State and Strategies of International Adjustment," *World Politics,* 39 (October 1986): 53–77.

70. It is possible that convergence in styles and institutions of industrial society could itself fuel conflict. The notion is that becoming more similar makes the two parties more directly in competition with each other.

71. Jackson, J. K., "American Direct Investment in the European Community," in "Europe and the United States: Competition and Cooperation in the 1990s," Committee Print of the U.S. House Committee on Foreign Affairs, June 1992, pp. 271–92.

72. See Wallace, W., "The USA and Europe in the 1990s," pp. 26–27.

73. See Strange, S., *States and Markets* (New York: Blackwell, 1988).

74. European Commission, "The European Commission is Proposing a Coherent Industrial Policy Concept for the Twelve," news release, Brussels, 30 October 1990.

75. This is a major argument in Olson, M., *The Rise and Decline of Nations* (New Haven: Yale University Press, 1982).

76. See Rose, R., "What is Lesson-Drawing?" *Journal of Public Policy,* 11 (1991): 3–30. See also Rose, R., *Lesson-Drawing Across Time and Space* (Tuscaloosa: University of Alabama Press, forthcoming).

77. See Jackson, J. J., "American Direct Investment in the European Community."

78. See Mann, M., "Citizenship and Ruling Class Strategies," *Sociology,* 21 (August, 1987): 339–54.

II
———

The Purposes of Public Action

5

Purposes of Public Action: Provision of Collective Goods and Redistribution of Wealth, A European View

Susan Strange

A general European view on the proper relations of state to economy and society is, of course, an impossibility. Over the past two years, European opinions have seldom, if ever, been more divided. The Germans wanted to recognize Croatia; the French wanted to keep Yugoslavia united. In the Persian Gulf War, the British were enthusiastic allies of America; the Germans wanted no active part in it. Most Europeans do not want the whales killed; the Norwegians still refuse to stop their fishermen from doing so. Most Europeans want interest rates lowered to get growth going again; the German central bank stubbornly refuses any but trivial cuts. And there have been defections from several cooperative enterprises. Germany withdrew from the development of a new European fighter aircraft. Philips withdrew from the European Community's ESPRIT research program. Even on a practical venture like the Channel Tunnel, President Mitterand cannot resist jeering at the British. Opening the new TGV link from Paris to Lille he said passengers would be able to race across northern France and through the tunnel, "and then be able to daydream at very low speed, admiring the English landscape and countryside" on their way to London. It was a good example of divergent opinions in Europe on the responsibility of governments for financing hi-tech infrastructure.

About the only thing, these days, on which Europeans still agree is that they wish to remain different. They want a Europe united in peace and friendship, with minimal barriers between countries. But except for a small minority of federalist enthusiasts, they do not want a centralized, homogenized United States of Europe. It now seems that the Europtimism of the mid-1980s, after the adoption of the plan for a Single European Market (SEM), was premature. So, probably, was the American revival of interest in the European Community since 1986. All over the United States university centers of European studies were set up and student courses initiated in anticipation of big changes in the political landscape of Europe. Such changes, it now seems, are going to be slow in coming.

Now, although the Commission of European Communities claims that most of the 234 directives called for in the Single European Act have now been approved by member governments, everyone knows that implementation is something else, especially in the southern members of the European Community. And, paradoxically, some of the current Europessimism is due precisely to those directives concocted by Brussels. Just the same industrialists whose businesses were being hindered by national barriers and who were therefore the most important allies of Cockcroft and Delors in getting the SEM launched, now complain bitterly about the arrogance of the Eurocrats and the frustration and irritation caused to industry by their "pettifogging" regulations. The Brussels philosophy, observed one CEO, appears to be summed up in the motto, "If it moves regulate it; if it doesn't move regulate it."[1] A special New Year edition of the *Financial Times* devoted to the state of the European Community carried a leg-pulling article headlined, "Fishermen Must Wear Hairnets," listing some real and some apocryphal directives coming out of Brussels.

All I can do, therefore, is to offer a personal view, as a European, on the subject of European and American perceptions of the appropriate relations between government and the market economy. I make special reference to the provision of collective goods and the redistribution of wealth.

In reality the differences between America and Europe are not as divergent as many suppose. The differences are more in the minds of Americans and Europeans than in the nature of their respective policies toward agriculture or industry, trade, investment, or finance. Americans, for instance, liked for a long time to think that they did not have an industrial policy; now they concede that international competition may oblige the government to adopt a "strategic trade policy," which amounts in practice to much the same thing. It follows from this that transatlantic differences of view on state's market relations, such as do still exist, are not the real problem. In my estimation, the real problem—for governments, for firms, and other social associations—is the growth of uncertainty over the locus of authority in a market economy. In the days when national economies were much less interdependent, much less penetrated by outside influences on their trade, investment, and information than they are today, the authority of government (at least in most states for most of the time) was clear enough. Today, that authority in most states and on many highly political issues is compromised and unclear.

There are therefore three preliminary points to be made that reinforce this contention. The first point is that opinions on this subject have tended to differ more sharply over time than over space—not only across the Atlantic but also for that matter across the Pacific or the Equator. Certainly in all the advanced industrialized countries, there seems over more than a century to have been a kind of cycle of opinions, first for and then against state intervention in the economy. The cycle has affected both Europeans and Americans.

The second point is that the shift in opinions has often been more extreme than the shift in actual policies. There is a kind of built-in resistance to change in institutions, in statutes, and in bureaucracies that tends to moderate the cyclical shifts in prevailing opinions.

The third point is perhaps more fundamental and more controversial. It is that these shifts over time may seem to have been the result of political debate and intellectual argument within each country or continent. But in reality, they are much more the product of structural change in the world market economy and world society. These changes have affected the four major structures of the international political economy—the structures of security, production, finance, and of knowledge, including in the latter both the content—ideas and beliefs—of knowledge and the technological means of its creation, communication, and dissemination. Thus, changes in the knowledge structure reflect changes in the security structure, in the production structure, and in the financial structure of the world economy. Each can be conceived as a separate structure within which indirect power is exercised over governments, society, and operators in the market. These structural changes—what the French refer to rather imprecisely as the "force des choses"—produce pressures on society and government to which, in America and in Europe, both managers and public policymakers are obliged to respond.

I would define structural power as the ability of some persons, groups, or institutions to influence the ways in which others conduct their business, private or public, or to influence the way others manage their social and political relations so that there is a significant change in the options open to these others. Their range of options may be extended or restricted; or it may be extended in one direction and at the same time restricted in another. Either way, these others are still formally free, but the costs and/or the risks of going outside the defined range of options will be unacceptably high. Structural power can be, and often has been, exercised by states or the agents of states, especially when interstate agreements are made or institutions established. For example, airports controlled by states have at any given time a limited number of slots or parking bays for incoming aircraft. These are allocated by the airport authority. Competing airlines can be allocated slots or they can be excluded. Competition in the sector can be increased or limited through structural power.

Structural power can thus be exercised negatively, by not acting, just as much as it can be exercised positively. An example is the intervention by central banks, or their failure to intervene, in foreign exchange markets. Exchange rates affecting business prospects and personal losses and gains can be treated to "benign neglect" or to active intervention. It is worth noting, however, that structural power in this case has significantly shifted as a result of the negative exercise of power by states in abandoning Bretton Woods rules of fixed rates and allowing freer movement of capital away from central banks and toward the markets and market operators.

Structural power can also be delegated to or left in the hands of nonstate authorities. The management of the production, sale, and purchase of diamonds for a hundred years was left to a private cartel, run from South Africa but accepted as a legitimate authority even by the old USSR. It can also be exercised unconsciously, without deliberate intent to cause pain or harm to others. An example would be the 1934 Silver Purchase Act passed by the U.S. Congress to relieve the plight of the western silver states. Its deflationary consequences for China and the Latin American states with silver-based currencies were much greater than any good it did for a few American silver mines, but none of these external consequences was ever anticipated or intended.

Increasingly, because of the ever-increasing complexity and power of world markets, states are delegating authority that they are either unable or unwilling to exercise themselves to professionals in the private sector—to lawyers and accountants, management consultants, insurers, and risk analysts, and to scientific and medical experts of many kinds. If we recall the definition of structural power over outcomes as the ability to change the range of options open to others, there can be little doubt that in the world market economy, nonstate agents of many kinds now share this power with the agents of states.

The nature of power—an apparently abstract and philosophical matter—actually has important practical implications. So it is worth emphasizing that almost all the theorists in political science and in sociology as in philosophy proper have made a distinction between direct or coercive power and indirect or contextual power. I have called the first relational power and the second structural power. Michael Mann calls the first authoritative power and the second diffused power (Mann 1989). Stephen Lukes distinguishes three levels of power of which the last two can both be called structural or contextual. But the labels are less important than the simple point that power can be exercised by direct force or threat, whether explicit or implicit, and through a structure, a way of organizing social economic or political relations between people.

The argument I make (Strange 1988; Stopford and Strange 1991) is that four structures of the world system, or international political economy (the structures of security, production, finance, and of knowledge), are necessarily interdependent, each being influenced by changes in the other structures.[2]

This, however, is only prologue—necessary but incidental—to the main purpose of this chapter. This chapter argues the case for a new, transnational framework of analysis of the world system. Instead of the statecentric one that is still conventional both in the study of international relations and of international economics we need one that looks at the international economy in terms of world society and world markets. The conventional approach sees the problem in terms of what Government X should do, or not do, in relation to the national economy of Country X. A political economy approach analyzes situations not only in terms of states but of authorities of all kinds. The basic assumption is that the problems facing different states are increasingly common problems. The solutions to be found are also likely to be common solutions—transnational solutions. They may be found through bilateral negotiation—as in bilateral investment treaties. Or they may be found through multilateral intergovernmental agreements, institutions, or "regimes"—as in the case of the air transport and traffic management. The basis for the solution may be coordination and standardization of national policies, such as by everyone adopting a metric system of weights and measures or a standard system of classifying traded goods. Or it may be by "follow the leader" behavior in which other states copy the solutions chosen by the more powerful ones. Or it may be through governments allowing some nonstate authority to coordinate action in support of a solution—as with the choice of venue for the Olympic Games.

What we need, in short, is a conceptual framework in which we ask not only what needs to be regulated in an integrated world market economy, and why—on what grounds—but also who or what authority is actually intervening, or should intervene—in market or society—and by what means. Much current discussion of the formation of trade blocs, or of the coming clash of civilizations misses the point. Blocs and civilization are both largely myths of an imaginative faculty unable to rise above the conventional notions of international, statecentric problematics.

This chapter seeks to raise this question of the paradigm that is appropriate to the debates and the issues of our times. For it is impossible to discern the issues and thus to design research projects and programs if we are bound by an obsolete and inappropriate paradigm, whether of international relations, international economics, business management, or sociology. Before we get to this question, however, let me begin by expounding the reasoning behind my three preliminary points.

CYCLES OF OPINION

The first point is that opinions in industrialized countries have varied more over time than they have varied over distance. For a start, recall the degree to which opinion in the United States accepted "socialist" policies during the World War II. Advancing far beyond the policy changes brought in by Roosevelt's New Deal, the U.S. government created an economy that was very largely state-directed and state-controlled. By the first quarter of 1945, no less than 42 percent of total production in the country was for the federal government. Between 1941 and 1945, the federal government added 12 million Americans to its payroll. Large sections of industry were state-owned and controlled. This included half the total capacity for production of aluminum, half the added capacity in the steel industry as well as a large part of the shipbuilding business. In synthetic rubber, for which capacity was vastly expanded, almost all was entirely financed and owned by the government and leased back to the operators at a peppercorn rent—a dollar a year (Vatter, 1985). Market forces were suppressed as the government introduced price controls, including rent controls (Galbraith 1958). At the same time, as in the USSR or Germany, labor was directed and much stricter rules imposed on employers regarding working conditions, the right to organize unions, wage negotiations, and safety standards. All these policies were apparently endorsed by American voters in the 1944 elections.

It may be objected that the exigencies of war were exceptional, and that these explained the very great extension of state control over the economy. But that is to concede that policies are contingent on structural change in the arrangements to provide security and that therefore there are no absolute rules or principles regarding the appropriate relation of government to economy, either in America or in Europe or Japan. If war is justification enough for state intervention, we may argue that conditions loosely described as "trade war," in which competition is fierce between the economies of industrialized countries, also call for more state intervention in matters of trade (Richardson 1991).

At any rate, the more general point is that the high point of state intervention in the United States in 1945 was only the peak of a cycle that ran from about 1920 to about 1980. Starting after World War I, state intervention began to increase in the 1930s, and began to decrease after 1945. But even in the 1950s, a great deal of New Deal regulation—of banking and labor relations, for example—persisted. And parts of the infrastructure of power and water supplies remained in federal hands, as did effectively large parts of industry working for the U.S. Department of Defense.

Meanwhile, the return of economic decision-making to the private sector after 1945 was mirrored by a similar though lesser retreat by European governments. Recall that while the British postwar Labor government had nationalized the Bank of England, it was a Labor President of the Board of Trade who, not long afterward, took the far more significant decision to reopen the City of London as a marketplace for commodities and for credit instruments. A market for capital being the core element in a market economy, this was a significant retreat from a wartime peak of state control in which the city functioned mainly as a vehicle for the sale of government securities. And in the rest of Europe, encouraged admittedly by the Economic

Cooperation Agency set up under the Marshall Plan, European governments steadily retreated from their control over trade, progressively turning over more and more of it from government to private hands.

One could point, moreover, to an earlier cycle beginning about the 1870s on both sides of the Atlantic and leading by the turn of the century to the agitation by the muckrakers and trustbusters in the United States for greater public control over the excesses of private business. In Britain, there was a parallel move, begun perhaps by Disraeli with educational reform in the 1870s, and reaching its crescendo in the early 1900s when the Liberals and the founders of the Labor Party acted to restrain the powers of privilege exercised by the House of Lords, to reform safety standards in industry, and to lay the basis of a public welfare system.

In short, it almost seems as though in all market economies, there is a recurrent tendency for policies to oscillate between underregulation and overregulation. At one point, the unacceptable face of capitalism leads to demands that public authority be used to bridle and restrain its excesses in society. Then at the opposite point in the cycle, there is a cry to loosen the handicaps perceived to be hindering efficiency and competitiveness in business; and regulation gives way to deregulation.

POLICIES LAG OPINIONS

The second point is that the swing in the pendulum of opinion is usually longer and stronger than the swing in actual policies. As noted earlier, the swing to socialism in postwar Britain stopped short of state allocation of credit as practiced in Japan or, later, South Korea. It stopped short of closing private secondary schools or abolishing the monarchy as the keystone holding up the British class system. And in America the postwar swing away from socialism looked much more violent than it really was, mainly because the outbreak of the Cold War with the Soviet Union allowed the associates of Joe McCarthy freely to conduct their vicious witch-hunt against New Deal liberals and "pinkos." Yet New Deal regulations on banks, industrial relations, and other matters stayed, as did the TVA and the powers of the department of the Interior.

Again, in Britain when the tide started to turn against Labor in the mid-1950s, the result was a compromise, known as Butskellism, in recognition of the welfare achievements of Prime Minister Gaitskell and the educational reforms of Conservative Rab Butler. Such lags of policy behind opinion suggest that many of the hopes of radical social and fiscal reforms under the Clinton administration are destined for disappointment.

LA FORCE DES CHOSES

The third point is perhaps already implicit: that opinions resulting in policy changes are themselves often the response to structural changes in the external environment. It may be the change from peace to war in the security structure, or from growth and prosperity to recession and stagnation in the production structure. To preserve the social consensus sustaining the political authority of the state, policy has to change to meet the challenge. The American sociologist Gary Hamilton has developed a similar sort of explanation for the variation in economic development strategies between the East Asian Newly Industrialized Countries. Policies, he explains, are chosen in response to whatever threat seems greatest to the cohesion and survival of the state. In South Korea, it is the threat of military attack from the North; to arm society adequately against the threat, industry must be export-oriented to earn the dollars needed to buy arms. In Taiwan, the greatest threat, at least for most of the 1950s and 1960s when the main lines of development policy were laid, was the threat of conflict between islanders and mainlanders. Growth through export-orientation was part of the answer, but creating an open competitive market in which the state—unlike Korea—had no favorites was the other part.

It could be that a similar approach to the variation of opinions in Europe may help to explain apparent differences—as between France and Germany, or France and Britain, for example. It is my contention, however, that such differences are less now than in the past. Integration into the competitive world market economy has reduced the insulating walls of national policy. As they have gotten thinner, the vulnerability to structural change in the external environment is more equally experienced. Policy responses to structural change also then tend to converge, even more than in the past.

But, and here is the connection between the third point and what follows, just because national insulating walls have gotten thinner and less effective, these policy responses are also less and less effective. All over the industrialized world, we observe ministers and heads of state getting elected with promises to cut unemployment, reduce fiscal deficits, restore competitiveness to national industries, and maintain stable money and the exchange rate. And all over the industrialized world, we see them failing to keep their promises. Quite often, despite their failings, we also see them getting reelected, simply because the voters see little chance that their opponents will do any better. This common incompetence among national governments is in striking contrast to earlier times when it did seem possible for states to use economic levers to manage demand while maintaining sound money and a fiscal balance. That so many governments should be having difficulty in delivering on their promises cannot be a coincidence. It cannot be due entirely to purely local causes, such as the decline in the standards of public service as perceived by Paul Volcker for the United States,[3] or to the costs of reunification as perceived by some Germans, or to decades of unchecked political corruption as in Italy. It is more likely that there is a common denominator at work in all the industrialized countries—structural change in the international political economy.[4]

My structural explanation of this rising level of incompetence or impotence rests on three propositions. From these follow the conclusion that the question of political authority and markets has to be addressed in a new and different way—not on a state-by-state basis, but on a global one, looking at the relation of authority to world society and world economy, as it is and as it might be.

The first proposition is that the governments of most nation-states have been losing power upwards, downwards, and sideways. That is to say, that, thanks to change chiefly in the production and financial structures, they are having to share authority in limited respects with other states, with international organizations, with nongovernment authorities of various kinds, and with regional and local authorities inside their borders. Their ability, therefore, to govern and to implement policy decisions is increasingly compromised. They may still be more powerful as authorities than their rivals above and below, but their monopoly of willing obedience is no longer what it used to be.

The second proposition is that this loss of power is very uneven and that consequently the asymmetry between powerful states and weak states, between rich ones and poor ones, those with influence over others and those unable to resist the influence of others, is growing year by year. The assumption of international relations that the international political system is made up of unitary actors called states is visibly creaking under this growing asymmetry. If the unitary actors vary as much as do Japan and Vanuatu, Nigeria and the Gambia, Germany and Luxembourg, how can we conceive of a theory based on the fundamentally statecentric assumptions of international law and international relations that satisfactorily explains the behavior of both?

And the third proposition is that between the sharing of state authority with others and the asymmetric distribution of power in the political system, great gaps have opened up in which there is no effective political authority over a powerfully integrated world market economy. There is none capable or willing to provide the political scaffolding that nation-states used to provide for their national economies and can no longer sustain, but which is still needed to allow a stable and efficient world market economy to grow and flourish.

Proposition one is perhaps more palpable in Europe than in America—although the attempt in California to impose unitary taxes on foreign-owned firms on the basis of their global profits is one indication that ideas about the territorial limits on state authority may be changing there too. In Europe, national governments are becoming acutely aware that their authority in certain issue-areas is now shared with the institutions of the European Community, notably the Commission acting in the name of the Council of Ministers. They are also more aware of the rival claims of regional authorities acting sometimes in collaboration with Brussels and sometimes in collaboration with regional authorities in other countries.

There are a number of examples of the power shared with the European Commission. One is over property rights as defined by European, not national, patent law, and administered by the European Patent Office in Munich. This effort at standardizing rules clearly has the backing of industry for whom the complications of registering patents in 12 different countries was wasteful and time-consuming. Another is competition policy, where the Commission has been effectively backed by the European Court of Justice—judged by some observers to be the "motor of integration" in the European Community (Shapiro 1992). By the famous Cassis de Dijon case, the Court "came very close to saying that each importing state must defer to the product standards of the producing state unless it can give the European Court a convincing reason for enforcing its own standards on the goods seeking entry."[5] Though the competition directorate of the Commission still has some big battles on its hands—against the European airlines, for example, and against the restrictive practices of car dealers—it has already shown itself prepared to face down protectionist interests in the member states in ways that national governments have not been able to do. And, as Tsoukalis observes, "The Community legal framework is arguably what most distinguishes the EC from traditional international organizations" (Tsoukalis 1993, 34).

In many matters, the success of the European Community in filching authority from national governments is only partial. Taxation is an example. Despite much talk of tax harmonization ever since the 1960s, there remains much more diversity of tax rates on corporate profits, and on petrol (gasoline), alcohol, and cigarettes than there is between different states in the United States. And the Commission's 1987 proposals on the extension of Value Added Tax (VAT) payments to cross-border sales, and the standardization of rates within two bands—14 to 20 percent for standard items and 5 to 9 percent for reduced-rate items—came up against resistance from national governments and had to be modified. The compromise results came into effect last January, and a minimum standard rate of 15 percent is now supposed to operate throughout the European Community.

The heart of the Community has from the beginning been the Common Agricultural Policy (CAP). It remains so, and the extraordinarily complex administrative details devised last year in Brussels for payment of set-aside subsidies to farmers were faithfully carried out this spring by national ministries of agriculture, acting as agents of the European Community.

Generally speaking, it would seem that while in Europe the trend, however slow and limited, has been to shift at least some authority from the state to the soi-disant supranational institutions, there has been no comparable loss of authority by the U.S. state to any international body. The arbitral powers of dispute settlement panels under the U.S.-Canada Free Trade Agreement may prove to be an exception, but it is probably too early to say. What both the Europeans and the Americans share is some new assertiveness by local and regional authorities. In both continents, there is much local rivalry to attract Japanese companies to invest in manufacturing, whatever the opinions of central government. In America, California authorities have tried to institute a unitary tax on foreign-owned firms; and even local authorities like San Francisco have effectively legalized marijuana in clear disregard of federal government policy.

The results of such comparisons lead to the second proposition, which is that there is growing asymmetry between the authority of states in the international system. Just as the European states have lost power both downwards to their regions and cities, and upwards to the institutions of the European Community, so they have continued to lose some powers sideways to the U.S. government. On matters of defense, this was always true among the European members of NATO, who time and again had to defer to U.S. decisions on the command structure and troop deployment, just as they also had to on strategic trade embargoes coordinated through the COCOM. This latter issue has also shown how much greater was the transnational reach of the U.S. government was than those of others.

In the gas pipeline case, for instance, the British government was unable to provide statutory protection for its national firms accused by Washington of transgressing its directives; it could try, but under threat of exclusion from all U.S. government contracts in the future, the firms had no alternative but to comply with the United States.

Another example can be found in the effective regulation of shipping. When it comes to environmental safety standards for ships, it is not the International Maritime Organization in London, where each member government has equal legal rights, that matters. It is the port authorities of the United States who lay down the minimum standards that must be reached by any ship wishing to dock and load or unload there. Because of the importance of the U.S. market in world trade, an estimated half of the world merchant fleet now conforms to these port authority standards. In this case, the U.S. rules are tougher than those of others. In other cases, in financial market regulation for example, they may be looser. The point is simply that the integration of the global financial and production structures is slowly increasing the asymmetries of state power. And the trend is probably accelerated by the expansion of the UN to include mini-states whose claim to autonomy is so slender that the gulf between the authority of the General Assembly and that of the five permanent members of the Security Council is now greater than it was in the 1950s.

For our purposes, it is the third proposition that is really most important. This, remember, was that the market economy, which is busily transcending national borders, now lacks the political scaffolding that held up a capitalist system in the past and that was so carefully and laboriously built up by each of the industrializing states. Some late-comers, like Turkey or Japan, saved themselves a lot of trouble with their scaffolding by simply copying existing models, such as the Swiss legal code for companies. Others, like Korea, developed their own variations of an American model. But whether they were so-called weak states with a robust social constitution, or strong states ruled by iron fists and draconian punishments, all the models were made up of the same basic components. All worked well so long as what went on within the national economy was more important than what went on in the world economy for most members of society.

That has now changed as a result of the structural changes, especially in production and finance, that were mentioned earlier. What goes on in the world economy is now more important for most of the societies of Europe, America, and Japan than what goes on within each national economy. This I believe to be true even though it is not yet universally recognized. It follows that the fundamental problematic for all students of international political economy is how in the future to adapt a political system based on the supposed authority and autonomy of territorial states to cope with those few but indispensable needs of an economy that overspills and indeed largely disregards their territorial borders. More specifically, it is how to arrange for the provision of those collective goods found by experience to be necessary in the long run for the functioning of a stable and efficient market economy. It is also how to substitute on a global scale for the sustaining social cohesion and consensus achieved by the modern state through a redistribution of wealth by rules and resource transfers for the benefit of those left underprivileged and defenseless by the operations of the market.

These questions must be further broken down into subsidiary questions. For the first, we must decide what collective goods are not only necessary but would also be sufficient for the successful operation of a market economy? Secondly and thirdly, how and by whom could they be provided?

The answer given for the nineteenth-century state by the classical political economists was that only three—possibly, four—things were both necessary and sufficient: the defense of the realm; the value of the currency; the sanctity of property and contract; and the administration of justice. First of all, the kingdom or republic had to be defended against foreign attack or invasion and against civil rebellion, riots, and disorders. It needed an army, or an army and a civil police force, because neither production, trade, nor investment was possible without credible guarantees against both external and internal sources of violence and disruption. Does it follow then that a world market economy cannot work for long without a collective security system and an international army/police force? Undoubtedly, it would work better if it had both. But there are enough examples of market economies continuing to function—if not optimally, at least adequately— despite no-go areas for the forces of law and order, areas such as Catholic Belfast and Derry, most of Sicily and parts of Calabria until very recently, the Persian Gulf during the Iran-Iraq War, Malaysia during the civil war of the 1950s and the riots of the 1960s, quite large parts of Sri Lanka, and the Burma-Thai borders. The occurrence of more and more such bad patches in the global security structure look rather probable during coming years. But unless they include the centers of major cities, it does not follow that the market economy cannot function.

Similarly, the second collective good identified in the classical literature—the provision of stable money—is highly desirable. But a market economy can surely continue to function—not optimally but adequately despite a somewhat unstable monetary system. Even in Germany in 1922-23, and in Argentina or Brazil in the 1980s, the economy did not totally seize up like an overheated petrol engine. For a while, the momentum of custom kept shops open, people at work on farms and in factories, public services running—even though workers, rentiers, and pensioners were being paid in currency that was almost worthless. Recall those who argued in the inflationary 1970s that world trade and international business could not survive the demise of fixed exchange rates. It turned out they could. The momentum of demand and supply in world markets forced market operators to find new ways to manage the attendant risks (Mikdashi 1990).

The third essential collective good mentioned by the classical writers was the legal protection afforded to buyers and sellers and to those investing capital in trade or production. Here, more than in the security structure or the financial structure, past experience suggests the possibility that, instead of the unitary state acting as the sole provider of collective goods, they may be provided by a multiplicity of authorities—moral as well as political, private as well as public. In the nineteenth century, the moral and social authority of the churches, and of the social peers in the capitalist classes, heavily reinforced the authority of the government against theft, dishonesty, fraud, and deception. Of course, all of these were still actively practiced; victims continuously suffered the consequences—but not so much, nor on so huge a scale as to bring down the whole edifice of capitalism. The scaffolding, in short, was made of diverse materials. It rested on pride as well as on fear; on precapitalist moral codes and peer pressure as much as on the courts and systems of formal law.

The decay of such multimaterial scaffolding seems to me to be one of the striking weaknesses of the contemporary world market economy—except possibly in Islamic—and maybe in Buddhist and Confucian—cultures. The impunity of too many financial criminals at the hands of impotent or inefficient national legal systems, the thin line distinguishing their behavior from those of recognized pillars of society, the widespread practice of preferential information-giving and of insider dealing, the repeated excuse that "everyone does it" can critically undermine the system.

So much for the basic collective goods thought by the classical writers to be necessary and sufficient for the functioning of a market economy. But times have changed since Adam Smith's day. The very success of market economies in creating wealth has brought with it two new problems, and two new perceptions of necessary state intervention. Because wealth was created, the gap between rich and poor widened and put new strains on the social structure. By the end of the nineteenth century, the first attempts to use state authority to redress this inequity in the system began to be seen, and by the middle of the twentieth century, at least in Europe, it had become generally accepted that some kind of state-financed welfare system was a necessary condition for social peace and political stability in a market economy. Secondly, the success of market economies imposed on many classes in society the pains of adjusting to the business cycles—the alternation of booms and slumps—that were characteristic of market economies. Again, by the middle decades of the twentieth century, countercyclical intervention to modify the severity of economic depression was accepted as necessary. Political debate for most of the last hundred years has been on how much welfare was necessary and how to finance it; and on how much countercyclical demand management in recession was either feasible or desirable.

CONCLUSIONS

Thus, to sum up, we have three old and two new items on the agenda of collective goods—five responsibilities for political authority of some kind necessary for the smooth and successful operation of market economies. But since, as generally agreed, we no longer have discrete national market economies connected tangentially to one another by trade and some cross-border mobility of people and capital, but one world market economy functioning despite the coexistence of national authorities—states—the crucial question is how and by whom these five responsibilities can be fulfilled. As pointed out earlier, we need not necessarily look for complete, optimal fulfillment. The market system can tolerate shortcomings from the ideal of political management without breaking down. And the management need not be in the hands of one single authority but can be shared, yet still be sufficient.

On all five counts, we can discern some recognition emerging in the course of the past 50 years of the need for change and innovation in the relation of authority to society and economy. But recognizing a need is only the first step. Satisfying it comes next and is more difficult. Briefly, we can see in the UN Charter and its proposed system of collective security under the joint management of the five permanent members of the Security Council, a recognition of the need for a framework of security. We can see in the Bretton Woods agreement, supplemented by the BIS's Basle Concordats on banking regulation, and by the London and Paris clubs on debt rescheduling, recognition of the need for arrangements to secure sound money and stable rules on the creation of credit and the management of debt. Not ideal arrangements, maybe, but at least an acknowledgment of the problem. And for the third collective good of a framework of law and morality, we can see again some minimal development of public and private international law, and the proliferation of organizations, nongovernmental as well as intergovernmental, for standardizing practice.

As for the fourth and fifth collective goods necessary to developed market systems—wealth redistribution and countercyclical intervention—these have been the subject of two of the big debates that have occupied intellectual circles in the United States, Europe, and beyond. The lesser developed countries' call for a New International Economic Order and the North-South debate at least addressed the question of economic justice even though the outcome was negligible. And the academic discussion of hegemonic stability theory, though it may have seemed arcane to a wider public, was actually addressing the right question. To safeguard the system against the dangers of world economic depression, does the system need a dominant political authority both able and willing to maintain the flow of international credit, to keep open a market for distress goods, and to act as lender of last resort to the banking system? From a European point of view, it has been unfortunate that the debate became sidetracked into a discussion of how, why, and whether American power had declined and what the United States, in its national interest, should do about it. In the process, the much larger question of how an interdependent world market economy could conceivably be managed has tended to get lost.

Where both debates have stopped short—indeed, have reached something of an impasse or dead end—therefore is in being conducted almost exclusively in terms of states and their potential as both redistributive and countercyclical authorities in the market economy. This chapter is a plea that both debates—indeed, debates on all five collective goods—should be reopened in a new, wider format that introduces nonstate sources of authority in society and economy—manufacturing enterprises, banks, insurance, accounting and law firms, and many transnational organizations of a professional or unofficial nature. A wider debate is needed to see whether, despite the limitations of intergovernmental organization, some combination of authorities cannot among them begin to provide the bare minimum of collective goods necessary for the successful survival of the world market economy.

ENDNOTES

1. Angus, M., ex-chairman of Unilever, chairman of Whitbreads, "The Bureaucracy that stifles Europe," *Financial Times,* May 20, 1993.
2. An idea I tried to express in *States and Markets,* 1988, by presenting the four basic structures as four planes of a single pyramid, separate but touching each other.
3. His Commission on the Public Service, which was trying to draw attention to the problem, was paradoxically one of the first victims of President Clinton's budget cuts.
4. See Stopford and Strange 1991, Chapter 2, in which an explanation was given of the nature of these structural changes, affecting both the rivalry of states in the international political system and the rivalry of firms in the world economy.
5. See Shapiro 1992. The Danish government did in fact succeed in giving such good reasons—of environmental protection—in the Danish beer bottle case, contested by German breweries exporting beer to Denmark in cans.

REFERENCES

Galbraith, J. K. *A Theory of Price Control.* Cambridge, MA: Harvard University Press, 1952.
Mann, M. "Power and Knowledge: The Case of Contemporary South Africa." *Public Administration,* vol. 67 (Summer 1989): 265–78.
Mikdashi, Z., ed. *"Banking and Public Authorities" Management of Risks.* London: Macmillan, 1990.

Richardson, J. D. "The Political Economy of Strategic Trade Policy: Review Article." *International Organization,* vol. 44, no. 1 (Winter 1990): 107–35.

Shapiro, M. "The European Court of Justice" in A. Sbragia, ed. *Europolitics.* Washington, D.C.: Brookings Institution, 1992.

Stopford, J., and Strange, S. *Rival States Rival Firms: Competition for World Market Shares.* Cambridge: Cambridge University, 1991.

Strange, S. "The Future of the American Empire." *Journal of International Affairs,* vol. 42, no. 1, (Fall 1988): 1–18.

Tsoukalis, L. *The New European Economy; The Politics and Economics of Integration.* 2nd edition. Oxford: Oxford University Press, 1993.

Vatter, H. *The U.S. Economy in World War 2.* New York: Columbia University Press, 1985.

6

Markets, Governments, and Policy Congruence Across the Atlantic

Robert T. Kudrle

INTRODUCTION

For several years commentators have discussed the emergence of three economic blocs, the so-called Triad (see, for example, the United Nations 1991). However oversimplified this characterization, it highlights the central international economic policy issue facing policymakers in Europe, Japan, and the United States. Is there sufficient agreement about what is fair and efficient across the three regions to allow for the present level of cooperation and to permit increasing integration among these critical parts of the world economy?[1] This chapter discusses a subset of issues bearing on this larger question. It will examine the uses of market outcomes as opposed to other alternatives—particularly highly regulated private provision and state production—as a means of organizing social activity. It focuses on differences and similarities between the United States and Europe and occasionally calibrates policy distances by comparing those regions with Japan.

Although the potential for cooperation and conflict drives much of the interest in the way markets and governments interact globally, another dimension to global relations must be considered: imitation and benchmarking. The global political economy—or at least the developed parts of it—seems unprecedentedly open to new ideas and policy innovation. If fresh approaches seem to work in one state or region, converging perspectives and improved information flows make them much more likely to be tried elsewhere than in earlier times. Furthermore, politicians and both private and public managers in one region are increasingly held to standards of performance attained elsewhere.[2]

Differences between the United States and Europe can be partially addressed by asking whether the purpose of public action is to provide public goods, to redistribute income and wealth, or to do something else. The question itself raises some interesting theoretical issues. Economists tend to divide goods into public and private on the basis of two characteristics: excludability and exhaustibility. Both characteristics are present in a pure private good and both are absent in a pure public good (Head 1962; Weimer and Vining 1992, 41–62).[3]

Public policies of all kinds (and the services of public institutions, as well) may be regarded as providing intermediate public goods that, in turn, may yield both public and private goods to various parties. Mancur Olson's original example of a public (he uses the term *collective*) good can be construed to illustrate this way of viewing public policy. Olson (1965, 47) posits a set of landowners who lobby the government for a tax rebate that they value for the exhaustible, excludable goods that it can buy. Olson fails to make explicit the impact on the rest of the community, however. If the landowners are paying lower taxes, others are paying more (or government services are reduced), and the impact on them is just as real—although more diffuse—as on those who engineered the public good for their own benefit.[4] The tax rebate is a "public bad" for the rest of the community because it redistributes the capacity to consume private goods.

Other redistributive policies may produce still more complex results. If the behavior of beneficiaries of government redistribution is altered in a way that negatively affects the rest of the community beyond its money cost—as some allege to be the case of U.S. welfare policies— negative externalities for the broader community would weigh against possible psychic income to those taxpayers who value increasing the material income of the poor. In turn, these valuations need to be added to those resulting from the shift in private purchasing power and its direct impact on the welfare of the two groups. In short, any public action that unavoidably affects the utility of members of a group— positively or negatively—is a public good for that group.

This excursion still leaves the more ordinary use of the term *public good,* as in cancer research or weather forecasting, as a category of market failure providing a possible justification for government intervention—in addition to those government activities that even Adam Smith would approve of, such as the military, the police, and the courts.[5] Market failures, of course, provide the theoretical justification for government intervention in private markets in neoclassical economic theory. In addition to public goods (valued by the community at large and including various kinds of information), these include direct external effects (positive or negative), natural monopoly power, and "unnatural" monopoly power (for example, the ability of a small group of firms to charge above cost as a result of concentration and barriers to entry).[6]

These problems can be regarded as providing a prima facie case for government action, although as Nobel Laureate George Stigler has argued, automatically assuming that government intervention will actually improve social welfare is equivalent to declaring the second singer in a vocal contest the winner—after hearing only the first singer. More formally, Charles Wolf has argued that "government failure" should be considered from the very outset in the design of public policy. A tendency toward inflated costs, arbitrary or self-serving maxims, unintended secondary effects, and inappropriate accretions of power and prestige must be set against the market's failings that intervention aims to correct (Wolf 1988). In addition, all government action not fully financed by fees introduces distortions into the economy through taxation. Such distortions also result from an important government intervention in all economies: taxation and expenditure for redistributive purposes. While not always regarded as a "market failure," an unaltered market distribution of income would be unacceptable in almost any polity.

AN APPROACH TO POLICY DETERMINATION

Because this chapter speculates about future developments, a definite approach to policy determination is employed. The approach used here is closely related to public choice theory and the new institutional economics (Furubotn and Richter 1990). The fundamental unit of analysis is the individual—whether that person be a private-sector worker, a property owner, or a government employee.[7] Unlike some versions of this approach, however, policy preferences in the scheme employed here are not based solely on specific calculations of personal material gain or social position. A citizen's utility function contains explicit arguments related to major government-provided public goods and allows for both ideal and self-interested valuation.[8]

In an earlier work, the author (with Davis Bobrow 1982: 1990) has considered goals to be served by government in its conduct of foreign economic policy and found that they can be satisfactorily reduced to four: security, autonomy, prosperity, and assertion.

- Security refers to the avoidance of threats to the country's physical safety from external aggressors.
- Autonomy resides in the self-consciousness of a group and expectations about its character that are historically determined at any given time. The goal may range from the minimal desire to maintain a distinct identity for the group (by avoiding submergence into another cultural environment) to the demand that the group (usually the nation-state) be purposely insulated from the activities of other groups.[9]
- Prosperity refers to physical welfare and is roughly approximated by income and wealth.[10]
- Recognition is the fourth goal. Groups gain psychic income from the admiration and imitation of others or their subordination, and much foreign policy behavior, particularly by large states, can be plausibly explained on these grounds (for further discussion, see Kudrle and Lenway 1990; Kudrle 1991a).[11] Policies and outcomes enhancing recognition somewhat resemble those concerning security because greater achievement of both goals usually involves zero-sum (relative standing) elements.

Foreign and domestic policy are considered. Strange (1988) simplifies state action by assigning a great deal of state activity to the goals of freedom and equality. Prosperity may be linked to both of these goals, mainly through their impact on efficiency. This linkage illustrates a possible trade-off (prosperity and equality) or synergy (prosperity and freedom) among goals, which may vary over time and among states.[12]

One way of considering these goals is to regard them as influencing individuals' postures toward policy—absent the particular personal stake that forms the usual basis for policy reference in public choice models. A policy's apparent fit with general goals may be called *ideological consonance*. The belief that one general policy direction has served one or more of the goals successfully creates an uphill fight for an alternative approach.

The clarity with which an individual sees the actual result of policy is termed *impact transparency*. Some policies have a fairly straightforward apparent relation to the general goals or an individual's self-interest, in other cases the relation may be quite murky. Political leadership may play a particularly pivotal role where the impact transparency of outcomes is low, yet groups can be persuaded to accept a certain interpretation of policy.

The *distribution of apparent costs and benefits* is a third policy determinant. This factor drives conventional public choice analysis; the stakes per agent are frequently assigned a major role in predicting policy outcomes because of their influence on the likelihood of political group formation, cohesion, and effective action.

Finally, the *institutional setting* powerfully conditions policy outcomes. Where settings are somewhat similar among states or within the same state over time, a discussion of policy can sometimes focus on the other determinants.

Lest the first and the fourth policy determinant assume critical issues away, it should be stressed that the same basic approach employed here can be used to trace—and predict—the development of ideology and institutions over extended periods of time (North 1981; Furubotn and Richter 1990).

AN APPLICATION TO THE COMMUNITY'S DEVELOPMENT

This scheme can be used to interpret the development of the European Community to 1993. An interpretation of this period not only illustrates the theory, but it also broadly traces the evolution of European attitudes toward the use of the price system.

The 1950s through the 1970s

Those who conceived of European unity saw a web of mutual economic gain between France and Germany as a powerful force to discourage future armed conflict in Western Europe as well as a source of general prosperity and a promising economic bulwark against the East. An important objective of the expanded European markets was increased competition; even early studies did not anticipate large gains simply from economies of scale. Such qualitative economic change was not just accepted but purposely sought, as the history of European competition policy illustrates. Sections 85 and 86 of the Treaty of Rome bear resemblance to U.S. antitrust law and went well beyond the domestic laws of any of the six founding states. Their enforcement aimed eventually at dislodging those entrenched national monopolies not already shaken by the competition of American multinational corporations (which took advantage of greater trade freedom earlier than did most European firms).

Influentials and much of the attentive public in all six states generally saw the uniting of Europe as a means of serving their prosperity, security, and recognition goals. The decolonization process endured by four of major European states (three of whom signed the Treaty of Rome in 1957) was at best orderly and at worst humiliating, and it profoundly affected the recognition goal and greatly accelerated a willingness to consider global influence from a European perspective. Many citizens of all countries increasingly believed that both prosperity and recognition implied an effective competition with the United States and Japan that was possible only in a United Europe (Kudrle, 1991a). Nonetheless, fears about autonomy and assertion rendered France ambivalent about many aspects of European unity, and bred de Gaulle's vision of *Europe des patries*. Similar fears together with considerable misgivings about the prosperity implications of disrupting established trade patterns with Commonwealth countries, which were also related to recognition, contributed to British ambivalence about the entire project.

After Britain agreed to find an accommodation in Europe and after the global economy had been severely disrupted by the quadrupling of oil prices, obvious modifications of previous national policies seemed to generate mediocre prosperity outcomes at best. Throughout the common market, and beyond, growth rates were lower and unemployment rates higher than in the 1960s. If "integration as usual" was working against stagnation, the effects were far from impressive. Détente removed some of the apparent necessity for tight coordination with the United States on security grounds. National autonomy remained under assault, but some semblance of a trans-European popular culture developed.

The Recent Period

These first two phases of development were sketched as if they operated uniformly across nation-states and as if the policies pursued reflected calculations made by technocrats on behalf of their societies. In fact, the observed outcomes mainly reflected the results of interest group leaders attempting to link specific European bonds—or their absence—to the self-interest of their constituents, while reinforcing those appeals with parallel interpretations of the relations of preferred policy directions to more general national goals.

By the late 1970s, Europe was still well behind the United States and was being surpassed by Japan in an increasing number of key sectors. Strong initiatives toward a unified European economic base as a necessary condition for effective competition with the other members of the "Triad" gained adherents. Unusually market-oriented governments were elected in Britain in 1979 and in the United States in 1980. The French Socialist government elected in 1981 began by pursuing an independent demand expansion policy and extensive nationalization, but it was so thoroughly thwarted by contrary global forces that it reversed course and pursued a generally liberal line over the rest of the decade.

In this context, the leaders of European business not only persuaded their governments of the necessity of rapid unification, they also frequently won over union leadership and large parts of their workforces as well. Many Socialists regarded the initiative as an extension of capitalist domination, but they saw no viable alternative.

Interpretation

The shift to greater emphasis on European unity based on wider and less fettered markets can be explained in terms of the model presented earlier. Security concerns dominated the initial postwar phase, while greater prosperity was promised by most of the same measures that served the security goal. Autonomy appeared threatened by the onslaught of Americanization, symbolized by the visibility of successful U.S. corporations in Europe. Subsequently, a more thorough affront to recognition appeared as Japan moved between Europe and America in an increasing number of technology spheres, a development equally foreboding for long-run prosperity.

The drive to 1992 was spearheaded by self-interested business acting with the general acquiescence of the rest of society. It was built on two major pillars, both of which are critical for this discussion. It bound Europe far more tightly by removing barriers, and it forcefully pushed the price system forward as the central organizer of the more open economic space by insisting on market-driven outcomes in areas previously regulated by member states for their own purposes.

Europe now faces the future from an unprecedentedly market-oriented position. In broad outline, the mix of state and private action in its economies more closely resembles that of the United States than was the case earlier in the postwar period. Nonetheless, while there is some variety within the United States about the way governments and markets are employed, there is much greater variety in Europe. In general, markets are relied upon more heavily in the United States, but one or more European states now sometimes pursue sectoral policies that are more market-driven than those in America.

Factor Markets

One approach to this subject is to focus on policy responses to traditional market failures in Europe and the United States. But because natural monopoly, competition, public goods, and externality concerns play special roles in particular factor and goods markets, it makes sense to look at these markets separately.

Land Markets

Land-use controls of various kinds are employed in Europe far more than in the United States. Historically, the differences probably stem more than anything else from the interaction of population density with a desire for preservation. The combination of high population density and the desire for control of a substantial part of available land for natural amenity or historical protection has limited both housing and roadway construction far more than has been the case in the United States. This has increased the appeal of public transportation, which in turn affects settlement patterns.

European land-use controls are justified on grounds of externalities or public goods. The control of noise, air pollution, and the visual alteration of the countryside can be regarded in terms of the creation or avoidance of certain externalities. Historic preservation can be seen as a public good. European practices have generated considerable imitation in the United States, where many visual controls, in particular, have been propelled by unfavorable comparisons with Europe.

From the standpoint of European-U.S. interaction, the most important manifestation of the difference may be the relative difficulty of establishing competitive distribution. Although data are not available, the United States almost certainly exceeds Europe in the ease with which a typical seller can establish a variety of channels to serve a population group of any given density. In Britain and the Netherlands, for example, high-density areas in which planning and building restrictions control large outlets are surrounded by "greenbelts" that are off-limits to large stores.

Differences in the stringency of land-use controls probably lie behind a major contrast between European and U.S. competition law: "vertical restraints" are much less tolerated by competition authorities in Europe because they are so much more difficult to work around. In the United States (since the Sylvania decision of 1977), the courts have generally been sympathetic to a manufacturer's desire to control the conditions of resale to promote service and investment by distributors. In Europe such agreements are far more likely to be regarded as foreclosing marketing channels for others. Thus one kind of interference in the market, as in land-use controls, bred another, public regulation of restrictive practices in the distribution chain (Rosenthal 1990, 310). Both U.S. and European commercial situations stand in sharp contrast to Japan where land-use controls are combined with vertical restraints that have not yet been effectively hindered by legal challenge. This combination contributes to the great difficulties that new sellers, most notably foreigners, have in penetrating Japanese markets (Ito 1992, 385–404).

Externalities relating to agricultural land use have been cited as an important ingredient in the conflict between the United States and Europe over the Community's Common Agricultural Policy (CAP). Some suggest that the character of the European countryside would be altered by lower farm prices. In fact, however, complete liberalization of farm prices is estimated to result in only a 10 to 15 percent reduction in farming jobs. Moreover, lower use of fertilizers and pesticides, which fell by 50 percent when New Zealand agriculture was liberalized, would reduce pollution. In some areas, unfarmed land would also provide a visual improvement. On the other hand, such reforms face an enormous political obstacle. Land prices, which absorb a huge fraction of the impact of subsidies, would tumble with liberalization, wiping out the savings of small holders.[13]

Arguments for agricultural protection based on "food security" are also suspect. Complete liberalization would only lower agricultural production in Europe quite modestly, while the ability to produce under all emergencies would require heavy protection of an array of support industries, which no one is proposing.

CAP policies are a source of positive externalities to the public, but net externalities are almost certainly negative. Costs now exceed 7 percent of the income of a French factory worker (Carr 1992, 7). Nonetheless, industries identifying with familiar and respected values are in decline. Their impact transparency is low, and their distribution of costs and benefits favor producer dominance,[14] particularly in the institutional context of agricultural influence in many European political parties. The greater tenacity of agricultural protectionism compared with many other trade controls also rests on agriculture's relatively small direct effect on concentrated economic fortunes.[15]

Agricultural protectionism on both sides of the Atlantic is based on a similar public misunderstanding, which may be eroding. No principles are blocking substantial liberalization. The pace of change in both regions nonetheless remains a major issue in the foreseeable future because Americans are determined to gain a more favorable trading position.

Trade barriers between the United States and Europe are generally quite low, but unsurprisingly, other major trade issues between them involve agricultural products. The dispute over U.S. hormone-beef imports into the Community illustrates the way that health and safety issues can be manipulated for protectionist intent. Regardless of the merits of that case, however, this dispute does not identify a consistent underlying issue in U.S.-Europe differences in the reliance on markets: In other health or safety spheres, the players' positions could be reversed. Instead, the dispute underlines the need for greater restraint and collaboration on standards that affect trade.

Considering all land-related issues, the treatment of legitimate externalities provides a fairly sharp contrast between U.S. and European land market practices but should not produce important disputes between them.

Capital

Highly developed and relatively unimpeded capital markets have emerged across Europe as they had generally done much earlier within each domestic market and in the United States. Internal controls on capital flows now apply almost entirely to ownership changes (discrimination against foreigners per se will be considered later; here only general impediments are considered). Many countries have legal impediments to the takeover of firms by outsiders, but the ownership of large blocks of stock by banking and insurance companies in Germany makes takeovers far more difficult than in Britain, regardless of takeover legislation. The German pattern rests more fully on market forces than does the situation in countries such as the United States where claims about the unique functions of the banking system have generated legal restrictions on the range and intensity of bank investment.

Foreigners have increasingly complained about antitakeover legislation at the state level in the United States (Fry 1991). Although it does not discriminate on the basis of nationality, U.S. legislation, and much of its counterpart in Europe, appears based on arrogation by "stakeholders" who have used the political system to protect existing ownership on the assumption that it is more likely to retain local production, pay higher wages, give more money to charity, or perform some other service. The restrictions rest on alleged externalities for the community as a whole but appear as a form of interference with ownership changes. Getting rid of such impediments implies increasing control by both the U.S. federal government over state policy and greater control by the Community over national prerogative (Kline and Wallace 1991), an unlikely development both because of the political cost of an assault and because such restriction is likely to be quite self-limiting on both sides of the Atlantic. If a takeover is denied to a determined entrant, that entrant may well come into another jurisdiction within the open market, a move that could ultimately disadvantage the protected firm.

Externally, planners in the postwar period saw trade liberalization as a high priority; capital controls, however, were regarded as a minor impediment to prosperity and an important tool for the control of exchange rates. Even after direct investment liberalization, general capital controls were often retained. They were employed temporarily by the United States in the 1960s for balance of payment reasons, and Britain did not abandon them until 1979. France removed most controls only in 1988 as mandated by the Single European Act.

The decline of capital controls does not warrant an elaborate political analysis. Like so many developments in financial regulation, it has generally developed at a technical level with broad-ranging but exclusively high-level political support. While politicians in general were quiescent, writers on the left have often decried the mobility of capital as an obstacle to the exercise of state sovereignty—especially in the service of socialism. In fact, the fit between national ownership and national deployment of capital has remained rather tight. In recent years no country has financed more than 15 percent of its investment from abroad and no country has sent more than 10 percent of its domestic savings abroad (Feldstein 1992, 62). So whatever the size of the investments, the physical assets used within a state are almost always overwhelmingly home owned, and the assets owned by individual citizens are within the jurisdiction of the state.

Some believe that the instability of the world financial system dictates a reintroduction of general capital controls (*Economist* 1992c). Where such an initiative would involve cooperation between the United States and the European Community, the initiative would probably involve government conflict with parts of national business more than a transatlantic quarrel.

Labor

Over the entire postwar period, differences in labor market practices— both traditional and legally mandated—have provided one of the sharpest contrasts between the United States and Europe. Organized labor was stronger and covered a much larger part of the labor force much earlier in a number of European countries than was true in the United States. In addition, laws concerning such issues as layoffs and information for workers have traditionally been far more stringent in Europe. For example, when the United States introduced 60-day compulsory employee notification of plant closure as part of the 1988 Trade Act, it was among the last industrial countries in the world to adopt such legislation. Moreover, the European state typically takes a much larger role in wage setting than in the United States. In France, for example, the only OECD country with a lower percentage of private-sector unionized workers than the United States in 1990 (13 versus 17 percent), the government plays a central role in setting minimum wages that heavily influence individual plant outcomes. In Germany, since the *Mitbestimmungsgesetz* of 1976, workers have claimed a particularly strong role in the management of industry with workers' representatives sitting on boards of directors. In most of Europe, notably excepting Britain, works councils deal with issues that are typically the sole prerogative of management in the United States (Freeman and Rogers 1993).

In the United States the high tide of European-style thinking that "labor is not a commodity" came under Lyndon Johnson's Labor Secretary, Willard Wirtz. For a time a group in the Labor Department advocated abandoning the use of the term *labor market* in all of its publications. Cooler heads prevailed. Indeed, probably the most important markets in any economy allocate its labor, and price regulation produces predictable secondary effects. In particular, government and union wage policy appear to have contributed to systematically higher levels of unemployment in most of Europe than in the United States over the period since 1980 (Freeman 1988).

American firms opposed the codetermination law in Germany as well as the Vredleing proposal of the early 80s that would have mandated U.S. multinational corporations in the Community to share considerable information and consult with their workers (Bobrow and Kudrle 1984). Even today U.S. firms systematically prefer operations in the United Kingdom to elsewhere in Europe, in substantial part because of looser labor constraints (a preference they share with the Japanese). Britain—at least under Conservative government—appears determined to retain this competitive advantage, as evidenced by its rejection of the Social Charter of the Maastricht Treaty.

The substantial difference in labor practices between most of Europe and the United States may have little effect on business operations. Most experienced firms in Europe reckon the additional labor constraint of a works council between a very small minus and a substantial plus in the efficiency of their operations (Freeman and Rogers 1993, 26). Some have doubted the survey evidence upon which such claims are made because of the concentration of German firms in such U.S. right-to-work states as the Carolinas. Nonetheless, American firms can choose to site their European operations in a range of countries with quite varied practices, and they have few substantial complaints. In fact, European national practice faces unprecedentedly severe constraint. If payment or shared authority structures seriously damage one EC country in competition with the others—or in global competition more broadly—there will be pressure for modification. Indeed, this very phenomenon is being observed in Germany today. Non-German European counters are pressuring Germany to modify its domestic financial policies and business practices to be more in line with European stability and competitiveness as an objective rather than as pure German interests.

State support for trade unions and other restrictions on labor markets are usually defended on equity grounds, an admitted market limitation. In Europe, moreover, the results of such interference may have a more systematically defensible impact on the overall distribution of income than in the United States. The wage premium attaching to unionism alone in Europe is quite modest, while in the United States it can be 25 percent or more. The comprehensive, central bargaining in which much of European unionism is engaged takes into account vertical and horizontal equity issues and even general unemployment problems exactly because unions are often far more "encompassing groups" (Olson 1983) than in the United States, where isolated unions are much more likely to practice *sauve qui peut* (every man for himself).

Overall income distribution by household quintiles as reported by the World Bank shows the United States to be somewhat more unequal than the average of its European counterparts.[16] In general the states with higher labor union density have greater income equality by these measures, but the relation is fairly loose and causality remains unclear. Because trade unionism has traditionally been associated with egalitarian attitudes, a decline in unionism—a trend throughout Europe— might be compensated for by increasingly redistributive taxation in some states.

Organized labor was investigated using the scheme developed earlier. Ideological consonance among those not most directly affected depends largely on whether union activity serves some general concept of social justice. Impact transparency is very low. In this context opponents stress contributions to inflation, unemployment, anomalous wage structures, and stultifying work rules while unions concentrate almost exclusively on "sharing" by stockholders, leaving the implication that the rest of society is largely exempt from the impact of successful unionism except as it gains from productivity-enhancing consultation and information-sharing within the firm.

These last arguments are critical for public sector unions (which remain powerful in America) because there cannot be too much confusion about where the money comes from. But the United States is both a natural laboratory and an open economic space; some states encourage unionism while others make it difficult, and many nonunion states have thrived largely at the expense of their more unionized neighbors (Crandall 1993). Years of federal hostility and unfavorable economic change has greatly eroded labor's traditional base and reduced private unionization to a level lower than before the first permissive federal legislation was passed in 1935. And many of the growing sectors of the economy are placing great emphasis on payment for individual or small group productivity—a reward system antithetical to traditional union norms. Some have predicted that private sector unionization in the United States may drop below 5 percent by the beginning of the new century (Freeman and Rogers 1993).

Similar economic changes are taking place in Europe, where the levels of union membership vary widely. The European experience in the immediate future should bear some resemblance to that of the United States. National industries with highly unionized workforces will suffer increasingly from competition—both within the Community and without—unless higher productivity can match any union-enforced wage premium. This challenge will increase in the face of greater capital and technology diffusion within Europe. As such competition and other changes reduce the level of unionization within a state, organized labor's views may become less "encompassing" and, partly as a consequence, an increasing share of the politically active population may come to see organized labor as just another "special interest" with objectives distinct from its own. This would tend to accelerate organized labor's demise by eroding support for special legal protections.

Predictions for Europe based on the U.S. experience should not be made too hastily because the ideological consonance of various measures to deal with equality issues may differ considerably. In recent response to the question, "Which is more important, equality or freedom?" those favoring equality in the United States, Britain, France, and Germany were 20, 23, 32, and 39 percent, while those favoring freedom were 72, 69, 54, and 37 percent. The response to the question, "Is it the government's responsibility to reduce income differences?" in the United States agreement was 28 percent; in Britain, 63 percent; and in West Germany, 56 percent (*Economist* 1992b). Such attitude differences fail to produce serious transatlantic incompatibilities in dealing with labor, however, and no changes increasing such problems are foreseen.

Economists have traditionally treated equity issues largely as matters of income and wealth distribution. In the United States in recent years, however, some attempts have been made essentially to redistribute social positions with income and status attached. Quite apart from antidiscrimination legislation, private organizations with public encouragement have developed hiring and promotion practices favoring female candidates and those from certain racial and ethnic minorities. The rationale offered has included compensation for past discrimination (or current discrimination elsewhere in society) as well as the desire to provide inspiration for others in the same demographic categories. The policies are usually declared to be temporary measures that will be reduced or removed as groups become less "underrepresented."

So far, private practice and official legislation in most of Europe appears to concentrate mainly on the avoidance of discrimination, and European firms operating in the United States have not been systematically accused of operating counter to U.S. practice—as the Japanese so conspicuously have been (Glickman and Woodward 1989). Practices that go beyond the avoidance of discrimination, as well as the standard of proof in discrimination cases, remain contested issues in the United States. Generally, they are treated as purely domestic matters. Some commentators, however, have tried to stress their possible detriment to American global competitiveness.

Cosmopolitan economists frequently lament that enthusiasm for free trade has never included the free movement of labor. In particular, many find it regrettable that, even though the labor force of Western Europe will soon shrink significantly, little tolerance can be found for substantial immigration even from Eastern Europe, let alone less ethnically similar areas. While the failure of most EC governments to develop wage structures, which allow absorption of the native labor force, certainly explains much of the current opposition, the problem is much deeper than that. Recent German events are deeply troubling and underline the inadequacy of the usual economic approach to immigration. In Germany immigration has primarily been considered in economic terms: marginal products, taxes paid, and public expenditures absorbed. New entrants are simultaneously workers and neighbors, however, and most elements of the second category are at the same time beyond the reach of the state (North 1981, Chapter 3) and a very important element of daily life for many nonimmigrants through direct, nonmarket interaction.

However parochial or unfair, the immigration experience in several countries has been sufficiently unsatisfactory over an extended period. Immigration appears to be more unpopular in Europe now than perhaps at any previous time. Moreover, this is an issue about which voters will probably show little deference to "expert" opinion. The impact that counts politically is likely to be the one that is most transparent: the presence of the immigrants and their general behavior. Immigration is unlikely to be substantially liberalized anywhere in Europe in the foreseeable future and may be substantially tightened.

The situation across the Atlantic is harder to judge. Americans probably accept more racial and ethnic diversity than most Europeans. Moreover, while many immigrants have entered the United States illegally, it remains unclear how much national commitment can be focused to enforce laws of pressing importance to only a few geographic areas where "excessive" immigration has caused a strong negative reaction.

Other migration issues can be forecast. Economic theory predicts that real remuneration by occupation should start to converge among countries within the Community in coming years and that this convergence will be strongest where the cross-elasticity of supply is highest. Other things being equal, this will occur where practitioners for various reasons feel more at home in different countries and where the actual tasks performed are the most similar. Such immigration will provide a policy challenge for governments because it will create pressure to alter domestic relative incomes. Oxford and Cambridge, for example, are apparently still regarded as the best universities in Europe. Over the postwar period through the 70s, however, average British incomes dropped relative to those elsewhere in Europe, and, although general British economic performance improved during the 80s, the Thatcher government tightly controlled university subsidies. Relative incomes for outstanding British academics must now rise or immigration should increase to North America as well as the rest of Europe. Overall, migration within the community has been modest so far. Only a few million workers of all kinds have yet taken advantage of the essentially free movement of labor.

A less-pronounced manifestation of the same phenomenon will emerge back and forth across the Atlantic where high real wages will increasingly tend to draw recruits from throughout North America, the Community, and beyond. "Leveling" will again be most pronounced among the most cosmopolitan professions performing the most internationally similar work. This interdependence should not create serious conflict, however, because wage structures should change rather slowly.

Markets for Goods and Services

Four issues will be treated in this section: the changing boundary between public and private in the production and distribution of goods and services, the issue of cultural industries, the role of competition policy, and the emerging problem of investment related trade measures.

Privatization

Privatization in many forms has taken place in both Europe and America since the early 1980s (although many of the French nationalizations of the early Mitterand period are being undone only now). From the standpoint of deductive economic reasoning, the trend cannot be a surprise. Much public ownership—beyond the operation of natural monopolies—was originally justified as placing what the British Labor Party called "the commanding heights of the economy" under public control. Just what fresh vistas or strategic advantages supposedly accrued to public ownership of such industries when they would otherwise have been "workably" competitive often remained unspecified.

The disadvantages of many such nationalizations soon emerged. Unions had frequently found the deepest pocket of all, and the maintenance of employment often became a major objective of nationalized firms (an "internality" in Wolf's lexicon [1988, 85]), at least for management's appointed by governments committed to public ownership. Global competition increasingly revealed the inadequacies of state monopolies as sellers of both inputs and final products, while firm losses increased government budget problems. Thus, one European trend over the past dozen years and more has been the privatization of industries that were large and apparently important but that had no significant "market failure" characteristics. This kind of privatization has brought the ownership patterns of Europe ever closer to that of the United States which, outside the defense sector, has had a negligible state production of goods and services beyond traditional natural monopoly. The European privatizations have also increased market opportunities for foreign firms.[17]

The traditional state sector—frequently justified initially on the basis of either natural monopoly or externalities—has also been considerably altered on both sides of the Atlantic. There are at least five identifiable cases:

1. The replacement of state ownership by regulated monopoly (as in British Gas, Rail). This turned on the realization that, whether regulated or not, the profit motive properly employed could put continuous downwards pressure on costs and perhaps encourage product innovation in a way that was virtually impossible with state ownership. Opposition to these schemes has generally concentrated on modes of regulation; there is little sentiment in most countries to move these firms back to the state.

2. The vertical "disintegration" of a natural monopoly (such as private contracting for services by British NHS hospitals). This rests on the recognition that natural monopolies need not run deep. A hospital may have monopoly power, but it may be able to get its halls cleaned more effectively by hiring private firms.

3. The contracting out of services (as in refuse collection by private firms instead of government employees in many parts of Europe and the United States). Many state employees have traditionally produced private excludable goods that can be obtained more efficiently if purchased through intermediaries. Objections to this approach, as to the previous one, usually turn on the pay and conditions of work for the employees involved and not on disputes about quality or efficiency.

4. The replacement of state monopoly by competitive suppliers (for example, primary and secondary education in parts of Germany, Denmark, and the United States). Recognition that some publicly provided or financed services might better be offered under conditions of choice has become widespread. Education in America, where government monopoly control has been as strong as anywhere, provides a prime example. Those choosing private education for their children must pay twice: once through local and state taxes for a place not taken and then again for the complete cost of the private education. This system has been deemed unsatisfactory by a broad range of Americans, but two alternatives contend: the use of what amounts to a voucher for either public or private education or a choice only among alternatives staffed by public employees. In most of Europe experimentation is easier because the systems have been more mixed historically, with private, often church related schools receiving various levels of tax support.

   The issue of educational improvement can only grow in urgency on both sides of the Atlantic. Policymakers, taking their cues from popular academic writing (see, Reich 1991; Thurow 1992), increasingly envision a kind of two-factor world in which immobile labor within the United States or the European Community must attract internationally mobile packages of complimentary resources. This simple model, and others of greater realism and complexity, come to essentially the same conclusion: Human capital is the single strongest contributor to national economic success, and educational policy is the major lever available to the state for its creation.

5. The abandonment of national protectionism disguised as natural monopoly (for example, European telecoms). Some industries, notably electricity generation and telecommunications, have been operated as public monopolies in large part to maintain national discrimination in equipment purchasing (Rosenman 1988;

McGowan and Thomas 1989). This motive calls for reciprocal liberalization—exactly what the Community has largely achieved and that is being considered in the GATT and in bilateral bargaining with the United States.

Does privatization represent a permanent shift or merely a fad? Some privatized industries have already experienced tighter regulation as the result of politically unsustainable profit levels stemming from residual monopoly elements. Nonetheless, the ideological impulse toward state ownership has been abandoned by most of the European left, leaving ownership and control to evaluation largely on pragmatic grounds. Impact transparency is fairly high, and the evidence so far confirms common sense. The World Bank recently completed a careful study of 12 privatizations, 11 of which produced a substantial average net social gain of 26 percent of firm turnover in the year before privatization (*Economist* 1992a, 73). (Only excessive optimism in equipment purchasing by a privatized Mexican airline produced a loss.)

In the absence of a strong ideological commitment to state ownership, societies gain from privatization. Moreover, while pressure to retain public ownership includes all of the original beneficiaries, privatization, which usually involves a sharp drop in employment, scatters much of the original constituency to the four winds. Unless there is a major recommitment of the left to state ownership on grounds other than efficiency, the probability of renationalization will remain low. A nationalized sector appears to place certain parts of the labor force in an especially secure position at the expense of the real income of most employees, who will typically face the need for ever greater adaptability to the vicissitudes of the global economy. Even if some states decide essentially to "drop out" of the race for higher material living standards (now seemingly unlikely as publics are bombarded with widely publicized information about how each national economy is doing in the league tables), this avenue of retreat toward the objective of employment stability might not be among those chosen.

One issue often considered in equity terms deserves careful scrutiny: The argument that globalization militates against the government provision of social services and the specific contention that the expansion of U.S. federal responsibility for health care will diminish U.S. competitiveness. Several scenarios can be developed. First, even before the suggestion of an expanded state role, many U.S. firms complained that increasing health care costs had diminished their ability to compete.

This only makes sense if they allowed those costs to increase wages beyond what they otherwise would have been. In a nonunion environment, increased health care costs would be substituted for money wages unless there was a market reason for raising the real wage. Similarly, under unionization, it is not clear why the real wage achieved through bargaining would be any different because of rising health care costs; additional wage costs should simply come as health benefits rather than money wages.

The impact of any expansion of public responsibility would depend on the situation of the firm and the means of finance; it could increase or lower firm costs. For example, if the new system were financed entirely by a payroll tax, some firms might be left almost completely unaffected. In general, the firm's competitive position will turn on the extent to which any necessary price increases differ from those of other firms in the economy—particularly its immediate competitors. But if the new government scheme raises the prices of all firms roughly proportionately, the impact on firm demand will be minimal.[18]

What happens in *international* competition? With flexible exchange rates and a national macroeconomy essentially stable in real terms, the price increase should simply cause a compensating devaluation of the domestic currency with no real effect. What many commentators envision, of course, is an impact on the competitiveness of individual firms and even industries in international competition when price-raising effects are *not* economywide and the prices of foreign competitors must be viewed at a fixed rate of exchange. Because piecemeal, differential gains characterize North American trade unionism, and Canada is more highly unionized than the United States the special opposition of Canadian organized labor to freer trade with North America is easy to understand.

The central point can be put in a somewhat different way: How the average citizen takes the same real income as a combination of government benefits and private purchasing power makes little difference to the country's immediate competitive position. On the other hand, increased competition from abroad at a given exchange rate can be expected to stiffen employer resistance to any cost increases—whether wage increases or higher taxes. In particular, if the fiscal system tries to increase the burden on capital earnings for some social initiative, the country's attraction as a site for activity is diminished in a world of capital mobility. Home firms are more likely to leave, and foreign firms less likely to come. As William Niskanen has pointed out, this capital mobility has reduced the revenue-maximizing tax rates of nearly all governments. This has many implications for policy, including the increased means testing of social welfare programs to reduce costs and hence taxes.

Cultural Industries

Many states interfere with the market to promote autonomy through domestic culture, and the means employed can sometimes be offensive to foreigners. The United States employs no discriminatory measures on cultural industries, but it acceded to a broad set of Canadian controls on trade and direct investment in the Canada-U.S. Free Trade Agreement. The Community has declared its interest in having a majority of broadcast programs "European where practicable" (discussed in Acheson, Maule, and Filleul 1989).

While it may or may not be possible to manipulate the communications system in such a way that a majority of programs are European by some measure, there is no way to assure an audience. Modern cable and satellite technology have produced such a variety of offerings from which only a very few are chosen by any one consumer that the national (or regional) content of most cultural *consumption* has already largely moved beyond the reach of government.[19] Policy can continue to encourage local production with subsidies, but the ability of price manipulation to encourage consumption is limited because money price is typically such a small part of the full price (time as well as money). The impact transparency of cultural protection is necessarily very high, and no matter how concentrated producing interests are, protection can be expected to be tightly constrained by consumer-voters. At the end of the day, it may also be difficult to distinguish European (as opposed to national) popular culture from the broader "Atlantic" category.[20]

Competition Policy

An ambivalent attitude toward competition prevailed over much of Europe when the Treaty of Rome was signed. For example, many argued with the traditional live- and let-live attitudes of large domestic firms toward smaller firms in the same industry. Nonetheless, both the Commission and many national authorities have developed policies in the period since that led one American authority to conclude that "gov-

ernment officials and the informed public have accepted that a paramount competition norm will generally produce the best long-term
public welfare results" (Rosenthal 1990, 301), a statement that would
also accurately characterize the present U.S. situation.

There are certainly differences in procedures and emphasis between
the United States and Europe. In particular, European policy emphasizes consultation and agreement over litigation far more than is the
American norm. Nonetheless, an earlier European policy concern for
the welfare of small- and medium-size businesses appears to be in
decline. In fact, contemporary Community policy aims at increasing
consumer welfare largely by permitting industry consolidation while
guarding against excessive concentrations of market power.

United States policy has moved in recent years from an extremely
simple view of antitrust, based largely on concentration, to a much
more sophisticated approach, which employs operational market definitions for concentration measurement and entry barriers (Salop 1987).
Current views on competition in the United States and Europe are
closer than they have ever been before, and in September of 1991 an
agreement was signed between the Justice Department and the Commission that includes provisions for notification, consultation, coordination, and mutual consideration of interest. The agreement may be
particularly important in avoiding extraterritorial claims that each set
of competition laws may extend into the jurisdiction of the other
(United Nations 1992, 78–79). In sharp contrast, while some have
advocated cooperation between U.S. and Japanese competition authorities (Kudrle 1991b; Bergsten and Noland 1993), the U.S. agenda in
such matters would clearly be an extension of the earlier Structural
Impediments Initiative: to encourage the Japanese to enforce more vigorously the competition policies that are already on the books and to
influence the substance of that enforcement.

Investment-Related Trade Measures

Regardless of GATT developments, trade barriers between Europe and
America are likely to continue to fall. Some issues, such as the application of "unfair" trade laws to exports from each side, may persist
for many years, but the disadvantage that protection of import competing industries poses for purchasers who must resell in global markets will provide a continuing political impetus for transatlantic
liberalization. The United States and Europe are both quite open to

incoming foreign direct investment except in a few sectors that may see liberalization in multilateral or bilateral bargaining. A current policy dispute across the Atlantic involves something close to the opposite issue: the use of government policy to entice direct investment. Just as the Uruguay Round considered trade related investment measures (TRIMs) as essentially trade performance requirements for foreign investors, governments can also employ various threats concerning market access to encourage local production. Although investment in Europe has seldom been explicitly expressed to be a quid pro quo for selling in the Community, many American firms have gained the impression that their prospects are much brighter if they add substantial value locally.

One area in which onshore activity has been an explicit requirement for participation is seen in some Community-wide research and development consortia such as ESPRIT or Eureka, which aim to increase the volume and effectiveness of the European Community's research and development. Support for the public good of research and development has been increasingly emphasized by Community countries. Germany now spends 2.88 percent of GDP on R&D (higher than most of its partners) by comparison with 2.82 percent in the United States (and 2.98 percent in Japan). The comparison looks much worse for the United States when nondefense R&D is considered: 2.75 percent for Germany and 1.97 percent for the United States (OECD 1992, 52–55).

The Community's approach to some consortia contrasts with the more nationalistic approach of the United States. For example, the U.S. semiconductor R&D consortium, Sematech, which operates with partial funding from the Defense Department and antitrust variances, includes only U.S.-owned firms. Some additional agreement between the United States and Europe could prevent future conflict in this area. Both sides should acknowledge that a certain volume of local production related to publicly subsidized R&D may be legitimately demanded as a quid pro quo for the subsidy. With such an understanding, the United States should be willing to allow foreign participation in its consortia. On the other hand, the United States should insist that pressures on its firms to locate production in Europe be removed along with its own discriminatory "Buy American" provisions that pervade government procurement. Unfortunately, this problem may become more severe before agreement is reached. States may compete more intensely to entice certain activity to their territory to capture rents and externalites seemingly promised by high-technology research and development and fabrication. Fundamental developments in many industries may be confined to only a few firms, and luring such activity from one state to another may create significant perceptions of gain and loss by both (Ostry 1992; Kudrle 1993).

Atlantic relations are complicated by the special concern of the Europeans with inadequate local activity by Japanese exporters and their attempts to manipulate Japanese trade and investment partly to gain greater access to the Japanese market. (Americans should remember the congressional push for "local content" in Japanese auto exports during the early 80s).

On both sides of the Atlantic, little special treatment is needed for industries especially critical for defense. Access and cost reduction should be paramount objectives in the post–Cold War world where extraordinarily expensive dual-use technology increasingly prevails, and "spin-on" from civilian to defense use is replacing the earlier pattern of "spin-off" the other way (Tyson 1992).

CONCLUSION

My argument is that public policies can be considered intermediate public goods and that, in most policy areas dealing with the relation of government to markets, policy directions on both sides of the Atlantic have converged. This partial convergence has primarily resulted from the rapid development of more market-oriented relations among the EC countries than would have been predicted during the early 80s. This simple, modified public choice model predicts little reversal to previous practices.

By implication, this argument accepts a role for the state that is quite limited in the economic sphere: providing a basic institutional framework and compensating for market failures, especially in terms of human capital formation and research and development efforts. Although issues of social justice were touched upon, especially in discussing income and status distribution issues, the more critically important policies regarding social relations were completely untouched. In particular the role of the state in inculcating values was left unexamined, even though many commentators have declared that such an activity is growing in importance. Such concerns, while perhaps more important than the issues examined here, await other research and probably another author.

Commentary: The Role of the State and Public Action

Georges Vernez

In their excellent chapters, Professors Kudrle and Strange provide two different perspectives on the topic of public action.

Professor Kudrle's presentation amplifies the debate over the extent of convergence in market practices between the United States and the countries of the European Community. He compares in detail the trends in market practices for each major factor of production (land, capital, and labor) as well as trends in privatization and public investments for research and development and concludes there has been growing convergence in the relationship of governments to markets between America and Europe. On both sides of the Atlantic the trend is toward greater reliance on markets and toward a more limited role for the state.

His is an "optimistic" view of convergence seeing little reason for major conflicts arising in the relationship between governments and markets, certainly not any that could not eventually be resolved. In reaching this conclusion, he does not consider the relationship between governments and society and between markets and society. Had he done so, I think his optimism would be tempered.

Take agriculture policy for instance. Through his American lens, Kudrle finds the "food security" argument for protection of agriculture to be suspect because a complete liberalization of trade for farm products would result in a minimal reduction in farming jobs in Europe from 10 to 15 percent. To the French, though, the "character of the European landscape" and of the "security of its food supply" are seen as an integral part of French culture. Viewed as an issue concerning the relationship between markets and society, it is not surprising that the controversy over liberalization of trade for agricultural products reached a salience in GATT negotiations very much out of proportion with the more narrowly conceived impact on farm jobs.

As another example take labor/immigration policy. Nowhere is the potential conflict between markets and society more acute than in this area. When it comes to decisions to emigrate, individual "market" decisions for job opportunities, family reunification, and/or individual welfare and safety prevail. This is one reason why governments in Europe and North America find it so difficult to control flows of immigration, particularly undocumented immigration. But when it comes to the question of "assimilation" of immigrants in the receiving countries, the issue is viewed primarily from a societal "cultural" perspective, not from an individual private perspective. Can and are immigrants willing to learn our language and embrace our values and social and cultural norms? The threat of immigration to the dominant cultures of Europe and the United States may be minimal even at today's rates of immigration, yet it hits at the heart of people's identity and their concept of society in all disproportion to that threat. And it goes a long way toward explaining why increases in immigration (combined with low employment growth), have generated a backlash in nearly all industrialized nations that is seemingly independent of the proportion of foreign-born in their midst and independent of whether a nation regards itself as a country of immigrants (as Australia, Canada, and the United States do) or not (as most European countries do).

Potential conflicts between markets and societal norms and values may also go a long way toward explaining why the international liberalization of movements of labor has not accompanied liberalization of exchanges in all other areas including trade, capital, technology, and information. Indeed the trend with respect to movements of labor seem to be going in the opposite direction and may well be diverging across nations. On issues dealing with the relationship between markets and societies, economic considerations may not be the most important ones.

These illustrations raise the question of what the role of the state is when market interests rub shoulders and seemingly conflict with the strong views a society holds of itself, for example, what is the role of the state with respect to shaping values as well as maintaining distinguishable cultural identities among ethnic groups and/or nations? This issue is particularly salient in the context of the trend noted by Kudrle toward privatization of education, including primary and secondary education. Here I am reminded of Jacques Delors's recent remarks that he would have started with education if the construction of the European Community was to be redone.

In contrast to Kudrle's optimism regarding convergence among nation-states, Professor Strange essentially argues that major structural changes in market relations between states require a paradigm shift in what, how, and by whom market economies should be regulated. She suggests that growing integration, and hence interdependence of the world competitive market will bring with it several critical consequences: (1) a loss of control by nation-states over their own affairs not only in economic matters but in social matters as well; (2) a loss of power upwards to other states or international organizations and downwards to regional and local authorities; and (3) the creation of a vacuum in which there is no effective political authority over a powerfully integrated world market. A stable and efficient world economy requires the latter to be filled, however.

My interpretation of Professor Strange's arguments (and I recognize that I may have not done them justice) raises a couple of questions. First, what is the real extent of the loss of control by nation-states? In his chapter, Kudrle notes that foreign investments in any one country does not exceed 15 percent of total investments, that no country sends more than 10 percent of savings abroad, and that the physical assets used in any one country are almost always home-owned. These are hardly statistics that suggest a loss of control by individual nation-states. However, it may well be that what matters here is less an issue of averages than an issue of what is happening at the margin, thus leading to a second question: In what critical spheres of relations, and by what mechanisms, are structural changes occurring that fundamentally impact on control by individual nation-states? The appropriate level of policy intervention may well differ depending on the answer to this question. Let me illustrate.

Liberalization of international exchanges is one major structural change taking place in all areas but one, the movements of labor as noted earlier. Indeed, nation-states' policies toward international migration seem to move in the other direction toward greater restrictions. Policy persistence in this direction may make individual states focus on upgrading education and training of labor (the last factor of production that remains "immobile") seeing it as the primary way to develop and/or maintain a nation's comparative advantage as suggested in Kudrle's chapter. But it also raises two more basic questions: How to then deal with the distribution of wealth across nations, most particularly between the northern and southern hemisphere, and whether liberalization of exchanges of trade and other areas can actually be sustained in the absence of a similar liberalization in the flows of people?

One mechanism through which nation-states may be losing control is through the development of "transnational networks" facilitated by the ease and the low costs of information exchanges via continuing technological advances. According to various observers, these networks are becoming the dominant form of international integration through business alliances in the economic arena and through alliances of issue-specific or nongovernmental organizations in areas, typically in the "public sector," such as the environment, human rights, and even immigration. In addition to a potential redistribution of power between governments and these formal as well as informal transnational networks, one consequence of this trend may be the development of new institutions designed to mediate between governments and these new forms of organizations.

In supporting her views of asymmetry among nation-states, Professor Strange argues that European countries have lost power to the United States government. But rather than a divergence of relative power, there may just be a leveling off within which any single nation is having increasingly greater difficulties imposing its will on a broad range of issues including trade and national security issues: a kind of "cooperative competition" among nation-states within which no one can unilaterally impose its will.

Professor Strange also perceives a downward loss of power of central governments to regional/local authorities within nations. I cannot speak for the nations of the European Community, but I do not perceive this to be the case in the United States. Within its federalist system, there has been periods of greater and lesser federal interventions at the state and local levels at the margin. But I cannot point to any trend in the distribution of responsibilities between the federal government and state/local governments that would point toward a structural change in this regard.

One trend that may be significant in the United States though, both domestically and internationally, is the ascendance of a western region of the United States centered in California that is increasing its cultural distance from the rest of the nation and that sees its economic future directly linked with Mexico, Latin America, the Pacific Rim, and eventually China rather than seeing it being linked with Europe. Managing this diverging regional interest between the western part of the United States and the rest of the country is looming as a significant challenge to the relations between the United States and Europe.

A final comment: to deal with the international structural changes she identifies, Professor Strange sees the need for international institutional building to deal at a global scale with the same kind of issues market-oriented nation-states have been dealing with—security, value of the currency, administration of justice and conflict resolution, welfare and distribution of wealth, and countercyclical interventions. However, she does not address the question of what kind of institutions need to be invented or established beyond what is "naturally" evolving. This leaves begging the question about the long-term stability of such a system, of the limits of integration, and of what kind of "world vision" ought to direct the development of these institutions.

ENDNOTES

1. An alternative question could also be asked: Does any one of the three have sufficient resources to succeed in economic conflicts with the other two, singly or together?
2. These points are related to the recent "lesson-drawing" literature, see Rose 1991 and 1993.
3. In recent years, political scientists have come to use the term *collective goods* to refer to a package of publicly provided goods that may be excludable and exhaustible, see, for example, Benjamin 1980; Benjamin and Peters, 1993. This approach has merit, but the way of viewing a combination of state-provided goods employed here retains the two original defining characteristics, while stressing the unique character of public policy.
4. The case is thus quite different from the classic textbook lighthouse, where all costs and benefits are confined to actors explicitly considered in the problem.
5. It is not accidental that these examples have a coercive character. One definition of the state involves its role as the sole repository of legitimate violence, see North 1981.
6. This list differs considerably by author. Wolf, 1988, for example, lumps information imperfections into a generally malfunctioning price system and treats public goods and externalities together.
7. Although the new institutional economics is distinguished in part by its rejection of organizations as unitary actors, the following discussion will typically treat firms, interest groups, and bureaus in the usual way when there is no compelling reason for further disaggregation.
8. Despite her skepticism about much of economics, Susan Strange's 1988 basic approach to international relations, beginning with individual aspirations that are aggregated (and distorted) through institutions, is precisely the starting point most economists would adopt to address the same issues, compare North 1981, Chapter 3.
9. Special problems arise when impulses for autonomy fail to correspond to boundaries for effective public policymaking or when large numbers of individuals shift group identification and disturb a previous consistency

between group and political boundaries. These issues will not be treated in this chapter, but they are responsible for today's Balkan horrors and promise continuing conflict.

10. Under the current American administration an ill-defined concept called "economic security" is being used. Within states this phrase has typically been associated with something akin to the assurance of material minima under various contingencies, such as old age, illness, or disability. But in the terminology used here, economic uncertainty at the state level—whether considered in a global context or not—is simply an aspect of the prosperity goal. Security is reserved for safety against the physical predation of a malign "other."

11. Some would argue that additional goals are necessary, even as a first approximation. A sustained and relatively pure concern for the welfare of persons in other countries may one day make the list; for now, however, foreign assistance faces great political obstacles in most countries—even where it is justified on the basis of its service to one of the primary goals. Another contender might be environmental preservation. For most persons, however, this concern appears to be a component of human living standards, as in prosperity. Only those seemingly intent on reviving a kind of animism insist on the preservation of the environment for its own sake.

12. Many have argued that Japan's postwar foreign policy bought security and prosperity at a modest autonomy price through its reliance on the United States. In sharp contrast, Americans maintained maximum autonomy through a security policy that exacted a considerable prosperity price and also bought a great deal of recognition.

13. The general inflation of land values resulting from protection may sometimes complicate the establishment of new competitors in broader markets for goods and services. This is certainly the case in Japan where agricultural protection is estimated to increase land prices by 200 percent (Carr 1992, 8).

14. Peter Lindert of the University of California at Davis has estimated that the peak of influence and cohesion in agriculture comes when it employs 3 to 4 percent of the workforce.

15. Food ingredients are a rather modest and inelastically demanded element of final food sales to customers. Hence the opposition of resellers is reduced. Moreover, agricultural protection is bolstered by the support of the industries that provide supplies to agriculture.

16. The United States is recently reported to have a somewhat smaller share of total income going to the lowest quintile than the next country (Denmark) and a higher share going to the top 10 percent than all except Italy

and France, see World Bank 1991, 263. Data are for various years in the 1980s, however, and are otherwise not entirely comparable.

17. Nikos Christodoulakis and Theo Peeters have reminded me that an important motive for some privatizations has also been the once-for-all positive impact on the government budget when the assets were sold. Deficits and accumulated public debt are a serious problem and a political issue on both sides of the Atlantic, see Franklin 1993, 14.

18. The higher prices should be compensated for by higher employee non-health purchasing power in money terms if the volume of real resources devoted to the health care system remains fixed.

19. Some cultural nationalists refer to broadcast satellites as "death stars."

20. This point was made many years ago by André Malraux; for a general discussion of cultural protectionism, see Acheson, Maule, and Filleul 1989.

REFERENCES

Acheson, C., Maule, C., and Filleul, E. "Folly of Quotas on Films and Television Programmes." *World Economy,* vol. 12, no. 4 (December 1989): 515–24.

Benjamin, R. and Peters, B. G. "The Democratic State and Public Policy." Mimeographed, 1993.

Benjamin, R. *The Limits of Politics: Collective Goods and Political Change in Post-Industrial Societies.* Chicago: University of Chicago Press, 1980.

Bergsten, C. F., and Noland, M. *Reconcilable Differences? United States-Japan Economic Conflict.* Washington, D.C.: Institute for International Economics, 1993.

Bobrow, D. B., and Kudrle, R. T. "MNE Disclosure Alternatives and Their Consequences." *Journal of World Trade Law* (September-October 1984): 437–54.

Carr, E. "Grotesque: A Survey of World Agriculture." *The Economist,* vol. 325, December 12, 1992: psurv 1–18.

Crandall, R. W. *Manufacturing on the Move.* Washington, D.C.: Brookings Institution, 1993.

"Escaping the Heavy Hand of the State." (World Bank—study on privatization.) *The Economist,* June 13, 1992(a): pp. 73–74.

Feldstein, M. "The Budget and Trade Deficits Aren't Really Twins." *Challenge* (March–April 1992): 60–63.

Franklin, D. "A Rude Awakening: A Survey of the European Community." *The Economist,* vol. 328, July 3, 1993: psurv. 1–20.

Freeman, R. B. "Evaluating the European View that the U.S. Has No Unemployment Problem." National Bureau of Economic Research, Working Paper no. 2562, 1988.

Freeman, R. B., and Rogers, J. "Who Speaks for Us? Employee Representation in a Non-Union Labor Market," in Morris Kleiner and Bruce Kaufman, eds. *Employee Representation: Alternatives and Future Directions.* Madison, WI: Industrial Relations Research Association, 1993.

Fry, E. H. "Foreign Direct Investment in North America: Political and Legal Considerations," Chapter 1 in Earl H. Fry, and Lee H Radebaugh, eds. *Investment in the North American Free Trade Area: Opportunities and Challenges.* Provo, UT: Brigham Young University, Kennedy Center, 1991.

Furubotn, E., and Richter, R. *The New Institutional Economics.* College Station, TX: Texas A&M University, 1990.

Glickman, N., and Woodward, D. *The New Competitors: How Foreign Investors Are Changing the U.S. Economy.* New York: Basic Books, 1989.

Head, J. G. "Public Goods and Public Policy." *Public Finance,* vol. 17, no. 3 (1962): 197–220.

Ito, T. *The Japanese Economy.* Cambridge, MA: MIT Press, 1992.

Kline, J. M., and Wallace, C. D. "EC-92 and Changing Global Investment Patterns: Implications for the U.S.-EC Relationship." Washington, D.C., Center for Strategic and International Studies, International Business and Economics Program, mimeographed, 1991 .

Kudrle, R. T. "The Challenge Within: Foreign Direct Investment in Europe and the United States," Chapter 2 in Earl H. Fry, and Lee H. Radebaugh, eds. *Investment in a North American Free Trade Area: Opportunities and Challenges.* Provo, UT: Brigham Young University, Kennedy Center, 1991a.

———. "Some Suggestions For Improving U.S.-Japan Relations Through Increased Attention to Competition Policy." Paper prepared for a conference at the University of Pittsburgh, September 3–4, 1991b.

———. "Regulating Multinational Enterprises in North America," in Eden, Lorraine, ed., *Multinationals in North America: Location and Regulation of the Top 1000.* Ottawa: Investment Canada, 1993.

Kudrle, R. T., and Bobrow, D. B. "The G-7 After Hegemony: Compatibility, Cooperation, and Conflict." Chapter 7 in David Rapkin, ed., *World Leadership and Hegemony.* International Political Economy Yearbook, vol. 5. Boulder and London: Lynne Reinner Publishers, 1990, pp. 147–67.

————. "U.S. Policy Toward Foreign Direct Investment." *World Politics* (April 1982): 353–62.

Kudrle, R. T., and Lenway, S. A. "Progress for the Rich: The Canada-U.S. Free Trade Agreement." Chapter 7 in Emanual Adler, and Beverly Crawford, eds., *Progress in Post-War International Relations.* New York, New York: Columbia University Press, 1990.

"Life, Liberty and Try Pursuing a Bit of Tolerance Too." *The Economist,* September 5, 1992(b), pp. 19–20.

McGowan, F., and Thomas, S. "Restructuring in the Power-Plant Equipment Industry and 1992." *World Economy,* vol. 12, no. 4 (December 1989): 539–56.

Nelson, M. M., and Ikenberry, G. J. *Atlantic Frontiers: A New Agenda for the U.S.-EC Relations.* Washington, D.C.: Carnegie Endowment for International Peace, 1993.

North, D. C. *Structure and Change in Economic History.* New York: Norton, 1981.

Olson, M. *The Logic of Collective Action.* Cambridge, MA: Harvard University Press, 1965.

————. *The Rise and Decline of Nations.* New Haven, CT: Yale University Press, 1983.

OECD (Organization for Economic Cooperation and Development). *OECD In Figures.* Supplement to the *OECD Observer,* June/July 1992.

Ostry, S. "The Domestic Domain: The New International Policy Arena." *Transnational Corporations,* vol. 1, no. 1 (February 1992): 7–26.

Reich, R. *The Work of Nations.* New York: Knopf, 1991.

Rose, R. "What is Lesson Drawing?" *Journal of Public Policy,* vol. 11 (1991): 3–30.

————. *Lesson-Drawing In Public Policy.* Chatham, NJ: Chatham House Publishers, 1993.

Rosenman, D. "Towards a GATT Code on Trade in Telecommunication Equipment." *World Economy,* vol. 11, no. 1 (1988): 135–49.

Rosenthal, D. E. "Competition Policy." Chapter 6 in Hufbauer, Gary Clyde, ed., *Europe 1992: An American Perspective.* Washington, D.C.: Brookings Institution, 1990.

Salop, S. C. "Symposium on Mergers and Antitrust." *Journal of Economic Perspectives,* vol. 1, no. 2 (Fall 1987): 3–54.

Strange, S. *States and Markets: An Introduction to International Political Economy.* New York: Basil Blackwell, 1988.

Thurow, L. *Head to Head: The Coming Economic Battle Among Japan, Europe and America.* New York: William Morrow and Company, 1992.

Tyson, L. D. *Who's Bashing Whom? Trade Conflict and High Technology Industries.* Washington, D.C.: Institute for International Economics, 1992.

United Nations, Transnational Corporations and Management Division, Department of Economic and Social Development. *World Investment Report, 1991, Investment in the Triad.* New York: United Nations, 1991.

————. *World Investment Report 1992: Transnational Corporations as Engines of Growth.* New York: United Nations, 1992.

"The Way We Were." *The Economist.* October 3, 1992(c), p. 71.

Weimer, D. L. and Vining, A. R. *Policy Analysis: Concepts and Practice,* 2nd Edition, Englewood Cliffs, NJ: Prentice Hall, 1992.

Wolf, C., Jr. *Markets and Governments: Choosing Between Imperfect Alternatives,* Cambridge, MA: The MIT Press, 1988.

World Bank. *World Development Report: The Challenge of Development.* New York: Oxford University Press, 1991.

III

Social Structures and the Demand for Public Sector Intervention

7

The Demand for Public Sector Intervention in a European Welfare State

Kees P. Goudswaard, Victor Halberstadt,
and Hans M. van de Kar

INTRODUCTION: MARKETS AND SOCIETY, AN ECONOMIST'S VIEW

The traditional starting point for a (public sector) economist when addressing the relationship between markets and society is the possible causes of market failure. He analyzes the outcome of the market system when it is inefficient or otherwise undesirable and determines how the government can correct or compensate against the undesirable outcome.

The normative public finance approach first analyzes market failure, since Musgrave's treatise, by distinguishing between three different aspects of government action: allocation, distribution, and stabilization[1]. This chapter focuses mainly on the first two aspects since the contemporary European welfare state is characterized by redistribution (in cash and in kind) and by intervention using regulation, taxes, subsidies, and other price instruments in the production, provision, and consumption of many goods and services.

Currently, there is a serious debate in many countries about the sustainability of this modern, but very costly, welfare state.[2] This debate often occurs in industrialized democracies in an atmosphere of possible drastic policy changes and panic. However, several reasoned examinations are needed to determine what the industrialized state should be doing for its citizens in the twenty-first century and how the state's actions can be financed.

This debate would be needed even if the fiscal positions were healthier. This particular debate, however, was largely initiated by the weakened condition of public finances. Demographic developments imply that current spending programs are unsustainable in the medium term. Moreover, changing lifestyles and individual tastes and aspirations also require a greater variety in the patterns of provision.

For both policy analysts and policymakers these developments require a revisit of the principles behind the welfare state, which was set up as protection for those who through poverty, illness, unemployment, or old age cannot, or cannot adequately, help themselves. To achieve these objectives, the European welfare states provide cradle-to-grave social security, health services, low-rent housing, and free education.

The provision of health and social security reflect the circumstances of the Western European postwar societies in which all but the wealthiest needed such support. The solidarity of wartime experiences in fact gave birth to a welfare state into which almost all contribute and out of which many draw. In such a case, demographics can be largely ignored.

The principle of social solidarity remains important. Any welfare state must command the support of those who contribute to it as well as those who most need its help. An increasing proportion of people can (wholly or partly) provide pensions, health care, housing, and education for themselves. However, there remain large groups who depend on the safety nets of welfare states. Yet paradoxically, various studies suggest that it is often the middle classes who get the most out of the welfare state, which leaves too little for those who lack alternative means.

The crucial question is whether the balance between collective and individual provisions is currently correct. In a sense, the welfare state acts as a savings bank, with people paying in when times are good and drawing out in times of need. A much larger portion of these savings bank functions could easily, with appropriate regulation, be undertaken by the individual through private provision.

For some welfare state services, however, efficiency may be best served by maintaining a large, important role for the state. In health, for example, international experience suggests that some sort of state role is essential to maintain a reasonable overall bill and ensure cost-sharing between different groups. But in the health services of all welfare states, many people want and would be prepared to pay for premium levels of service.

In addition, to understand the economic rationale of the welfare state concept, the traditional theoretical analysis of market failure should be reviewed. The first source of market failure is the existence of pure public goods and involve an allocative role of the government. A pure public good technically cannot (or cannot efficiently) exclude beneficiaries. Thus free riding is immanent. A pure public good is also nonrival in consumption. Therefore, the marginal cost of adding another person to consume the good is zero. In this case, market principles should not be applied. Moreover, goods and services are sometimes nonexcludable, but rival in property resources: the fish in the sea, clean air, the ozone layer, or the common meadow in David Hume's *Tragedy of Commons*.

In many cases, but not always, pure public goods are provided for by a public budget. This does not necessarily imply public production. The government may sometimes subcontract the production of a public good to a private producer. On the other hand, public production does not imply the production of public goods. Many goods and services produced in the public sector have the nature of private goods or are mixed goods. In practice, most goods and services do have a mixed character: exclusion is possible and consumption is rival but the consumption or production also involves externalities or spillovers.

Externalities are social costs and benefits that are not reflected in the market prices. Thus, prices are too low when negative externalities (pollution) occur and too high in the case of positive externalities (education). Price correction through taxes or subsidies is the classical response to externalities.

Nonexcludability, nonrivalry (which also includes cases of decreasing-cost industries or natural monopolies), and externalities are the traditional allocative domain of government.

In the modern welfare state this traditional allocative domain is supplemented and often overgrown by the distributive role of government. In practice, the distributive role often includes the provision of merit goods.

The distributive role focuses on the social justice of the distribution of incomes and wealth, and not with the efficiency of the market system. Redistribution can be executed through cash transfers or through the subsidization of specific goods and services (education, health care, welfare services, housing, passenger transport). Subsidization involves income support in kind. The merit good is often used for justification, for example, when the government wishes to overrule individual preferences. Thus the general rule of consumer sovereignty is not followed.

In light of the current debate, this chapter will describe the public finance of a modern welfare state and examine the past and probable development of relevant categories of public expenditure by using the Netherlands as an illustration. The Netherlands is a good example of a European welfare state in transition. Demographic assumptions as well as changes in social structures and economic scenarios are included.

The second section, titled "Trends in General Government Expenditure," provides insight into some trends in general government expenditure and a summarized international comparison of the size and scope of public sector activity.

The third section, titled "The Public/Private Mix in Selected Policy Areas," illustrates various roles of the government through relevant outlays. It also reviews changes in the role of the public sector in the Netherlands. Outlays in specific sections of the welfare state are analyzed and changes in the private/public mix for financing these expenditures are discussed.

In the fourth section, titled "Long-Term Scenarios," possible policy reactions are addressed considering the expected demographic changes and the changes in social structures, such as the shift from the family to the individual as the relevant policy parameter. The different scenarios are reviewed.

In the fifth section some general observations and conclusions are provided.

TRENDS IN GENERAL GOVERNMENT EXPENDITURE

It is quite difficult to assess the quantitative role of the public sector in the economy. Public sector activity extends beyond expenditures and revenues. The OECD, however, divides public sector activity into five categories:[3]

- general government transactions in goods and services and transfers of income and capital;
- economic activities of public enterprises and institutions;
- tax expenditures;
- public sector lending and loan guarantees to private borrowers;
- government regulation.

Government expenditure represents the most important activity, and is generally well documented. However, when making international comparisons, measurement difficulties and institutional differences may blur the picture. For example, in some countries government child support is provided through tax allowances, while other countries provide direct cash allowances. Although the end result may be the same, figures for government expenditures and revenues strongly differ under the two regimes. These and other differences should be kept in mind.

Table 7.1 presents data on total government outlays in OECD countries.[4] The level of total expenditure relative to GDP in 1990 ranged from approximately 30 percent in Japan, Switzerland, and Turkey to 61.5 percent in Sweden. Belgium, Denmark, the Netherlands, and Norway are positioned closely behind Sweden. Government expenditure in Europe is on average more than 11 percentage points higher than in the United States. Moreover, the difference between the United States and the Northern and Western European welfare states is much larger (some 20 percentage points).

Table 7.1 also shows that the government expenditure share increased on average by 8.4 percentage points between 1970 and 1990. The growth of government in Europe (12 percentage points) has been much more pronounced than in the United States (5.3 percentage points).

The data also shows a break in the upward trend of the public expenditure ratio in 1982. In 1990, spending ratios were in most countries below their 1982 values. This change in the trend can partially be attributed to business cycle effects, but also to a rather fundamental policy change. In 1982, expansionary fiscal policy was abandoned and most OECD countries chose strategies to reduce the size of the public sector: "Concern over the effects of a continuing expansion of the public sector on private sector performance and a greater appreciation of the social costs of higher taxation produced broad agreement on expenditure reductions. This was to be accompanied, at the microeconomic policy level, by a reduction of government intervention, particularly where it distorted price signals or impeded market forces."[5]

In table 7.2, government expenditure is decomposed by economic category. It should be mentioned, however, that the OECD has drawn these data from different sources, which seriously hampers intercountry comparisons. Thus, only some broad observations can be made.

Expenditures on public goods, the traditional domain of public activity, are a relatively small part of total public outlays in most

Table 7.1

General government outlays[a] as percent of GDP

	1970	1979	1982	1984	1989	1990
United States	31.7	31.7	36.5	35.8	36.1	37.0
Japan	19.4	31.6	33.6	32.9	31.5	30.7
Germany	38.6	47.7	49.7	48.1	45.4	46.0
France	38.5	45.0	50.4	52.0	49.5	50.4
Italy	34.2	45.5	47.4	49.3	51.7	53.2
United Kingdom	38.8	42.5	46.9	47.2	40.9	42.9
Canada	34.8	39.0	46.6	46.8	44.3	46.4
Total[b]	32.1	36.5	40.4	40.0	38.9	39.7
Australia[c]	26.8	33.5	37.0	38.5	34.8	36.4
Austria	39.2	48.9	50.9	50.8	49.6	48.6
Belgium	42.2	58.1	64.2	62.8	55.5	54.7
Denmark	40.2	53.2	61.2	60.3	58.7	57.5
Finland	30.5	38.7	39.1	39.8	38.2	40.8
Greece	22.4	29.7	37.0	40.2	47.7	50.4
Iceland	30.7	32.8	34.2	32.1	39.8	—
Ireland	39.6	46.8	55.8	54.0	48.8	44.5
Luxembourg	33.1	52.5	55.8	51.8	—	—
Netherlands	43.9	55.8	61.6	61.0	56.0	58.3
Norway	41.0	50.4	48.3	46.3	54.6	55.1
Portugal	21.6	38.2	43.0	44.4	41.7	—
Spain	22.3	30.5	37.6	39.4	41.8	41.9
Sweden	43.3	60.7	66.3	63.5	60.1	61.5
Switzerland[d]	21.3	29.9	30.1	31.4	29.9	—
Turkey	—	25.8[e]	26.4	25.5	28.8	30.4
Total[b,f]	33.6	43.6	48.8	48.9	47.4	47.9
OECD Europe[b,f]	36.9	45.3	49.3	49.6	47.6	48.6
North America[b]	31.9	32.4	37.4	36.8	36.8	37.8
OECD[b,f]	32.3	37.4	41.5	41.2	40.0	40.7

[a]Total outlays consist mainly of current disbursements plus gross capital formation.

[b]Averages computed using 1985 purchasing power parities.

[c]Fiscal year beginning July 1.

[d]Current disbursements only.

[e]OECD Secretariat estimates.

[f]Excluding Iceland, Luxembourg, Portugal, Switzerland, and Turkey.

Source: OECD National Accounts and OECD Economic Outlook 49. See Table 7.2 for method.

Table 7.2
Structure of general government outlays by function[a]
(percent of GNP/GDP)

	United States			Japan			Germany			United Kingdom			Australia[b]		
	1979	1989	Change	1979	1989	Change	1979	1989	Change	1979	1989	Change	1979	1989	Change
I. *Total expenditure*	32.1	36.3	4.2	31.1	31.6	0.5	48.0	46.8	-1.2	42.8	41.2	-1.6	33.7	34.8	0.9
Traditional Domain															
II. *Public goods*	7.7	9.1	1.4	3.9	3.7	0.2	8.3	8.2	-0.1	8.4	8.3	-0.1	6.6	8.3	-0.2
1. Defense	4.9	5.9	1.0	0.8	0.9	0.1	2.8	2.6	-0.2	4.5	4.1	-0.4	2.2	2.1	-0.1
2. General public service	2.1	2.5	0.4	3.1	2.8	-0.3	5.5	5.6	0.1	3.3	3.6	0.3	4.3	4.2	-0.1
3. Other functions	0.7	0.7	0.0	-0.0	0.0	0.0	0.0	0.0	0.0	0.6	0.8	0.0	0.0	0.0	0.0
The Welfare State															
III. *Merit goods*	6.2	6.1	-0.1	11.3	10.9	-0.4	13.3	12.7	-0.6	13.6	12.8	-0.8	11.8	11.8	0.0
1. Education	4.5	4.6	0.1	4.6	3.5	-1.1	5.0	4.3	-0.7	5.2	4.8	-0.4	5.8	5.1	-0.7
2. Health	0.9	0.9	0.0	4.5	4.9	0.4	6.1	6.5	0.4	4.6	5.0	0.4	4.6	5.1	0.8
3. Housing and other	0.8	0.6	-0.2	2.2	2.5	0.3	2.2	1.9	-0.3	3.8	3.0	-0.8	1.5	1.6	0.1
IV. *Income transfers*	10.8	11.7	0.9	—	—	—	18.4	17.5	-0.9	11.9	12.9	1.0	7.5	7.4	-0.1
a. *Income maintenance*	7.6	7.8	0.2	6.3	7.2	0.9	16.5	15.8	-0.7	9.2	9.6	0.4	7.0	6.5	-0.5
1. Pensions	6.6	7.0	0.4	4.1	5.7	1.6	12.3	11.3	-1.0	8.4	8.2	-0.2	4.8	4.1	-0.7
2. Sickness benefits	0.1	0.2	0.1	0.2	0.1	-0.1	0.8	0.7	-0.1	0.4	0.3	-0.1	0.1	0.2	0.1
3. Family allowance	0.4	0.4	0.0	1.6	1.2	-0.4	1.2	0.8	-0.4	1.6	1.6	0.0	1.1	1.0	-0.1
4. Unemployment comp.	0.4	0.3	-0.1	0.4	0.2	-0.2	0.9	1.5	0.6	0.7	0.7	0.0	0.8	0.9	0.1
5. Other income support	0.0	0.0	0.0	0.0	0.0	0.0	1.3	1.5	0.2	0.1	0.8	0.7	0.2	0.3	0.1

Table 7.2 (continued)

	United States			Japan			Germany			United Kingdom			Australia[b]		
	1979	1989	Change	1979	1989	Change	1979	1989	Change	1979	1989	Change	1979	1989	Change
IV. *Income transfers (continued)*															
b. Administration and other spending	2.5	2.2	-0.3	—	—	—	2.5	2.4	-0.1	1.3	1.5	0.2	0.5	0.7	0.2
c. Other transfers (non-profit institutions and r.o.w.)	0.6	1.7	1.1	—	—	—	0.4	0.4	0.0	1.4	1.8	0.4	0.0	0.2	0.2
The Mixed Economy															
V. *Economic services*	4.5	4.5	0.0	6.6	5.5	-1.1	5.4	4.6	-0.8	3.7	3.0	-0.7	5.8	4.7	-1.1
1. Capital formation and capital transfers	1.6	1.7	0.1	4.4	3.9	-0.5	2.3	1.5	-0.8	1.1	1.0	-0.1	1.4	1.1	-0.3
2. Subsidies	0.4	0.6	0.2	1.2	0.7	-0.5	1.9	1.9	0.0	1.1	0.5	0.6	1.4	1.0	-0.4
3. Other	2.5	2.2	-0.3	1.0	0.9	-0.1	1.2	1.2	0.0	1.5	1.5	0.0	3.0	2.6	-0.4
VI. *Public debt interest*	2.8	5.0	2.2	2.6	4.0	1.4	1.7	2.8	1.1	4.4	3.6	-0.8	2.1	4.4	2.3
VII. *Balancing item*	0.1	-0.1	-0.2	0.4	0.3	-0.1	-0.1	0.0	0.1	0.8	0.6	-0.2	0.0	0.0	0.0
VIII. *Net lending*	0.2	-3.1	-3.3	-4.7	2.5	7.2	-2.8	-2.1	-0.7	-3.2	-0.1	-3.1	-1.4	1.7	3.1

[a]For a description of the methodology and sources used in this table, see source material referred to below. Because of the approximations made for some countries, cross-country comparisons should be made with caution.

[b]Fiscal year beginning 1 July.

Sources: OECD *National Accounts* supplemented by data for Item IV from national sources and OECD Social Expenditure Data File.

countries. The ratio of expenditures on public goods to GDP varies from 3.7 percent in Japan to 10.0 percent in the Netherlands. The United States is in second place (9.1 percent), reflecting high defense spending.

The differences in welfare state activities, such as income transfers and merit goods, as in education, health, and housing, are much more pronounced. Public expenditures on merit goods in the United States are less than 50 percent of the European level. This reflects the very low public health spending in the United States. In Japan spending on merit goods is not much lower than in Europe.

The share of income transfers in GDP is also almost twice as high in Europe as in the United States. The U.K. is an exception because at this point it is more comparable to the United States than to the rest of Western Europe. In Japan and Australia, income support is even lower than in the United States.

Most countries managed to stabilize or reduce spending on merit goods in the 1980s. Income transfer payments declined in the Netherlands and in Germany. The Nordic countries, however, still witnessed a substantial rise in expenditures on income transfers in the 1980s. Furthermore, in almost all countries debt interest payments were the main growing expenditure category in the 1980s.

THE PUBLIC/PRIVATE MIX IN SELECTED POLICY AREAS

Introduction

This section analyzes whether the relationship between government and markets has changed in the last decade.[6] There is an ongoing debate in the Netherlands and in many other countries on the role government should play in a market-oriented economy. In the late 1970s and early 1980s it was widely felt for economic and ideological reasons that the size and role of the public sector should be reduced. In particular, this section investigates how this changing view has indeed led to less public intervention in the 1980s in the Netherlands.

A survey directed at specific sectors that were largely affected by considerations of social policies was conducted in the Netherlands. The targeted sectors were: housing, education, old age pensions, the labor market, health care, and passenger transportation. The public/private mix is indicated, where and when possible, by the public sector share in total expenditures or by specific types of expenditures as a percent of GNP. In some cases not only direct subsidies, but also tax expenditures are considered. These indicators are quite rudimentary because government intervention in the economy extends beyond spending activities and tax facilities. In addition, various forms of regulation are also of great importance, but are not considered here. However, these data try to answer whether and to what extent the public/private mix has changed in the specified sectors.

Health Care

The Dutch health care system has its roots in the "Bismarck"-model of social security. This model features compulsory (public) insurance and is applied in countries like Canada, Japan, France, Belgium, and Germany. In contrast, the "Beveridge"-model provides social security benefits (including health care), which are paid for out of general public (tax) revenue. The health care systems of Sweden, Denmark, and the United Kingdom follow this model.[7]

Neither model applies to the United States. In the United States only 43 percent of the population (1985) receives health care, which is financed by collective means (public insurance and/or taxes). In the countries mentioned above the coverage is between 90 and 100 percent. In the Netherlands, however, the coverage ratio is somewhat lower: 70 to 80 percent.

Total health care expenditure has increased in the Netherlands from 6.3 percent GNP (1970) to 8.2 percent GNP (1980) and 8.4 percent (1985). In recent years this relative growth appears to have come to an end, with 7.9 percent GNP (1990).

The actual policy debate on the future of Dutch health care finance focuses mainly on two issues:

- the introduction of a uniform public insurance scheme with broader coverage;
- a reduced role of the government, mainly through deregulation.

The health care debate in the Netherlands has not yet lead to final conclusions and is rather complex. Demand and supply of health care are both characterized by strong government intervention. Since cost control and cost effectiveness score poorly in the health care sector the debate focuses on stronger financial incentives and increased competition to promote a better cost control. Moreover, the health care market is inherently imperfect, since supplier-induced demand is combined with a very low price elasticity. This feature impedes the proper functioning of the market mechanism.

The demand for health care is strongly influenced by demographic developments and by sociocultural factors.[8] Since demand is age-dependent, aging, or more specifically an increase in the number of people older than 80, has had a significant impact on health care consumption and costs. The influence of sociocultural factors is illustrated by the rapid growth of problems of mental health resulting from higher stress—a risk of an increasingly dynamic society. A related phenomenon is the preference drift of desired or acceptable health status. The growth of real income induces an upward shift in the desired level of health status. In addition, health care consumption by people under a public insurance scheme (ZF) is, on average, larger than the consumption of a privately insured person. Moreover, coverage in kind results in higher costs per capita than insurance schemes that refund doctor's bills, and so forth.

In short, the demand and supply-side characteristics obstruct cost containment in the health care section. This does not imply, however, that a radical change toward either more or less public intervention in the health care system will always lead to better cost control. Indeed, the U.K. National Health Service brings about a lower cost/GDP ratio than observed in "Bismarck" countries, but at the same time the waiting lists are much longer. On the other hand, the United States has a relatively "free" health care market, but at the same time one of the highest cost/GDP ratios.

To analyze the public/private mix within the Dutch health care system, a breakdown of the sources of finance is needed. The health care system in the Netherlands has five main sources of finance: two public insurance schemes ("AWBZ" and "ZF"), direct public subsidies, private insurance, and direct private contributions (user fees not covered by private insurance). In table 7.3 the last two sources are combined.[9]

Table 7.3
Sources of finance of health care, billion Dutch guilders

	1970	(percent)	1980	(percent)	1990	(percent)
ZF	3.0	(41.7)	11.9	(43.1)	15.8	(40.0)
AWBZ	1.2	(16.7)	7.4	(26.8)	11.9	(30.0)
Public subsidies	1.4	(19.4)	1.7	(6.2)	1.8	(4.5)
Private sources	1.6	(22.2)	6.6	(23.9)	10.1	(25.5)
Total	7.2		27.6		39.6	

Source: Central Bureau of Statistics; authors' computations.

In conclusion, the table indicates that although there have been some changes in the relative importance of the various sources of health care finance, the changes are mainly restricted to the public sources of finance. In addition, the public/private mix indicates only a slight movement towards more private funding.

Passenger Traffic

The Netherlands is the most densely populated country in the OECD area. In combination with a relatively high use of cars, the dense population causes severe congestion problems. The Dutch public transport system, including train, tram, and bus, is heavily subsidized by the government.[10] Total subsidies amounted to some 0.8 percent of GNP in the 1980s. Compared to other countries these subsidies are high. For urban transport, the subsidies amount to some 75 percent of total cost (the OECD average equals 45 percent). Railway subsidies are around 45 percent (the European Community average equals 35 percent). This ratio increased substantially in the 1970s and 1980s. In 1970 urban transport subsidies were up 48 percent and railways were up 30 percent.

Subsidization was advocated for many years because of its alleged positive allocational effects. The utilization ratio, however, of the public transport system remained relatively low. In practice, the substitution effect, in regard to the private automobile, turned out to be much less than expected. Nevertheless, the subsidization policy did not change.

Moreover, analysis indicates that increases in the costs of using automobiles discourages mainly "fun" nonbusiness driving. On the other hand, expanding the public transport system in itself does not reduce road congestion. Expansion might even induce a further increase in the demand for transport.[11]

Table 7.4 illustrates the public/private mix.

In conclusion, the public/private mix has remained rather stable.

The Housing Sector

The demand for housing depends structurally on the number of households. The number of households is influenced by demographic factors, such as population growth and shifts in the age structure of population; sociocultural factors, such as the growth of the "headship rate," for

Table 7.4

Sources of finance of public transport, billion Dutch guilders

	1981		1985		1988	
		(percent)		(percent)		(percent)
Private user charges	2.0	(43)	2.2	(40)	2.3	(41)
Public subsidies	2.7	(57)	3.3	(60)	3.3	(59)
Total	4.7		5.5		5.6	

Source: Central Bureau of Statistics.

example, the number of heads of household as a percentage of the number of persons in an age group; and economic factors, mainly the disposable income of households and the costs of housing.

The negative externalities caused by a structural shortage of proper housing were used to justify the subsidization of housing after World War II. Housing was also considered a merit good. Nowadays the housing market is more or less in equilibrium. However, in spite of the growth of real disposable incomes, housing subsidies did not diminish.

The motivation for current subsidies is mainly the provision of proper housing for lower income groups. Public spending for housing takes place via several subsidies and tax reliefs. The largest part of public spending in this sector consists of object subsidies on rental prices. However, the direct redistributional character of housing policies results from income-related individual rental subsidies, the second-largest public spending instrument.

Table 7.5 shows an increase to a rather high level in 1985 for both direct and tax subsidies. They are slightly reduced in the more recent years. Today, housing policies still involve budgetary provisions of approximately 3 percent of GNP.

Table 7.6 indicates that 71 to 84 percent of newly built houses were subsidized in the 1980s. However, this intervention has reduced slightly since 1985. Recent policies include relative rises in rents and taxes on rental values. The average relative private expenditure on housing has increased from 7 percent in 1960 to 13 percent in 1990. This is a result of yearly rises of (regulated) rental prices. The increase was strongest in the rented housing sector.

In conclusion, the public/private mix has slightly shifted toward more private expenditures.

Table 7.5
Direct subsidies and tax subsidies in the housing sector in percent GNP

	Subsidies[a]	Tax revenue forgone due to interest reduction[b]	Tax revenue forgone, net of tax on rental value[c]
1970	0.4	n.a.	n.a.
1975	1.0	0.8	0.6
1980	1.3	1.5	0.2
1985	2.2	1.5	1.3
1990	2.1	1.3	0.8

[a]Individual subsidies, object subsidies, and urban renewal subsidies.

[b]Interest payments on mortgages are fully tax-deductible; the revenue forgone is computed using a 50 percent marginal tax rate (income tax and social security premiums).

[c]The net rental value of owner occupied houses is taxable; in 1990, 1.8 percent of the value of a house in an occupied state is included in the tax base.

Table 7.6
The share of subsidized houses

	Subsidized rented houses in percent of total stock	Subsidized rented houses in percent of total newly built houses
1970	31	84
1975	34	79
1980	36	75
1985	38	85[a]
1990	n.a.	71

[a]1984

Sources: Ministry of Housing, Physical Planning and Environmental Protection; authors' computations.

Education

Together with health care, the largest proportion of merit goods spending in the Dutch public sector is on education. The share of education spending rose from 7 percent in 1970 to 7.5 percent of GNP in 1980. From 1980 to 1990 this share declined to below the 1970 level (6.4 percent in 1990).

Total spending does not, however, fully reflect the extent of government involvement in this sector, because the outlays are also influenced by demographic trends. To correct for demographic effects, spending per student can be analyzed. Recent research indicates that while manpower per student has remained stable, total real spending per student has declined by 8 percent between 1980 and 1990 (De Groot and Goudriaan 1991). This reflects a drop in relative wages in education. Demographic factors also reveal a much stronger decline in education expenditures than the actual decline. This is explained by the rise of participation-ratios in certain categories of schooling.

An indicator for the public/private mix in this sector is the share of tuition fees in the total outlays per student. Tuition fees for higher education for example amounted to only 5 percent of total exploitation costs in 1980. This percentage was around 10 percent in 1990. However, this indicator is very rough because private spending for education includes more than just these user charges.

In conclusion, the public/private mix for education is very low but has shifted slightly toward private spending.

Old Age Pensions

The Dutch pension system consists of two components. It is a public pension scheme with uniform, not income-related, benefits for every citizen starting at the age of 65. These benefits are financed on a pay-as-you-go basis. It also consists of supplementary private pensions. In most cases, these are a compulsory element in labor contracts. These private schemes are earnings-related and financed through a capital reserve system. Research has indicated that the public pension benefits for employees are relatively low in an international perspective. However, the private supplementary pensions are relatively generous (Petersen 1989).

Table 7.7 indicates that expenditures on supplementary pensions have increased more rapidly than expenditures on public pensions. However, part of the supplementary pensions is financed by a preferential tax treatment, which involves a sizable tax expenditure.

The public/private mix is expressed by the share of average supplementary pension shown in table 7.8.

The share of average supplementary pension has increased and will increase even further. It was 21 percent in 1980 and is estimated to

Table 7.7
Expenditure on old age pensions in percent GNP

	Public Pensions	Supplementary Pensions
1975	5.6	3.3
1980	5.8	3.5
1985	5.5	4.3
1989	5.5	5.0

Sources: Ministry of Social Affairs and Employment; Central Bureau of Statistics.

reach 39 percent by 2030. In conclusion, there is a tendency toward a larger private share in old age pensions.

Labor Market Related Income Transfers

Through a cumulation of rules and a variety of income transfers and subsidies, the Dutch labor market is characterized by strong market intervention. This intervention weakens the incentive structure of the labor market. There is a large wedge between labor costs and net income. In addition, net social security benefits are relatively generous and a large number of income related regulations and provisions have been implemented. As a result, market flexibility is lacking, which contributes to large structural unemployment in the Netherlands.

Public spending for the unemployed is concentrated more on income support than for employment search and training. Moreover, the implementation of labor market policies in practice has merged with the implementation of disability and sickness programs. Thus transfer programs related to the labor market are a large part of the welfare system.

Table 7.8
Average share of supplementary pension in total pension

1980	1990	2000[a]	2030[a]
21%	25%	26%	39%

[a]Estimates.
Source: Central Planning Bureau.

Expenditures on unemployment and disability programs rose rapidly in the 1960s and 1970s, primarily because of extended coverage and higher benefit levels. The number of beneficiaries has also rapidly increased because of several factors, such as an aging population, the economic recession, and the behavioral responses to the system described earlier.[12] Moreover, the general feeling that the operation of the disability programs is lacking control is growing.

Table 7.9 shows that spending for disability programs stabilized in the 1980s, despite the continued growth in volume. Stabilization and a substantial reduction in real benefits per recipient occurred simultaneously. Replacement ratios declined from 80 percent to 70 percent of previous wages. Moreover, wage-indexing was suspended from 1980 to 1989.

Unemployment and disability programs were partially reformed in 1986. Unemployment benefits are now based more heavily on work records. In addition, new partially disabled workers no longer receive full disability benefits. These measures resulted in significantly lower benefits. Real disposable income of an average disability recipient, for example, fell by 14 percent from 1983 to 1990. This is a clear sign of a changing policy direction.

The results of policy reform in this sector are however still disappointing because volume growth continues, especially in the disability programs. The large number of sickness and disability beneficiaries helps explain the relatively low labor force participation rate in the Netherlands. Other explanatory factors are the low participation levels of women and of older men. "Nonactivity" characterizes 46 percent of the population aged 15 to 64 years. This is still a top political concern.

In conclusion, public income transfers have been cut, but they have increased in volume, making the public/private mix harder to interpret.

Table 7.9
Labor market related income transfers in percent GNP

	1975	1980	1985	1990
Unemployment	1.5	1.7	3.5	2.5
Disability, Sickness	4.9	6.5	5.8	6.3
Total	6.4	8.2	9.3	8.8

Source: Ministry of Social Affairs and Employment.

Overall, the macro level of total public expenditures indicates that the role of the public sector was indeed reduced in the 1980s. This conclusion however, is not so evident from current public/private mix figures in various sectors. Public income transfers, both old age and labor market related, have been cut. On the other hand, the public share in expenditures on health care, transport, education and housing has reduced slightly but not significantly. The change in government activity is thus less fundamental than might be concluded at first sight.

LONG-TERM SCENARIOS

This section reviews the current condition of the Dutch welfare state and analyzes the challenges for the future welfare state. The structural weaknesses of the Dutch welfare state consist of a high tax burden (including social security taxes), a very high number of social security beneficiaries in relation to the working population, and an inflexible labor market. The incentive structure is unfavorable for three reasons: a large wedge between labor costs and net labor income, a small difference between social security benefits and lower wages, and many income-related subsidies and provisions. Labor force participation rates are low by international standards. Moreover without policy changes, these problems will be reinforced by current demographic developments.

Possible policy reactions to these developments are highlighted within the context of a recent study at the Netherlands Central Planning Bureau (CPB). The CPB has outlined three long-term scenarios for economic development until 2015.[13] Since economic theories have failed to produce a unanimous vision of the process of development, an eclectic position was chosen. A distinction was made among three schools of economic thought with three different perspectives on economic development.

1. The *equilibrium perspective* is primarily based on neoclassical economic theory, which presupposes the existence of a well-functioning price mechanism and rational economic subjects and assumes that everyone is well-informed and with rational expectations; uncertainty is therefore virtually irrelevant.

    In this perspective, the prosperity level depends on the available production factors and the state of technology. The government's role is limited to generating pure public goods and the correction of prices by means of taxes and subsidies to take account of negative external effects.

2. The *coordination perspective* is primarily based on the Keynesian school of thought. The main idea is that rational behavior on the micro-level may result in significant imbalances on the macro-level. These imbalances are primarily the result of uncertainty about the future, about which economic subjects must make decisions.

   In this view, not unlike postwar economic policy in Western Europe, coordination and cooperation can better stimulate economic development than the individual (and sometimes short-sighted) pursuit by economic agents with nothing but their own interests at heart.

   For this reason the government's role, and that of cooperation among other organized social groups, is extremely important, especially in periods when a common response must be found in changing circumstances and expectations.

3. Finally, the *free market perspective*. This scenario stresses that in a world of great uncertainty and imperfect information, entrepreneurs and their visions play the dominating part in economic development. Here a well-developed system of property rights, absence of political intervention, low taxes, and modest social security arrangements are essential conditions. Consequently, there is little appreciation for government intervention. Government policy is viewed as the outcome of a power struggle among many parties, each with its own interests, so that the economic rationale of government policies is in no way guaranteed.

The three perspectives therefore provide three different visions with respect to fundamental forces affecting the process of long-term economic development. The perspectives are to a large extent competitive, but are also in part complementary, since history has shown that total neglect of any one of the three is dangerous. The three perspectives are reflected in three long-term scenarios.

The *global shift* scenario is characterized by rapid technological development. The Pacific Rim nations benefit especially in this scenario because of their innovative strength and competition, which is reinforced by trade liberalization. Western Europe cannot match the strong growth that exists in the Pacific Rim region. Moreover, the process of integration stagnates and calls for protectionist measures. Africa and Eastern Europe are strongly affected by the negative economic development in their regions, which causes widespread migration to Western Europe.

In the *balanced growth* scenario economic growth is vigorous and sustainable, because environmental problems are tackled. Strong elements of the three perspectives, "equilibrium," "free market," and "coordination," are combined. Western Europe reinforces its incentive structures. Japan opens up its markets. The United States corrects weaknesses in the fields of education, infrastructure, and savings.

The *european renaissance* scenario is characterized by a strong emphasis on coordination. Technological development is less dynamic than in global shift, which provides Europe a relative advantage. The European integration process is successful. The economic incentive structure is also improved, but coordination and consensus are the elements.

Demographics is an important parameter in all three scenarios. The Dutch population is relatively young and projections indicate that the Netherlands will have the highest population growth within the European Community. However, as in other countries, "graying" substantially alters the demographic structure. "Graying" is when the projected average growth of the number of households exceeds the projected growth in persons. Particularly as a consequence of aging, there will be a substantial increase in the number of one-person households. The growth of real per capita income also is expected to push the number of households upward. These demographic changes and their respective consequences have to be accommodated by government policies.

All the scenarios describe changes in social policy and other policies in the "welfare" and "mixed economy" sector in the Netherlands, but with clearly differing scopes. See tables 7.10 and 7.11 for the public expenditures by function and other economic indicators for all three scenarios in the years 1973, 1990, and 2015.

In *global shift* the weaknesses of the Dutch economy become even more apparent. Initially, no effective reform of the social security system is implemented; benefit levels remain almost unchanged. Labor market rigidities are not tackled. Combined with the unfavorable economic development in Europe, a further increase in expenditures for income transfers results (see table 7.10). The aging of the labor force, shrinking employment, and high immigration cause increasing volumes in the disability and employment programs. All of this together with the rising number of old age pensioners leads to a sharp increase in

Table 7.10

Public expenditure by function in three scenarios: global shift (Gs), balanced growth (Bg), and European renaissance (Er), in percent net national income

	1973	1990	Year 2015 Gs	Bg	Er
Total public expenditure	47.5	59.2	58.8	44.0	56.5
Traditional Domain:					
• general public services	8.2	9.1	9.1	6.0	7.8
• defense	3.0	2.9	1.8	1.2	1.4
• infrastructure	2.6	1.5	1.2	1.3	1.2
Merit goods[a]:					
• education	6.3	5.0	4.7	4.9	5.4
• health care	5.0	7.4	9.9	8.8	11.9
Income transfers:					
• income maintenance	16.4	21.6	22.1	13.3	18.1
• subsidies	3.0	4.9	4.4	2.6	3.4

[a]Housing not included.
Source: Central Planning Bureau.

the inactivity ratio, as in the ratio of social security beneficiaries to the working population (see table 7.11). Public expenditures and tax burdens increase by more than 10 percentage points in the period 1990 to 2005. Therefore, by 2005, it is finally recognized that drastic changes are necessary to halt the relative decline vis-à-vis the Pacific Rim area.

Inevitable severe measures are taken. For example, general cuts are made in social security. These measures result in a sharp decline in minimum transfer incomes.

Housing policy remains generous until 2005. Rental prices are kept low and subsidy-outlays grow. After 2005, rental prices rapidly increase, but even by 2015 they do not cover full housing costs. An expansion of the stock of dwellings is necessary, in this and in the other scenarios, because of the decrease in the average size of households.

In this scenario education is in real trouble. Even though the European Community invests less in research and development compared

Table 7.11
Other economic indicators in three scenarios

	1973	1990	Year 2015		
			Gs	Bg	Er
Total tax burden[a]	47.0	52.2	54.2	39.1	51.4
Marginal tax wedge for model wage in percent	46.0	54.0	56.0	47.0	44.0
Inactivity ratio in percent[b]	51.0	86.0	106.0	85.0	81.0
Labor supply[c]	5.7	6.8	7.8	8.5	8.3
Employment[c]	5.5	6.3	7.2	8.2	8.0
Replacement rates					
• minimum benefit family/minimum wage	92.0	99.0	100.0	66.0	93.0
• minimum benefit family/modal wage	68.0	69.0	66.0	57.0	59.0
• minimum benefit single person /minimum wage	70.0	74.0	74.0	47.0	60.0

[a]In percent Net National Income.

[b]Social security beneficiaries as a percentage of the working population.

[c]Millions of persons.

Source: Central Planning Bureau.

to the Pacific Rim, there is still not a sufficient budget to improve the quality of education. This occurs primarily because the increased transfer expenditure crowds out other public spending.

Health care policy remains unchanged, and there is the same cost increase as in the 1970s. Demand and supply are not matched and waiting lists lengthen. Government regulation and public spending increase until 2005, when a sharp change of policy is inevitable. By 2005, stronger financial incentives and increased competition are introduced into the health care system.

More or less the same story holds true for public policies regarding passenger traffic. Initially there is no policy change, mainly because of a lack of consensus in the European Community on corrective excise taxation. The government, therefore, continues to stimulate public transport and subsidies grow. The result is an increase in public transport, but without a significant decrease in the private use of automobiles. Thus, negative externalities continues to grow. Drastic policy change occurs in 2005, when prices for both private and public transport are rapidly increased and some improvements are pursued.

Balanced growth shows a fundamental reassessment of the role of government within the framework of the free market perspective. There is more emphasis on primary government tasks,[14] streamlining regulation and privatization.

International competition, labor market rigidities, and sociocultural changes, such as increasingly emancipated and calculating citizens, necessitate a fundamental reevaluation of the social security system. Wage-related benefits are cut drastically. More importantly, a general and completely individualized system of negative income taxes is introduced. The basic benefit is 50 percent of the current social minimum for couples. However, the favorable economic conditions in this scenario make it possible for a single person living only from the basic benefit not to have to face a decline in real net income between 1990 and 2015. The gap between transfer incomes and wages sharply increases. The system of negative income tax stimulates labor supply and reduces labor market rigidity, because no benefits are lost when the individual or his partner accepts a job. The constant marginal tax rate on labor income is 44 percent. The pension system is also individualized by introducing a premium-reserve system.

Housing subsidies are eliminated by 2015, except for the income-related rent subsidies, which are maintained as a safety net. This net is considered necessary because of the low basic benefit of the negative income tax system. Nevertheless, these income related subsidies are of course an anomaly in the setting of this scenario.

In education more market conformity is introduced. Wages of teachers and tuition fees are differentiated. The priority given to the improvement of human capital is reflected in increased government spending on education.

Suppliers and consumers of health care are restrained by the gradual introduction of financial incentives. Competition between insurance companies and suppliers, however, is enhanced through regulatory measures taken by the government. As a result, a very moderate increase of health care costs occurs. More consumer sovereignty and better health care quality is achieved.

Sharp increases in the prices of passenger mobility reduce transport. The increased prices stimulate technological improvements, which further diminish negative externalities.

As a consequence of these changes, public expenditures and tax burdens are reduced substantially. Total public expenditures decline by

15 percentage points between 1990 and 2015. Despite the aging process, the inactivity ratio is slightly lower in 2015.

In *European renaissance,* the emphasis is on the coordination perspective. Society prefers to maintain high standards of social protection and a relatively equal income distribution. Many tasks are transferred to the European Community and, at the domestic level, to local governments. Labor market policies and social policies are especially decentralized.

The most important change in welfare state policies is the shift in emphasis from income guarantees for those without work toward an active and mobilizing labor market policy. There is consensus between government, employer, and trade union organizations to reintegrate the low-skilled unemployed and partially disabled persons. In addition, labor market related benefits are cut moderately. Priority is given instead to maintain generous old age pensions.

The allocation in the health care sector is controlled by cooperating insurance companies, backed by the government. Cost control is accomplished by implementing a cost ceiling for the insurance companies. As a result, the individual citizens and the suppliers of health care have less freedom of choice. Expenditures for health care continue to rise because the tighter control of health care consumption tends to be overcompensated by the impact of demographics.

The government takes on an important role in education. Priority is given to research and development, primarily through the European Community to attract high-quality economic activities.

The government continues to assume responsibility for providing adequate housing for large sections of the population. Externalities are the main argument for this public intervention. Nevertheless, housing cost-related subsidies are reduced because the Dutch level of subsidization is not in line with EC averages.

Direct regulation, not price instruments, is the main policy tool for passenger traffic, such as strict emission controls, limited parking and access to cities. Congestion is reduced and since automobiles are relatively clean in this scenario, environmental damage is limited.

These policies result in a stabilization of expenditures on income transfers. The inactivity ratio is reduced from 86 percent to 81 percent in 2015. Total public expenditures and the total tax burden only fall slightly. However, as a result of measures used to broaden the tax base, the marginal tax wedge in the labor market is reduced substantially. Tax rates are set in line with the European averages.

CONCLUDING REMARKS

In Western Europe there is an ongoing debate on the future of the welfare state.[15] Policymakers do not yet have a clear, common understanding of the nature of the interaction between the welfare state and economic performance, nor do they have a clear, common vision of how to improve economic performance while maintaining the gains in security and equity that a welfare state provides.

It is possible that the welfare state is now out of date. The demographic, labor market, family household, and economic conditions that existed when welfare states were designed in the early postwar period no longer exist. Already in the late 1970s it was widely felt that the existing structure of the welfare state had indeed contributed to current economic problems. There was a general commitment by governments to reduce the role of the public sector and especially the role of income transfers and merit goods. The key concepts were (1) more consumer sovereignty and (2) a return to the core tasks of government.

The experience of the Netherlands as a typical European welfare state, explored earlier, indicate that few fundamental reductions in government activity have yet occurred. Public expenditures were cut in the 1980s, mainly by reducing income transfer benefit levels, but the public/private mix in several key sectors did not change substantially as a result. The gap between plans and reality could be explained by the firmly rooted cooperative manner of managing most social programs. However, this could be a typically Dutch phenomenon (Goudswaard et al. 1992).

In the future, demographic and, to a lesser extent, social changes might even cause more, rather than less, government intervention in certain policy areas. The scenario study of the Central Planning Bureau in the Netherlands shows that these developments, combined with stronger foreign competition and rapid technological developments, require fundamental changes in the welfare state. In all scenarios expenditures on income maintenance transfers and subsidies are substantially reduced. These reductions primarily improve the functioning of the labor market. Government intervention in the merit goods sectors, however, especially in health care and education, is not expected to decline.

The scenarios indicate that the future relationship between markets and societies in Western Europe is characterized more by a "free market" orientation, but not necessarily less "coordination." In the scenarios, the role of the government and the role of cooperation among other organized groups are very important, especially in periods when a common response must be found in changing circumstances and expectations.

The United States, on the other hand, will probably face a shift to more "coordination" oriented policies to cope with structural budget deficits and weaknesses in the fields of education and infrastructure. Moreover, some determining factors of public sector demands, particularly demographic and social pressures, will be more or less analogous in Europe and the United States. This suggests some convergence between Europe and North America in economic arrangements and public policy orientation.

To conclude, in both Europe and the United States, the scenario approach, which compares a national economy in different long-term world economy perspectives, is a powerful tool for guiding policymakers to more rational thinking about future public sector intervention.

ENDNOTES

1. Musgrave, R. A., *The Theory of Public Finance: Study in Public Economy* (New York: McGraw Hill, 1959).
2. For an early discussion, see OECD, *The Welfare State in Crisis, an account of the Conference on Social Policies in the 1980s* (Paris: OECD Publication and Information Centre, 1981).
3. Saunders, P., and Klau, F. "The Role of the Public Sector—Causes and Consequences of the Growth of Government," *OECD Economic Studies,* no. 4 (Spring 1985): 27.
4. All data in this section are from Oxley, H., and Martin, J. P., "Controlling Government Spending and Deficits: Trends in the 1980s and Prospects for the 1990s," *OECD Economic Studies,* no. 17 (Autumn 1991): 145–89. See also a larger study, Oxley, H., Maher, M., Martin, J. P., and Nicoletti, G., "The Public Sector: Issues for the 1990s," *OECD Working Papers,* no. 90 (December 1990).
5. Oxley, H., and Martin, J. P., op. cit., p. 146.
6. This section draws from Goudswaard, K., Halberstadt, V., and Hans van de Kar, H. "Dutch Social Policy in the 1980s: A Changing Role of the Public Sector," *Atlantic Economic Journal,* vol. 20, no. 2 (1992): 21–9. Full references on data can be found there.

7. Centraal Planbureau, "Nederland in drievoud: een scenariostudie van de Nederlandse economie, 1990-2015," Den Haag, 1992, pp. 346–48.
8. Centraal Planbureau, op. cit. (1992), Chapter 4, Section 8.
9. The figures of table 7.3 do not include tax subsidies. Private expenditures on health care are, however, within certain limits, deductible for the personal income tax.
10. de Groot, H., and de Kam, C. A., "Jaarboek Overheidsuitgaven 1993", Den Haag, 1992, p. 59.
11. Central Planbureau, op. cit. (1992), Chapter 4, Section 7.
12. Wolfe et al., 1984, conclude that the increase in transfer generosity caused a yearly reduction in the number of hours worked by 2.7 percent during the 1970s. In the United States this reduction was only 0.65 percent.
13. The CPB first outlined scenarios for the world economy in "Scanning the Future: A Long-term Study of the World Economy 1990-2015," The Hague: Central Planning Bureau (1992). A further elaboration on the Dutch economy is in *Nederland in drievoud; een scenariostudie van de Nederlandse economie, 1990–2015* (The Netherlands in Triplo; A scenario study of the Dutch economy, 1990–2015, English summary), The Hague: Centraal Planbureau, 1992. This section draws solely from the CPB study.
14. The CPB includes education as a primary government task.
15. See Haveman, R., Wolfe, B., and Halberstadt, V., "The European Welfare State in Transition" in Palmer, J. L., ed., *Perspectives on the Reagan Years,* (Washington: 1986), pp. 147–73.

REFERENCES

Central Planning Bureau. "Nederland in drievoud: een scenariostudie van de Nederlandse economie, 1990-2015." (The Netherlands in Triplo: A Study of the Dutch Economy.) The Hague, 1992.

Central Planning Bureau. "Scanning the future: A long-term study of the world economy 1990–2015." The Hague, 1992.

Goudswaard, K., Halberstadt V., and van de Kar, H. "Dutch Social Policy in the 1980s: A Changing Role of the Public Sector." *Atlantic Economic Journal,* vol. 20, no. 2 (1992): 21–9.

De Groot, H., and Goudriaan, R. "De produktiviteit van de overheid." Schoonhoven, 1991.

———, and de Kam, C. A. "Jaarboek Overheidsuitgaven 1993." Den Haag, 1992.

Haveman, R., Wolfe B., and Halberstadt, V., "The European Welfare State in Transition" in J. L. Palmer, ed., *Perspectives on the Reagan Years*. Washington, D.C.: Urban Institute Press 1986, pp. 147–73.

Musgrave, R. A. "The Theory of Public Finance: A Study in Public Economy." New York: McGraw Hill, 1959.

OECD. "The Welfare State in Crisis: An Account of the Conference on Social Policies in the 1980s." Paris: OECD Publications and Information Centre, 1981.

Oxley, H., and Martin, J. P. "Controlling Government Spending and Deficits: Trends in the 1980s and Prospects for the 1990s." *OECD Economic Studies*, no. 17 (Autumn 1991): 145–89.

Oxley, H., Maher, M., Martin, J. P., and Nicoletti, G. "The Public Sector: Issues for the 1990s." *OECD Working Papers*, no. 90 (December 1990).

Petersen, C. "Economie en Pensioenen." Leiden, 1989; Saunders, P., and Klau, F. "The Role of the Public Sector—Causes and Consequences of the Growth of Government." *OECD Economic Studies*, no. 4 (Spring 1985): 5–239.

Wolfe, B. L., de Jong, Ph. R., Haveman, R. H., Halberstadt V., and Goudswaard, K. P. "Income Transfers and Work Effect: The Netherlands and the U.S. in the 1970s." *Kyklos*, vol. 37, no. 4 (1984): 609–37.

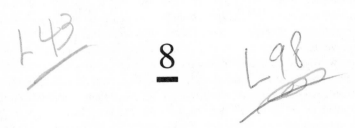

8

At the Crossroads of Markets and Governments: Public Utilities Regulation in the European Market—Lessons from America?

Christian Stoffaës

PUBLIC SERVICE IN AMERICA

Does Network Regulation in the United States Contain Lessons for Europe?

Over the past few years the pursuit of the Single European market has caused large industrial and commercial public services to change in accordance with the nature of the European treaties, which are inspired by the liberal ideas of free trade and competition. Moreover, the American experience provides insight for the Europeans on how liberalism devises and manages public services.

The American Constitution is based on individual freedom, in particular for free enterprise, so that economic intervention by local public authorities is reduced to the minimum. Federal government intervention does not exist. The postal service, for instance, was a rare exception to this since it was managed from the start by the federal government. In the United States, the regulation of network industries began with the activity of private firms and the operation of the free market; it was not based on the authority of the central state, and public intervention, in terms of regulation, was introduced to correct the negative effects of laissez-faire; in other words, it was to protect social and economic balances from the abuses of private monopolies.

The concept of public utility has its roots in the philosophy of Anglo-Saxon or common law and its aim is to establish a balance between the interests of the firms producing it and the interests of users buying and using the service. The modern idea of public service began in 1887 with the Supreme Court decision in *Munn* vs. *Illinois*. This case established two necessary conditions for public utility—necessity and monopoly—declaring that "when a private individual devotes his good to a use of interest to the public, he thereby confers on the public a special interest in the supply of this use: under these conditions this person must be subject to public control, for the common good."

The jurisprudence laid down the right of public authorities to control public utilities. Regulation began with local public authorities (city, county, and state authorities) and then moved to the central level of the federal government. This shift toward the federal level occurred as trade and investments developed throughout the North American continent, beginning with the Interstate Commerce clause of the Constitution of the United States (Clause 1, Section 8). Regulation in the United States was therefore based on principles of free trade, freedom of establishment, and access to markets and competition. The three branches of state intervention—legislative, executive, and legal—were designed to ensure that the general philosophy of the market and free trade was respected.

The general principle, guiding the creation and activities of the regulatory authorities, established that it was necessary to defend liberalism from itself, and to prevent the forces of liberalism from finally ruining the foundations of liberal society through its own excesses. Paradoxically, "public service" was built on the ideas of competitive markets and not in opposition to it. This historical evolution of American public service sheds light on the European Union's experience.

THE SOCIAL-COLBERTIST TRADITION OF PUBLIC SERVICE

In many European countries, particularly in France and in the Latin countries, industrial and commercial public service was most often built on the "kingly" state of public authority. Public authority was combined together with the interventionist actions of economic and technical ministries, such as public works departments, Post and Telecom administrations, energy, transports, and so on.

Networks, from the roads of the Roman Empire to the bridges and highways of the kingdom of France, from sea routes granted to charter companies to the Chappe military telegraph, and from oil pipelines to high voltage lines, were often devised with "imperial" concepts, instruments of national sovereignty and economic defense, and even direct military action. Public opinion in Europe generally considers the authority and action of the state as a natural part of networks.

Recently the philosophy of social law has been added to the "kingly" tradition of network management. In the spirit of "social law," public service consists of both an essential place for the arbitration of macrosocial conflicts, as for those between employers, management, workers, executives, and regions with different levels of development, and a privileged way of promoting social equality between both prosperous and impoverished regions and social classes with different income levels. Social law is currently valued as a way of reviving the economy and increasing investment through large-scale public infrastructure projects.

THE SPIRIT OF THE LAWS: COMMON-LAW VS. PUBLIC LAW

In Europe, the action of the state and litigation with the state are often under special legislation, known as public law, and sometimes under special jurisdiction: for instance, in France, it involves the Council of State and the administrative tribunals, In Europe the executive and the legislative elements of government have never wanted excessive development of the "power of judges."

The general legal philosophy in the United States, known as common law, involves both common law, where the state is subject to the same law and the same judge as the individual, and "customary law," which is derived from society and tradition, and not from the state. The rules laid down by the legislator, both laws and regulations, are only considered supplements or details to common law, which consists of unwritten regulations, previous jurisprudence, and preexisting traditions. This means that laws and regulations are only incorporated into the legal system after being interpreted and applied by the tribunals and legal courts. Therefore it is possible to refer to past jurisprudence decisions that apply to current laws and regulations.

Furthermore, the principle of separation of powers prohibits, or severely limits, delegation to the executive by the legislative. There is therefore no real distinction between laws and regulatory acts as found in the French Constitution, where the legislative field is strictly limited. The United States of America make up one federal state; thus, sharing competences among the various levels of public authority is necessary and permanent. Analogies exist between constituent treaties and the American constitutional principles of freedom, of establishment and trade, and the interstate commerce clause of the Constitution.

In contrast to Europe, network regulation in the United States is provided by so-called independent regulatory commissions. They are not directly related to the executive, legal, or legislative powers, but nevertheless they are instituted and controlled by acts of Congress.

These commissions,[1] or agencies, are specifically empowered by legislation to provide a triple function: 1) quasi-executive, to supervise inform, plan, and enjoin; 2) quasi-legal, at prejurisdictional level, to arbitrate or regulate conflicts before intervention and under the control of the tribunals and Supreme Court; and 3) quasi-legislative, to pronounce what would be called in French public law decrees or orders within the framework of their mandate.

AGAINST THE ABUSES OF THE DOMINANT POSITION

The American economy in the final third of the nineteenth century was marked by a vast movement toward technical development and economic growth. This movement is attributed to a number of fundamental technological innovations and the subsequently large firms, which were established in the context of a free market and "uncontrolled competition." The "monopolists," who extended their hold over transport infrastructure networks, imposed their discretionary service and price conditions on small producers and users. Multiple conflicts developed, and the courts were called upon to settle the disputes. Abuses of the dominant position held by the big businesses were strongly contested.

To put an end to excesses and to arbitrate conflicts between producers and users, the parliaments of the various states set up suitable legislation, as well as local public service commissions (PUCs), with regulationary power to set tariffs and to control the management of the operating companies. But after the 1929 crash, it was above all Roosevelt's New Deal, based on the social forces that were antagonistic to big business, such as trade unions, farmers in disadvantaged areas, and user associations, which massively developed the federal regulatory bodies.

REGULATION AND DEREGULATION

Opposition to the regulation system began in the 1950s. The opposition brought out the conflicts concerning interpretation and the contradictions between the two motivations for creating regulation commissions: fighting the trusts and preventing agreements versus placing them under public control. It was observed that public control may encourage monopolies by granting protected situations and exclusive rights to concessionary companies and by encouraging agreements or even legitimizing them with the seal of public action.

The slowdown in economic growth following the 1973 oil crisis exacerbated the disputes. With the rise in inflation, the fight against rising prices primarily involved reinforcing competition in protected and "cartelized" sectors. In some sectors, technological developments made the old regulatory framework obsolete.

The Carter administration was a Democrat administration particularly sensitive to the arguments of consumerist and ecological movements and to components of the new American left, trade unions and minorities. At the end of the 1970s, they initiated marked change in the deregulation of natural gas, electricity, ground transport, air transport, and telecommunications. The Reagan administration, beginning in 1981, continued the deregulation movement, but in a slightly different spirit. The Republicans did more than protect consumers from the abuses of big business; they also reduced the bureaucratic constraints that slowed down productivity and innovation in business.

In short, deregulation is not simply the result of eliminating regulation or of the regulatory authority establishing a competitive structure. In some sectors, regulation was certainly reduced, as in transport; while in other sectors, regulation was made more complex, as in telecommunications. Economic concentration was encouraged as a result of reinforced competition, as in air transport. Thus, the targeted objectives were diverted from their initial objective. For instance with electricity, new energy sources were rarely developed and deregulation benefited natural gas and cogeneration. It is therefore more accurate to speak of regulatory reform rather than deregulation.

Nevertheless, the results were often spectacular: profound change in air transport, including international traffic, regarding prices, commercial practice, and service qualities; prolific development of new telecommunications and satellite broadcasting (radiotelephone, cables, teledata, and so on); and rapid development of natural gas, especially for electricity generation. There was a new wind of freedom and innovation in sectors that had been a bit sluggish, which gave way to new initiatives but also created victims such as Pan Am, TWA, and other airlines.

PUBLIC SERVICE CHARTER IN EUROPE

The "American model" is a useful reference for the single European market as the European Union searchs for guiding principles. The American model is useful not because it is the ideal structure, but rather because the American model encourages modesty and pragmatism. The American model is not ideal for Europe because the technical and economic performance of public services in the United States, particularly in terms of tariffs, service quality, redistributed equity, and so on, are not always of the same standard as the models for public trusts in Europe.

A few common basic principles, with broad, adaptative, pragmatic, and diverse approaches, are provided by the American model. In addition, two approaches provide a forum for permanent deliberation on the respective advantages and drawbacks of public intervention and the play of the market.

The role of the regulatory commissions and the jurisprudence interpretation of the tribunals and the Supreme Court have varied over time. Some periods were more influenced by socialist and interventionist ideas while other periods were marked by liberal ideas, as a function of alternate policies and ideologies of American society. This observation has its price for Europe. The idea of European public service will also be based on texts and basic principles of treaties, such as free trade and competition, but they will also be based on choices made by the European societies. Thus for European public service to emerge, Europe must first express its choice in terms of a model for society; a "European society" needs to be constructed.

To specify a future orientation for network regulation directives to resolve conflicts of interpretation embedded in contradictory texts, to assist judges in Luxembourg, and to furnish long-term investment in the framework of institutional stability that it requires, the Union must specify founding principles for the future regulation of public services. Only this will dissipate the climate of uncertainty and legal insecurity that has been felt over the past few years in nation states and in the Single European Market.

ENDNOTES

1. The areas of intervention and the composition of the public utilities commissions (PUCs) of the federated states and the federal agencies vary. Their National Association, NARUC, consists of 95 bodies (11 federal, 63 state, and 22 other), with a total of 385 commissioners. The commissioners are appointed by the head of the executive (governors for the state public utility commissions; President of the United States for the federal commissions). Their appointment is submitted to the Senate for approval. The commissioners must not show majority membership of the same party. They cannot be removed from office for a period of six years on average. Decisions are collegial. Their powers are vast, within the strict framework limited by legislation on authorization, but the often allusive terms of this legislation ("reasonable prices," "honest profits," "unfair competition," and so on) do not actually constitute an obstacle to executive efficiency.

9

From Boiling Pot to Melting Pot: The Real Lessons of the American Experience of Immigration and "Assimilation"

Thomas Ferguson

The New Deal means a more sympathetic and humane consideration of his [the alien's] problems and a spirit of friendliness and helpfulness rather than one of antagonism and persecution.[1]

In the next few years, enormous streams of refugees and immigrants are likely to flow into Western Europe from both the east and the south. Not surprisingly, with xenophobia, racism, and anti-immigrant violence already flaring dangerously and economic growth very fitful, both policymakers and ordinary Europeans are on edge. All are looking hard at available policy alternatives.

No crystal ball is required to see that efforts to help stabilize Eastern Europe, North Africa, and the former Soviet Union are likely to form a vital part of the European Union's final policy mix in this area. Restrictive immigration legislation will also be an element of the EU's policy. But just as the Americans choked off immigration in the 1920s and left many fundamental questions about the relation of immigrants to American society unsettled, these measures recommended by the European Union will not resolve the current debates in the Old World about immigration and "assimilation."

For more than a hundred and fifty years, the great American "melting pot" has alternately fascinated and repelled Europeans. In the 1990s, as various members of the European Community reflect on their policy options, it seems safe to predict that some will find themselves wanting to take yet another look at the U.S. experience.

When they do, however, they may be in store for a disappointment. The writing on American immigration is copious, and some of it is brilliant. But most of this commentary describes what Europeans see as the key outcome and one that many of their forbearers, including such luminaries as H. G. Wells and Andre Siegfried, doubted was possible: the successful assimilation, in a distinctively "pluralist" sense not premised on rejection of earlier ethnic heritages, which occurred during and after the 1930s, of tens of millions of non-Protestant, non-Nordic, and—eventually, though far more equivocally—non-white immigrants and their children.[2]

The existing literature's nonchalance about elucidating the causes of the "Great Assimilation" is surprising, and motivates the present assessment. What follows attempts to explain this extraordinary development, which, for all its admitted shortcomings, is virtually without precedent in comparative historical terms. The argument is that the assimilation was the unintended product of another, more fundamental historical process: the mass mobilization of immigrants and their children alongside many "older stock" workers into unions and the Democratic party during the New Deal. Although the new, assimilated workers movements had to share power (quite unequally!) with the bloc of large, capital intensive, internationally oriented businesses that financed and dominated the New Deal's Democratic coalition, this "Multinational Bloc" itself was cosmopolitan, oriented strongly to free trade, internationalism, and anti-colonializing because it opposed preferential trading blocs. Its leaders also came from a wider array of ethnic and religious groups than the traditional WASP (White Anglo-Saxon Protestant) aristocracy that dominated the pre–New Deal Republican Party.[3]

For convenience, this chapter is divided into three major parts. The first is quite brief. It considers and rules out several plausible alternative explanations that state that the Great Assimilation can be explained simply by World War II or by the prosperity of the 1950s and 1960s. The next section then reviews the evidence in support of a rather obvious fact: For all the noise about the American melting pot, up to the very eve of the New Deal, the melting pot was better characterized as a boiling pot, in which any number of ethnic groups, races, and minorities battled each other while also struggling with the dominant WASP upper classes. The third section then lays out the main argument, sketching out the successive phases in the Great Assimilation, as the High New Deal deradicalized and the postwar boom commenced. The rather lengthy conclusion tries to distill the main lessons of this experience for contemporary European discussions. It also notes ominous signs that with the waning of the New Deal the great American melting pot is once again coming to a boil over the question of immigration.

SOME NONEXPLANATIONS

But is there anything here that really needs to be explained, or, as is so common in contemporary social science, are we simply inventing problems? A skeptic might, for example, plausibly suggest that World War II might have been the critical causal factor in bringing about the Great Assimilation. Did not the war, for example, help break down the differences between groups by providing poignant evidence that tens of thousands of immigrants and their children were just as willing as other citizens to die for their country? And did not the war lead millions of other Americans to cooperate—in some cases, for the first time—in joint activity in pursuit of a shared goal that easily became a basis for still more experiences of patriotic unity and common ground?

No less plausible on first hearing is another suggestion: that what really dissolved so many (certainly, far from all) of the social tensions that formerly divided immigrants from other groups was the postwar economic boom. Not the CIO, or Roosevelt, but Levittown, home appliances, and eventually, the great leveling experiences of suburbs and shopping malls were what finally brought (many parts, if not all of) America together.

Neither of these suggestions is foolish. Both point to real factors that any detailed account of the Great Assimilation must incorporate. But it is easy to show that neither by itself provides any sort of fundamental explanation.

For example, the suggestion that prosperity by itself led to the "Great Assimilation" can be dismissed out of hand. As everyone who has tracked the course of the American economy in recent years is aware, rates of economic growth were indeed higher in the 1950s and 1960s. But this fact is less helpful for the "prosperity" hypothesis than one might think. By no later than the mid-1950s many analysts—especially, perhaps, those caught up in the discussions of religious pluralism—were acknowledging the "Great Assimilation" as a fact. Indeed, they were celebrating and idealizing the whole process. But this leaves barely four or five years for prosperity to have transformed the boiling pot into the melting pot, since the immediate postwar years of demobilization, restructuring, and record strike rates were far more difficult than they now seem in the golden afterglow of memory. A transformation on this scale in such a short period is implausible on its face.[4]

Even more compelling, however, is the evidence, discussed later, indicating that critical changes in popular culture and official policies took place in the 1930s, not the fastest, but—here is a point that should interest contemporary Europeans—the *slowest*-growing decade in twentieth-century America. It may also be worth observing that the fact that America in the 1980s and 1990s is far richer in an absolute sense than in the 1940s has not prevented the idea of assimilation from once again coming under attack, though one might counter by trying to recast the argument in purely relative terms.

The suggestion that World War II explains the Great Assimilation is equally untenable. The experience of the war alone was not the underlying cause for the Great Assimilation. Even though World War I is similar in some aspects to World War II it does not explain why the Great Assimilation occurred. As in World War II, World War I yielded plenty of evidence that immigrants, or their children, were prepared to sacrifice their lives for the United States. Moreover, the conflict during the first world war also provided plenty of opportunities for Americans to cooperate in joint activity in pursuit of shared goals. Unfortunately, in many of these instances during both world wars, the joint activity preferred by many "old stock" citizens was the hounding and persecution of immigrants and their children, along with vigorous agitation for draconian (and outrageously discriminatory) legislation to restrict immigration. Therefore, World War II had an effect other than the experience of assimilation in the United States.[5]

There can be sympathy found in the suggestions that Nazi notions of racial superiority tended to put under a (slight) cloud the generally less virulent forms of racism that were very popular within the United States in the first decades of the twentieth century. It could thus be argued that the two world wars might not be comparable in regard to their implications for assimilation. But unless this observation is embedded in a more complex argument it is simply an interesting *aperçu*. The effect in question is simply too weak to explain an event on the scale of the Great Assimilation. Poll evidence from the early 1940s on public opinion in regard to civil rights, for example, show that American attitudes toward African-American rights clearly had not been much affected by invidious contrasts with Nazism. Major changes in opinion on these issues certainly did happen after the war. These, however, were clearly driven principally by events and social movements too well known to require comment here, save to note that they were obviously related to the career of New Deal, discussed later.[6]

While black-white differences probably represent an extreme, and singular case, the evidence suggests that before the war American public opinion in regard to Germany responded mainly to what a then sharply divided media and elites perceived as unambiguous threats to the United States. Otherwise, most groups in the population were, as usual, paying relatively little attention to events abroad.[7]

Also, timing is once again an awkward problem. If one concedes that the sea change in regard to immigrants started very early in the New Deal in quite tangible ways that are easy to identify, then the suggestion that Americans assimilated because comparisons to Nazism made them uncomfortable becomes outlandish. Suggestions that the war was the primary factor also slide past a fact often conveniently overlooked—that far into the 1930s both Hitler and Mussolini found many powerful defenders in America.[8] Proponents of this argument also tend to forget that criticisms of alleged German arrogance and exclusiveness were a staple of allied propaganda in World War I, so that few average Americans probably perceived how distinctively monstrous Nazism really was until well into, or even after, the war—too late to be a moving force in the Great Assimilation.

Let us acknowledge, accordingly, that neither war nor prosperity by themselves can explain the Great Assimilation, even if we also agree that both played significant roles in the broader picture.

THE PRE–NEW DEAL BOILING POT

This discussion of immigration in American life before the New Deal neglects many issues. But the existing literature is obviously in need of revision along the lines of the central point outlined here: prior to the 1930s, America was not a melting pot, but a boiling pot.

Long before the Civil War, of course, immigration and the role immigrants should play in American life had been bitterly controversial. Federalist sponsorship of the "Alien and Sedition" Acts, which were directed at immigrant constituencies supportive of Thomas Jefferson's new Democratic Republicans, played a role in the older party's loss of the White House in 1800. During the Jacksonian Revolution anti-immigrant and anti-Catholic (in largely Protestant America, the one usually implied the other) riots exploded in many cities, often in the wake of economic downturns and failed labor movements. In a money-driven political system that required—even then—quite fantastic amounts of campaign finance to mount more than purely local campaigns, both parties tended to be dominated by various coalitions of businesses and investor blocs. Such parties had no interest in organizing around unions, but they certainly needed to find issues that could arouse a passionate response from some segment of the electorate, particularly during business cycle downturns, when laissez-faire came under a massive challenge.[9]

Not surprisingly, virtually from the beginnings of the revival of party competition in the 1820s, one of the major parties—usually the Whigs, later the Republicans—typically specialized in appeals for "law and order," temperance (and, sometimes, Prohibition) and other issues designed to attract better-off "old stock" workers (a category that, by the Civil War, sometimes included non-socialist Germans as honorary members). By contrast, the other major party—normally, the Democrats—pointedly championed tolerance, or perhaps more accurately, the idea of tolerance, for those whose ancestors had not had the good fortune to land at Plymouth Rock.[10]

In the wake of the Irish potato famine and the failure of the Revolution of 1848 in Europe, immigration into the United States markedly accelerated. Many states briefly witnessed the rise of powerful nativist "Know-Nothing" movements. These uprisings, however, were unable to attract consistent support from the business community, which was all but unanimously convinced that immigration was essential for rapid growth. All quickly collapsed.

The immigration debate altered fundamentally during the Gilded Age. In the highly stereotyped terms of a celebrated French observer that well convey the feelings of many older stock Americans:

> After 1880, and especially after 1890, an entirely different immigration took place. Between 1880 and 1914 a veritable tidal wave carried to America almost 22 million immigrants. The important point is that their origin was almost entirely different from that of the earlier settlers. It was the Latin and Slav countries and not northern Europe (Germany, Scandinavia, and Great Britain) that now contributed. Instead of heading

for the great open spaces of the West, they now congregated in the Atlantic ports or in the industrial and mining centres of the East—truly a bewildered and inarticulate crew existing on the margin of the original civilization!

From the religious point of view the change was even more striking, for the majority of the immigrants were no longer Protestant. There were Jews from Russia or Poland, and Catholics from Italy and the Slav countries; and altogether their material and moral assimilation was slow and difficult. They formed solid indigestible blocks in the lower quarters of the big cities, and when by the second generation they had acquired an American veneer, they were out of sympathy with the spirit of the country and the Protestant and Anglo-Saxon traditions laid down by the Fathers of Independence.[11]

The effect of all this on the political system was predictable: Alarm spread through the elites of both parties and the "old stock" parts of the mass population. A particularly useful illustration for our purposes of the reaction that ensued is a pamphlet by Moorfield Storey. A prominent corporate lawyer and leader of the Boston Reform Democrats (and thus, note well, the recognized party of immigrants!), Storey was for decades a major figure in national politics, business, and philanthropy. His lifelong dedication to a variety of noble causes—anti-imperialism, antitrust, free trade, Booker T. Washington—has led a succession of biographers to treat him as though he had been carved from one of the planks of Old Ironsides. Here he surveys his hopes for the melting pot:

> The immigration of every year adds to the mass of poverty and ignorance in our country. The foreigners who seek our shores know little of our society, our methods, our history, or the traditions of our government. Their prejudices, their habits of thought, their entire unfamiliarity with American questions—in a word, their whole past, unfit them to take an intelligent part in our political contests, yet in a few years they become citizens and their votes in the ballot box count as much as our own. Their presence in our large cities has made the problem of municipal government infinitely more difficult, and they are today the most dangerous element in our body politic.[12]

This was 1881. While negative characterizations of universal suffrage had become common after the great strike wave of 1877, Storey rested his hopes in mass education—and aristocratic leadership.[13]

These ignorant voters, wherever they are found, are the natural prey of the demagogue and the corrupt politician. As they increase in numbers their prejudices are certain to be consulted by party leaders, and the tone of political discussion sinks lower and lower. Our most recent experience has shown us how possible it is that the policy of this country on a great economic question may be determined for years by a few thousand votes bought in the slums of a great city, or by some perfectly immaterial episode like Lord Sackville's letter. The only cure for the evils which spring from ignorance is education. We must either raise the lowest classes in the state or they will drag us down. If we would not be governed by Tammany Hall, we must reach their followers and lead them ourselves. The more difficult the task, the more it demands the attention of educated men.

Nor can anyone now say, as many have said in the past, that bad government does not affect him. The questions between labor and capital, between great corporations and the communities which they serve, between the public and the rights of private citizens are vitally interesting to us all. When a wave of popular excitement induces legislation which cripples railroads, every man and woman who owns a share of stock feels the loss of dividends. If the strike on the Chicago, Burlington, and Quincy railroad had extended to other systems, as at one time seemed probable, whole districts would have found themselves suffering. . . .[14]

Not surprisingly, however, others soon began to experiment with less high-minded—and expensive—shortcuts (that Storey seems finally to have decided he could live with). As C. K. Yearly has shown in his study of *The Money Machines: The Breakdown and Reform of Governmental and Party Finance In the North: 1860–1920,* the treasuries of northern cities were beginning to falter under the strains of that era's "welfare crisis." With city budgets, and therefore, tax rolls, swelling to meet new demands from America's growing numbers of poor and destitute, and immigration still soaring, men like E. L. Godkin, founder of *The Nation,* began to fear that "our modern experiment in Democratic government is really an experiment in the government of rich communities by poor men."[15]

What to do was obvious. As J. Sloan Fassett, an associate of Boss Platt's, who was then chair of the New York State Senate Committee on Cities, wrote not too long before he was implicated in the Ice Trust Scandal, America needed a "new form of ballot" that would pare down the number of voters. "Universal suffrage does not permit itself to be persuaded by failures but obeys prejudices."[16]

The result is now well understood, at least by those willing to take the trouble to look past the Rusk-Converse response to Burnham's earlier essays. Contrary to the folklore in which public policy aspired to introduce immigrants into the mainstream of public life as rapidly as possible, American elites began practicing "creative federalism." As table 9.1, reproduced from an earlier essay of mine, demonstrates, a striking wave of election law redraftings rippled through the various states. After 1890, the nineteenth-century trend toward the elimination of the property tax as a qualification for voting abruptly reversed. The number of states imposing other taxes on voters rose sharply. Residence requirements stiffened, especially at the ward level, although at the state level these had been tightening since the Jacksonian period. Registration requirements, exactly as Burnham noted, proliferated between 1890 and 1912, while educational requirements, almost unknown before the 1990s, became far more common in both the North and the South. Most striking of all for this argument, however, a complete reversal of attitude took place toward the common nineteenth-century practice of allowing aliens who declared their intent to acquire U.S. citizenship to vote.[17]

One writer in a series of "University Research Monographs" published during the 1920s laid bare the thoughts that motivated this last development.

But even worse, aliens tend to colonize in the great cities. The assimilation of this vast foreign horde seems impossible. The only safe national policy would appear to be the restriction of immigration. This affords at least an opportunity for the much-wished-for "Americanization" of our alien residents. It is evident that such a program will greatly simplify the foreign suffrage problem. . . .

Citizenship as a qualification for the elective franchise is not old. . . . when the tide of immigration was swelling and the much-needed settlers were pouring into the central part of the United States, states in that section began to offer extra inducements by allowing aliens to vote after taking out first papers. Wisconsin initiated this dangerous suffrage expedient. . . . other competing states followed her bad example. . . .

Since [1889] a countermovement has restored the citizenship test in all but one—Arkansas. The awakening of America to the danger of foreign influence during the World War will undoubtedly cause the elimination of the cheap makeshift which allowed aliens to vote. . . . every indication points toward continued sound future legislation at this point. . . .[18]

Table 9.1
Number of states with selected suffrage limitations

Restriction	Year							
	1789	1800	1830	1860	1890	1912	1928	1940
Specific property	6	7	8	3	2	9[a]		5(+6)[b]
Taxes	6	7	12	8	11	16[c]	14	8
Residence—state								
2 Years	—	4	6	5	3	7	4	5
1 Year	3	2	10	19	28	29	35?	32
6 Months	—	—	1	4	9	11	8	11
4 Months	—	—	—	1	1	—	—	—
3 Months	—	—	1	2	2	1	1	—
Residence—township, city, etc.								
1 Year	5	5	4	2	2	6		3
6 Months	2	6	9	10	11	14		9
5 Months	—	—	—	1	1	1		1
4 Months	—	—	—	2	1	2		2
3 Months	—	—	2	2	6	6		9
2 Months	—	—	—	1	7	5		—
1 Month	—	—	—	2	5	10		6(+1)[d]
10 Days	—	—	—	3	2	1		—
Residence—ward, etc.								
90 Days	—	—	—	—	1	3(+4)[e]		4(+7)[f]
60 Days	—	—	—	1	2	3		4(+1)[g]
30 Days	—	—	—	1?	9	10		14(+2)[h]
10 Days	—	—	—	3	3	5		6
Oath	3	4	5	5	10	6		
Serious crime	—	1	11	24	37	39		41
Alien (allowed)	—	—	1	5	15	8	1	—
Pauper, dependent, etc.	—	1	5	16	33	47		44
Indians	—	1	2	8	9	8		
Education	—	—	—	2	5	16	18	19
Registration	—	—	—	4	21	47	46	47

Note: A blank space equals no information; — equals zero as far as ascertainable.

[a]Includes two states in which property owners alone could vote on special tax and debt issues and one state in which they alone could vote on expenditures.

[b]The second figure (6) applies only to elections for bond issues.

[c]Includes one state in which tax requirement applies for votes on taxation and one in which it is required at state and county levels for votes on council and expenditures.

[d]One state required 40 days.

[e]Three states required 90 days; two required 6 months; and two required 4 months.

[f]Four states required 90 days; six required 6 months; one required a full year.

[g]One state required 40 days.

[h]Two states required 20 days.

On occasion a thousand words adds up to a revealing picture. Other sections of this essay illustrate another fundamental fact about America's "Boiling Pot" in this period: that separating issues of immigration from those of social class (or race) was a purely academic exercise.

> After the meteoric flight of Lenine [*sic*] and Trotsky, the dullest clod thrust into eminence and even into actual political and social prominence by some industrial upheaval may reach for power. . . . Whether we want to or not, we must consider the "stranger within our gates." The question is not what will we do with the foreigner industrially and politically, but what will he do with U.S. and our institutions. Americanization is a safety first program. . . .
> No one anticipated Bolshevism in Russia. With a communistic kindergarten in the I.W.W. and industrial unrest and disorganization widespread, nothing is impossible.[19]

The point is not simply that the colossal fall in voting turnout outside the South, where no one has ever suggested democracy was the order of the day, between 1896 and the New Deal is incompatible with traditional images of "Americanization." No less important is this turnout decline's quite obvious link to the labor-management conflict that roiled the period.[20]

Beginning in the mid-1870s, when a massive strike wave led to the first systematic efforts to collect reliable statistics, the pot never really

---

Source: Table 9.1 has been prepared from information supplied by many sources, including various state constitutions and statutes. But most of it comes from four large-scale surveys of state voting provisions: O.H. Fisk's *Stimmrecht und Einzelstaat in den Vereinigten Staaten von Nordamerika* (Leipsiz: Verlag von Duncker & Humbolt, 1896); The Legislative Reference Bureau of the Rhode Island State Library's *General Constitutional and Statutory Provision Relative to Suffrage* (Providence: Freemen, 1912); Richard Boeckel, *Voting and Non-Voting in Elections* (Editorial Research Reports, 1928); and Council Of State Governments, *Voting in the United States* (Chicago: Council of State Governments, 1940).

All summary efforts like these have problems stemming from minor variants among similar state laws and the occasional loopholes or special qualifications created by states. For example, in 1830 New York had a three-year residence requirement for the "man of color." Should New York figure in the table as a state with a residence requirement or not? My answer was no, on the grounds that this would be too specific a usage for a category that usually represents a far more universal disability. Similar problems attend some of the other categories, especially "serious crime" and "paupers." "Serious crime" is a catchall category that varies from state to state. Much state legislation barring the lowest classes from voting ("paupers") lumps them together with maniacs, alcoholics, or other types of "dependents."

I have attempted to standardize among the sources by checking likely exceptions and cases that stand out as anomalous between them, so the figures here sometimes differ from any particular sources. Where exact details about individual states became important, however, recourse should be had to each source's notes and the state's constitution and statutes, for more exceptions exist than are noted here.

It should be noted that several states' literacy requirements were waived for the occasional affluent illiterate, i.e., one could buy into the franchise if one could not pass the literacy test.

stopped steaming. Between 1880 and 1930, for example, the wrecking of strikes and attempts to organize labor unions by means of court injunctions developed into a fine art. Table 9.2, compiled from data in an old study of *Government and Labor Disputes,* shows a steep rise in injunctions until 1920, when the table thereafter could easily be mistaken for an effort to approximate a power series.[21]

Until the New Deal, public policy left employers free to attack their workforce with virtually any weapons money could buy. Almost all large firms maintained private armies. Some of these—the Pennsylvania Coal and Iron Police, General Motor's Black Legion, or the Ford Motor Company goon squads recruited by the notorious Harry Bennett—far outmanned local police forces. Firms too small to afford their own *Freikorps,* as well as larger units requiring additional, specialized assistance, regularly contracted out to any number of private consultants, including the Pinkerton Detective Agency, or banded together in specialized trade associations, such as the National Metal Trades Association.

When private resources proved insufficient, the government could provide a means of recourse. In the years between the Great Railway Strike of 1877 and the end of the century, the regular army was called out more than 300 times to deal with labor disputes. The National Guard, however, also labored tirelessly on this front.

From 1877 to 1892 a minimum of 30 percent of National Guard duty was connected with strikes. But state adjutants general used various euphemistic expressions in their reports—"suppression of riots," "repression of a mob"—which suggests that the real percentage was over 50. A careful compilation of instances of National Guard duty from 1886 to 1895 shows precisely 36 percent (118 of 328) to have been in connection with "riots consequent upon labor troubles." Again, ambiguous categories suggest that the true percentage approached 50.[22]

There were also many instances of plant seizures by the government, almost always on the side of management, to say nothing of myriads of local interventions by the police and Pinkertons.[23]

Because the point is so seldom made outside of specialized labor histories, it may be worth noticing that the private armor was good for more than merely strikebreaking in crisis. Commonly, such brigades also spied on the workforce and stood general guard duty. In the mid-1930s, a Senate Committee later estimated that more than 40,000 management spies honeycombed the workplaces of America.[24]

Table 9.2
The use of injunctions in labor disputes

1880–1989	28
1890–1999	122
1900–1909	328
1910–1919	446
1920 to May 1, 1930	921

Note: "Nearly 300" of the injunctions in the 1920-30 period were issued in conjunction with the railroad shops craft strike of 1922.

Source: E. E. Witte, *The Government in Labor Disputes* (New York: McGraw Hill, 1922), p. 84.

The 1920s—the very eve of the New Deal—was in many ways perhaps the most repressive period of all. By then, the first Great Red Scare and the National Association of Manufacturer's famous "American Plan" (for a "union-free" environment) had reduced organized labor to a virtual nullity. The (second) Ku Klux Klan was riding high, not only in the South, but in states such as Maine, Pennsylvania, and Indiana. Over the protests of many immigrant groups, the United States had also passed the Prohibition amendment to the Constitution, outlawing alcoholic beverages. Despite a long literature identifying this proposal with the cause of dissident rural interests, the measure was in fact championed by a virtual Who's Who of American industry, including Ford, Rockefeller, the Du Ponts, Alfred P. Sloan, S. S. Kresge, and Walter Chrysler.[25] Leading American financiers and industrialists were also promoting anti-Semitism and anti-Catholicism.[26]

And, of course, the United States had finally passed legislation slowing down immigration to a trickle, after a long period in which many leading business groups had gradually become far more anxious about the costs of immigration, and then, during the great strike wave of 1919-1921, had become very worried indeed about importing still more radicals.[27]

In what should be a fire alarm ringing in the night for contemporary Europeans, passage of the bill(s), with their notorious quotas favoring Northern Europeans, did little to calm the troubled waters. Instead, one controversy after another broke out in which public attitudes toward immigration figured prominently, including the trial of Sacco and Vanzetti, and the near-hysteria over Al Smith's Catholicism and urban background in the 1928 election.

THE NEW DEAL

The New Deal's curiously elusive political formula, at once daringly radical and venerably conservative, has perplexed analysts for almost two generations. To really come to grips with it, one has to break with most of the commentaries of the last 30 years. One has to go back to primary sources and attempt to analyze the political system as a whole.

Then what stands out is the novel type of political coalition that Roosevelt built. At the center of this coalition, however, were not the workers, African-Americans, and poor that have preoccupied liberal commentators, but something else: a new power bloc of capital-intensive industries, investment banks, and internationally oriented commercial banks.[28]

This bloc constituted the basis of the New Deal's great, and in world history, utterly unique achievement: its ability to accommodate millions of mobilized workers (enormous numbers of whom were immigrants) amidst world depression. Because they were capital-intensive, such firms were less threatened by labor turbulence and organization. Because (with the exception of the chemical industry, which could not compete with the Germans) these capital-intensive firms were world as well as U.S. pacesetters, they stood to gain from global free trade. They could and did, ally with leading international financiers, whose own minuscule workforce presented few sources of tension and who had supported a more broadly internationalist foreign policy and lower tariffs since the end of World War I.

This newer bloc enjoyed a variety of advantages, which helped overcome its relative numerical insignificance vis-à-vis the rest of the business community. It included many of the largest, most rapidly growing corporations in the economy. Recognized industry leaders with the most sophisticated managements, these concerns embodied the aggressively universalistic norms of professionalism and scientific advance that fired the imagination of large parts of American society. The largest of them also dominated major American foundations, which were coming to exercise major influence not only on the climate of opinion, but on the specific content of American public policy. And what might be termed the "Multinational Liberalism" of these internationalists was also aided significantly by the spread of liberal Protestantism; by a newspaper stratification process that brought the free trade organ of international finance, the *New York Times* to the top; by the growth of capital-intensive network radio in the dominant Eastern, internationally oriented environment; and by the rise of major news magazines. These last promised, as Raymond Moley himself intoned while taking over at what became *Newsweek*, to provide "Averell [Harriman] and Vincent [Astor] . . . with means for influencing public opinion generally outside of both parties."[29]

In the darkest moment of Roosevelt's first term, as the so-called First New Deal collapsed in 1935 amid rising public criticism and turmoil, this bloc came dramatically together. Its leaders were drawn from many of America's most prominent corporations; including Standard Oil of New Jersey, General Electric, IBM, Standard Oil of California, Pan Am, and ITT along with a host of prominent investment bankers (such as James Forrestal, Averell Harriman, and Sidney Weinberg) and too many Texas oil barons to be conveniently mentioned.[30]

By intervening in support of the Second New Deal's meliorative social policies (and, as I have recently shown in detail, helping to bankroll the President's 1936 reelection bid)[31] the bloc spared Roosevelt the choice between socialism and the termination of a constitutional regime—a choice then being forced on leaders of other countries with many fewer, capital-intensive businesses. It also provided the decisive impetus for the Second New Deal's historic break with the traditional Republican policy of high tariffs.

The part this bloc played in promoting the "Great Assimilation," however, quite transcended these roles. This new "multinational bloc" was far more open to Catholics and Jews than was the bloc of older industries that had dominated the pre–New Deal Republican Party and that continued to lead the opposition to the New Deal. More liberal in regard to both race relations and ethnic questions, it had both the resources and the willingness to subsidize fundamental challenges to the worldview and concrete public policies championed by its more conservative opponents.

Under Beardsley Ruml, for example, various Rockefeller foundations extensively supported research in anthropology and sociology that attacked the quite explicitly racist foundations of those disciplines. Other leading foundations affiliated with this bloc were also very active (see, Myrdal's famous *American Dilemma*, subsidized by the Carnegie Endowment).[32]

As the ferocious opposition to Roosevelt galvanized during 1935, and news from Europe became more menacing, parts of Hollywood joined with the foundations and pro-Roosevelt leaders in education and business to promote movies pointing up the folly of bigotry and prejudice. Some of these were well-reviewed and were seen by millions of Americans. They were also disseminated into high schools.

Sympathetic Church leaders, notably the Catholic Cardinal of Chicago (who, not accidentally, also joined a committee promoting the renewal of the Reciprocal Trade Act and was a leader in his church's efforts to end the practice of "national" parishes) also promoted tolerance.[33]

And, of course, while elites realigned, ordinary Americans by the millions—old stock, new stock, every kind of stock—flocked to join unions. In sharp contrast to most AFL unions, the CIO was willing to organize African-Americans along with everyone else in factories, including, of course, immigrants and their children. Both the unions and the administration strongly encouraged these new recruits to register and to vote—with the result that voter turnout soared, as immigrants really assimilated. In a delicate touch insufficiently appreciated by later historians, a banker whose endorsement of Roosevelt for reelection had created a sensation in 1936, and who vigorously championed assimilation, served as special adviser to the celebrated CIO political action committee during World War II.[34]

If space permitted, one could develop in some detail an account of the various stages in the Great Assimilation. Tentatively, at least three subperiods can be distinguished: The first phase, running from Roosevelt's first term to the end of the war, witnessed the rapid expansion of unions, major public campaigns for tolerance, the beginnings of (halting) official support for the rights of African-Americans, and most of the reforms of the High New Deal. In the more conservative second phase, running from about 1946 to the mid-1950s, unions ceased expanding, and the rise in voter turnout leveled off. After spiking to record levels right after the war, strike rates fell as employers recovered some, though far from all, of the ground they had conceded earlier.

The second Great Red Scare and the ensuing campaigns to purge universities and Hollywood furthered this deradicalization of the New Deal. So did the sharp reduction in wage and income differentials within the economy and the colossal rates of government-sponsored investment in human capital represented by programs like the "G.I. Bill of Rights" and the steady expansion of requirements for primary and secondary education in cities and states (the fruits of which definitely spilled over into the African-American community, even in the South).[35]

Appeals by business and political leaders to ethnic heritages became rather more overtly nationalistic, commercial, and heavy-handedly official.[36] Church groups (especially the Catholic hierarchy led by Cardinal Spellman of New York) cooperated with the multinational bloc to conscript immigrants, particularly from Eastern Europe, into the new crusade against the "worldwide" Communist threat. A new cohort of much more conservative union leaders, often from the older, and much more conservative American Federation of Labor, also came to the top of most unions, with much help from business and the government.[37]

The third phase of the Great Assimilation, symbolized by the merger of the AFL-CIO under terms that greatly favored the AFL and the legendary BOMFOG (Brotherhood of Man, Fatherhood of God) speeches of Nelson Rockefeller (previously FDR's Assistant Secretary of State for Latin America, later a sterling example of how far the new consensus reached) saw the move of millions of immigrants from the city to the suburbs. By breaking down, though not eliminating, ethnic enclaves in the big cities, this exodus weakened the fabric of support for ethnic consciousness and religious intolerance alike. In the long run, the decline of the enclaves also chipped away at the influence of the Catholic Church, the primary religious influence on American blue-collar workers. Though the Baptists were active in the South and West, most non-Catholic blue-collar Americans had been lost to the mainline Protestant denominations before the turn of the century. This development exposed the new suburbanites—and even more importantly, their children—to the full power of the new, standardized consumer culture that was the true ideology of the great postwar boom.[38] By then assimilation was all but universally regarded as a "good thing," which public discourse took for granted, and even most Republicans applauded. Though conclusive evidence is not yet in, I suspect strongly that this phase of the Great Assimilation will one day be reckoned a stage of ceremonial decay, as ethnic heritages receded into a nostalgic past, amid the triumphant advance of a great, leveling materialism.

CONCLUSION: WHAT EUROPE MIGHT LEARN FROM AMERICA

What then might contemporary Europe learn from the Great Assimilation? The most important lesson is all too apparent. In the United States grandiose talk of assimilation, melting pots, Americanization, and so forth had filled the air literally for a century. But all this in fact produced was towering irony—raw material for a long line of gifted writers from Dreiser and Dos Passos to E. L. Doctorow. What actually melted the pot was a series of concrete political movements that succeeded in bringing millions of previously scorned and largely powerless citizens into at least the antechambers of power. When this occurred, "assimilation" happened, under conditions that convinced nearly everyone—including heavy majorities of old stock nonimmigrants, that they were winners, not losers. The result was a vast liberation of energy and enthusiasm and the sudden creation of possibilities for far more productive organizations. And all this started, if it did not come to fruition, in the midst of the greatest economic crisis in history.

Thus, the greatest lesson for Europe is that there is a vast difference between talking about multiculturalism and (pluralistic) assimilation, and actually achieving it. For the latter, the prescription is straightforward, if rarely discussed and unlikely to be implemented in the Europe of the 1990s: give life to the European Community's "Social Charter" by unleashing I. G. Metall and its cognates.[39]

One should also note that the Great Assimilation owed next to nothing to official promotion of small business, ethnic chambers of commerce, and so on. The now much-touted process of "top down" assimilation via a widening of business opportunities for "minorities" had been extensively promoted for decades in the United States, but had added up to next to nothing. Mass industrial unionism created more real equality in ten years than the entire previous century of talk about "growth" and the "magic of the marketplace."[40]

Note, however, that earlier limitations on immigration may have promoted this development in a curious way. By reducing the inflow of immigrants, legislation of the 1920s almost certainly held down the percentage of legal aliens in the population as a whole. This may have been important when the New Deal finally arrived, for it ensured that most people working in industry had the legal right to register to vote and become fully active citizens.

From this standpoint, the efforts within the European Community to ensure that all residents have the right to vote in at least local elections sounds like a step forward. If nothing else, the American experience certainly provides vivid warning of what happens when economic disadvantage is combined with legal and extra-legal disability. The recent election of a native Turk to the board of one of the big German unions perhaps adds up to an even bigger step forward, if scarcely a new deal.[41]

The American experience may have another, more somber lesson for Europeans as well: History can go backwards. In the late 1970s, the balance of forces that sustained the New Deal party system and the public policies that defined it broke down irretrievably. Ever since then, public policy has breached both the letter and the spirit of the New Deal's confident policy activism.[42]

For most of the population, the New Deal is at best a nostalgic memory, rather like the Christmases of one's childhood. Unsurprisingly, with the collapse of the old form of popular politics and the great "right turn" to macroeconomic austerity, immigration is once again emerging as a major political issue. Whereas before the 1973-74 recession even fairly substantial flows of immigrants attracted relatively little comment, now a wide variety of groups are becoming interested in the question, including many subsidized by various foundations or wealthy investor blocs, as well as parts of organized labor.

At least since the air traffic controllers' strike in 1981, the federal government has pursued a conscious, if largely unheralded, low wage strategy to the neglect of other less laissez-faire oriented approaches to economic adjustment. On the premise that the "globalization" of markets for money, goods, and people is an irreversible process, American political authorities and most of the business community have not attempted to check the flow of immigrants into the United States. Instead, as a Mexican commentator has shrewdly noted, they have collaborated with the Mexican government to ensure that the legal status of the now vast numbers of Mexican migrant laborers working in the United States remains in a legal limbo.[43]

As the economic squeeze continues and it becomes increasingly apparent that the Clinton administration's differences with the Republicans in regard to both the wage question and relations with Latin America are largely rhetorical, unrest is growing within both the mass public and parts of the business community. Moreover, damaging stereotypes are widely circulated: a detailed study of the 1992 election showed that the population far overestimates the number of children born to out-of-wedlock mothers on relief. In California and lately in Congress, Republicans have been experimenting with explicit anti-immigrant appeals, while bi- or nonpartisan efforts to declare English the official language have won some support in a number of states. In a few localities, some voices have also been heard suggesting that Spanish should be declared a second official language. Lawsuits by fiscally strapped state governments to force the federal government either to crack down on illegal immigrants or pay the costs the influx imposes on states are proliferating. U.S. policy in the Caribbean now clearly reflects anxiety about additional waves of immigrants. It appears that what the New Deal once put "miraculously" together is now on the verge of breaking asunder, under unbearable pressure from a world economy in which most interest rates remain far too high, exchange rates are badly misaligned, and every major country dreams of producing and exporting, but not consuming.[44]

Commentary: A Comparative European Perspective

Jarig van Sinderen

Professor Ferguson's approach in his chapter, "From Boiling Pot to Melting Pot: The Real Lessons of the American Experience of Immigration and 'Assimilation,' " of drawing lessons for Europe from the rich history of the United States, especially with respect to assimilation (or integration as Europeans prefer to call it) and immigration is both stimulating and very informative. Immigration has become a very real policy issue in the Europe of the 1990s. In 1989 and 1990, for example, 10 percent of the German labor force migrated from East to West. Net migration into the Netherlands has risen from 8,000 persons in 1983 to approximately 60,000. Although Professor Ferguson's chapter deals primarily with the U.S. history of immigration, it should not be forgotten that the phenomenon is not new for Europe, as Pollard points out in his book *Peaceful Conquest.*[1] The current immigration problem differs from a century ago, primarily in terms of the character of the immigrants. Therefore, it is a pity that Ferguson's chapter concentrates on the New Deal and pays little attention to the more recent immigrant phenomenon in the United States. Migration is an important policy problem in the United States: as is stated in a recent paper by Richard Freeman,[2] about one quarter of the Puerto Rican population and 5 percent of the Mexican population have emigrated to the United States. Furthermore, the New Deal may not be the appropriate reference point for Europe in the 1990s. With these criticisms said, it is strictly how topically much of what was relevant in the early 1900s is still relevant. Many of his arguments are being voiced today in Europe.

Below are four general comments:

1. Europeans do not have a boiling pot but a pressure cooker. Communism for decades suppressed popular movements. Now that the old rule has ended, an unfortunate by-product appears to be that irresponsible populist leaders have increased the heat; the most vivid example is former Yugoslavia. But the same is true (albeit to a lesser extent fortunately) for former Czechoslovakia and the former USSR. Germany also faces problems today that were unthinkable ten years ago.

2. The extent of unionization is an important difference both across continents and in a historical perspective. Unions unite people

with different backgrounds and cultures. However, only giving immigrants a right to vote will not solve the problem of integration. Moreover, if micro-forces push wages up too high, employment for immigrants (often low skilled) may decrease, which certainly does not stimulate integration. Ferguson is probably right when he argues that employment in general increased in the 1930s despite the increase in capital intensive production, but this does not imply that in the present situation low-skilled labor will obtain a job easily.

3. Motivations of U.S. immigrants especially in the 1930s and of "modern immigrants" (both in the United States and in Europe) differ considerably. The former were often pushed by Nazi practices while the latter are often pulled by income differentials.[3]

4. In the present situation, migration differs a lot from that of the 1920s, because a lot of immigrants have low skills. The problem in the OECD countries is that low-skilled jobs are crowded out more and more by high-skilled ones. One reason for this is technological development, since technology increases productivity, requires flexibility, and demands higher education. Furthermore, high real-wage costs (especially important in Europe) are at the lower end of the wage scale. Minimum wages and the large wedge between gross and net income make it very difficult for immigrants to find legal jobs, because the wage costs for low productive jobs are sometimes higher than their expected output. This has a twofold effect. On the one hand, low-skilled legal immigrants can draw from the social safety net. . . . On the other hand, illegal immigrants work at a rate below official wages. Therefore, some of the low-skilled jobs are filled with illegal labor. Legal and illegal immigrants end up as competitors in the same segment of the labor market and one group tends to crowd out the other.[4] This problem is found in both Europe and the United States. However, Europe can learn from the United States: Flexibility at the lower end of the wage scale is necessary to create low-paid jobs and a welfare system should not be too generous.[5]

Overall, Ferguson's chapter is too optimistic about U.S. assimilation and is too pessimistic for Europe. Not being an expert on U.S. social and racial relations, I think Ferguson should have elaborated a bit more on what he means by "dissolved so many of the social tensions." Given what I hear from the media my impression is that in the United States there still exist many problems. Data show, for example, that many blacks still hold low-paying jobs and that two-thirds of black children visit schools in which all children are minority or immigrant. Moreover, although only 13 percent of the U.S. population is black, almost half of U.S. prisoners are black. This suggests that a large part of U.S. society has not "assimilated."[6] Of course, blacks could hardly be called immigrants, given U.S. history, but these statistics should be a warning as to what might happen to minorities if integration is postponed or prolonged.

In Europe the "assimilation" of the different European Union countries has not caused problems. As a result of the European community, migration between the different member countries has actually decreased. However, at the same time, in Europe people from the East Indies are integrating rather well. Nowadays the migration and integration problems are especially concentrated in terms of low-skilled immigrants and economic refugees, who for a large part end up on social welfare.

POLICY PROPOSALS

From an economist's perspective, it cannot fail to be observed that the main purpose and impact of the New Deal was to restore economic health. I contend that the melting pot has been a by-product of this new economic perspective. Hence, what Europe should probably learn from the American experience is that sound economic policies are a prerequisite to turn a boiling pot into a melting pot. A common policy is needed. The New Deal particularly increased the power of the federal government vis-à-vis the states, which can be an important lesson for Europe. If Europe is to be successful in implementing a common immigration policy, it must increase the policy coordination in Brussels. In the future the following should be pursued in Europe:

1. The economic health of the East and South in Europe should be a political concern for policymakers in the West. The economic policies, however, which are currently needed in Europe to further the integration of immigrants, may be quite different from those of the New Deal. For example, education and a more flexible labor market are crucial ingredients for Europe.

2. Migration at a very rapidly increasing scale should be prevented, because the risk of immigrants not finding a legal job is quite substantial. Investing in the sending countries and increasing in-

ternational trade, instead of importing, is a much better policy approach.

3. Coordination of international policies is needed; this is a very important lesson from Ferguson's paper. Coordination within the European Union is needed, but it is also needed outside of the European Union. If the sending countries do not join in the cooperation, it will be difficult to handle the inflow of their inhabitants.

4. Economic growth is important to restore the equilibrium within an economy. It is important that both the United States and the European Union feel responsible for pursuing a policy that restores the conditions for economic growth on a global scale.

ENDNOTES

1. D. W. MacCormack's statement is from his "The New Deal for the Alien," *Proceedings of the National Conference of Social Work* (Chicago: National Conference of Social Work, 1934), p. 465; quoted in Weiss, R., "Ethnicity and Reform: Minorities and the Ambience of the Depression Years," *Journal of American History,* 66 (December 1979): 567.

2. Most writing on American immigration accepts the general validity of the notion of "assimilation." See, for example, the discussion and wide-ranging literature review in Hirschman, Charles, "America's Melting Pot Reconsidered," in Turner, R., and J. F. Short, Jr., eds., *Annual Review of Sociology 1983* (Palo Alto, California: Annual Reviews, Inc., 1983), pp. 397–423. But the timing and historical limits of this process of assimilation are critical issues. A brief review of the state of the evidence about how various groups have fared over time may be helpful.

    Around 1900 the evidence is very strong that "old stock" Protestant Americans from northwestern Europe fared far better than so-called new immigrants from southern and eastern Europe, African-Americans, or immigrants from the Orient in regard to incomes, high-status occupations, choice of residence (i.e., not limited by spatial segregation), and education. See, among many sources, Stanley Lieberson's very impressive reconstruction of the quantitative evidence in regard to the disparities among all these groups in his *A Piece Of The Pie: Blacks And White Immigrants Since 1880* (Berkeley: University of California Press, 1980). Also especially instructive is Hershberg, T., Burstein, A., Ericksen, E., Greenberg, S., and Yancey, W., "A Tale of Three Cities: Blacks and Immigrants in Philadelphia: 1850–1880, 1930 and 1970," *Annals of the*

American Academy of Political and Social Science, 441 (January 1979): 55–81.

Not surprisingly, intermarriage rates between the WASPs and the other groups, and between the other groups themselves, were very low. See, for example, Pagnini, D. L. and Morgan, S. P., "Intermarriage and Social Distance Among U.S. Immigrants at the Turn of the Century," *American Journal of Sociology* 96, 2 (September 1990): 405–32; McCaa, R., "Ethnic Intermarriage and Gender in New York City," *Journal of Interdisciplinary History,* 24, 2 (Autumn 1993): 207–31; and Peach, C., "Ethnic Segregation and Ethnic Intermarriage: A Re-examination of Kennedy's Triple Melting Pot in New Haven, 1900–1950," in Peach, C., Robinson, V., and Smith, S., *Ethnic Segregation In Cities* (London: Croom Helm, 1981).

By, say, 1970, the situation was radically different. For all the (extensively subsidized) noise about "unmeltable ethnics" that accompanied the early years of the Nixon administration and the halcyon days of the old "Coalition For A Democratic Majority" championed by Democrats such as Senator Henry M. Jackson, disparities between "old stock" and "new ethnics" in regard to education, occupational success, or housing and a real segregation had virtually disappeared. Indeed, in some instances, the "new ethnics" now placed microscopically ahead of WASPs on some of dimensions. Religion now accounted for virtually no variance in these outcomes and, with important qualifications noted later, intermarriage was common. In addition to the sources just cited and Hirschman, "Melting Pot," see, for example, Alba, R. D., and Golden, R. M., "Patterns of Ethnic Marriage in the United States," *Social Forces,* 65, 1 (September 1986): 202–23.

It should also be noted that if one is concerned with explaining variation in some attitudes and patterns of behavior (rather than the dimensions of socioeconomic stratification referred to earlier), ethnicity may still play a role, though I believe that most studies along these lines lack sufficiently rigorous controls for both social class and less obvious economic variables such as "human capital" or sectoral variation within the economy. See Steinberg, S., *The Ethnic Myth* (Boston: Beacon Press, 1969) for a stimulating argument; also exceedingly instructive is Hobsbawm, E., *Nations and Nationalism Since 1780* (New York: Cambridge University Press, 1990). Note also the discussion of econometric misspecification in regard to the evidence usually mustered in support of the so-called ethnocultural synthesis of American voting behavior in Ferguson, T., "Party Realignment and American Industrial Structure: The Investment Theory of Political Parties in Historical Perspective," in Zarembka,

P., ed., *Research in Political Economy,* vol. VI. (Greenwich, CT: JAI Press, 1983), p. 69, no. 36.

There is no reason to overstate an already compelling case: A mild preference for marriage within the older groups remains, and older cities often continued to display obvious concentrations of ethnic or religious groups, as did suburbs in yet more attenuated form. Incautious statements of the "assimilationist" case, I think, have helped fuel a backlash that often appears to deny that anything has really changed. See, for example, Kantrowitz, N., "Ethnic Segregation: Social Reality and Academic Myth," in Peach, et al., *Ethnic Segregation.* Works such as this, however, overlook the obvious decline of "national" churches even in the old cities.

For this chapter, which focuses on the New Deal, Lieberson's—and, though limited to one city, Herschberg, et al.'s—cohort evidence about when the "new ethnics" began to catch up is interesting. Differences between the "new ethnics" and the WASPs, Lieberson suggests, melted very slowly, though steadily, from 1910 or even earlier. The truly dramatic changes, however, occurred within the lives of the cohorts born in 1925 and after. See, for example, Lieberson, *Pie,* p. 162 or p. 329. This is simply a sociological expression for the period of the New Deal, as broadly conceived in this chapter.

The relation of the New Deal coalition to African-Americans, Latinos, and other minorities is quite complex. Presumably no one familiar with my previous work on the New Deal will accuse me of idealizing it, so in this paper I will work with the stylized fact of the "Great Assimilation." But it is obvious that African-Americans, Latinos, Native Americans, and several other groups—such as the Japanese Americans whom the administration interned during World War II—benefited much less from the New Deal, particularly in its early stages. Here Lieberson's quantitative comparisons with the "new ethnics" and the WASPs are sobering. In many cities at the turn of the century, he suggests, African-Americans were actually less segregated than a number of the "new ethnic" groups (*Pie,* pp. 263 and following pages). But whereas the spatial segregation of most of the "new ethnics" increasingly broke down over time, the segregation of African-Americans in the cities increased markedly— a conclusion supported by Herschberg, et al., "Tale of Three Cities." Lieberson also documents large and persisting gaps between African-Americans and other major groups in regard to education, income, and occupational success (Lieberson, *Pie,* Chapters 6 to 11). Some of these gaps actually widen during the Depression as the "new ethnics" begin to race ahead.

Not all of the economic disparity between African-Americans and other Americans during this period can be traced to racism—some of this disparity appears to reflect the operation of a job "queue" in the sense of Thurow, L., *Generating Inequality* (New York: Basic Books, 1975) that would have operated to the disadvantage of whichever group happened to arrive last in the industrialized North (Lieberson, *Pie,* pp. 338–39). But Lieberson's data also demonstrate that differences in family structure, orientation to education, and other values cannot account for most of the difference (see inter al., pp. 186 and following pages, and Chapter 12) and that African-Americans plainly faced more intense and prolonged antipathy from the rest of society than did other comparatively disadvantaged groups. (See especially his chilling review of educational disparities in Chapters 6 to 8; a discussion that is also sensitive to gender differences.)

But even his results indicate that in the later stages of the New Deal system some aspects of life for African-Americans improved significantly: Educational differences began to narrow, as both the amount and quality of education improved somewhat (p. 145). Victories also began to be won in the long struggle to end segregation in higher education and open up professional schools (see, for example, p. 156—which indirectly witnesses to the role played by the New Deal's famous reorientation of the Supreme Court). In the very long run, even the income disparities lessened somewhat while the number of African Americans in business and the professions increased. See, for example, Amott, T., and Matthaei, J., *Race, Gender, and Work* (Boston: South End Press 1991; pp. 178–79) and, for the consequent changes in social structure within the African-American community, Vanneman, R., and Cannon, L. W., *The American Perception of Class* (Philadelphia: Temple University Press, 1987), Chapter 10. Spatial segregation remains very high, although some African-Americans have succeeded in breaking into certain suburbs. See Schneider, M., and Phelan, T., "Black Suburbanization in the 1980s," *Demography,* 30, 2 (1993): 269–79.

Rates of intermarriage with whites, while still very low, also rose slightly. Compare McCaa, "Ethnic Intermarriage," p. 212, and Pagnini and Morgan, "Turn of the Century," p. 430.

Though a powerful current of racism continues to flow in American society, over the long run there is little doubt that overt racism has declined and public opinion has shifted in a more liberal direction. See, for example, Page, B., and Shapiro, R., *The Rational Public* (Chicago: University of Chicago Press, 1992), pp. 67–81 and Schuman, H., Steeh, C., and Bobo, L., *Racial Attitudes in America* (Cambridge: Harvard University Press, 1985). Both of these works carefully consider the objections brought against this claim by a variety of critics.

It is apparent that many of these changes represent cumulative consequences of the New and Fair Deals (and are at risk of being rolled back in the 1990s). The "civil rights" movement of the 1960s (and similar developments among Latinos) had numerous institutional, ideological, and in many instances direct personal affiliations with the earlier social movements (and, as discussed later, leading foundations and businesses) of the High New Deal, whatever Roosevelt's own well-known limitations and equivocations. So did the landmark Hart-Cellar Act of 1965, which abolished the infamous national quota system for selecting immigrants. (Hart and Cellar were prominent liberal "New Deal" Democrats.) See also what follows on the efforts by business and leading Democrats to brake the radical New Deal. Assessment of the New Deal's relation to minorities should also remember that the mere decision to extend relief to minorities in the South was extremely controversial at the time.

An excellent review of other limitations of "assimilation" for particular groups is Daniels, R., *Coming to America* (New York: Basic Books, 1990). In regard to the New Deal, however, this fine work is somewhat eccentric. Daniels is right that FDR did not contemplate major changes in the law governing immigration. (Few public figures did—though, as indicated, this did not imply that they supported nativism or xenophobia.) I also agree with his criticism of the tardy U.S. response to the needs of refugees from Fascism. But he should also credit the immense long-run effects of the New Deal's policies.

For Wells on the future of the melting pot, see his *The Future in America* (New York: Harper, 1906); for Siegfried, see later.

On the "pluralist" and other senses of assimilation, see Weiss, "Ethnicity," pp. 568–69. This more flexible sense of assimilation does not suggest that "melting pots" imply that people forget their ancestry—a point that has often been used against the very idea that the United States ever became a melting pot, even during the New Deal. But such a strong construction is unreasonable and leads to neglect of important discontinuities in U.S. history.

3. See Ferguson, T., "From 'Normalcy' to New Deal: Industrial Structure, Party Competition, and American Public Policy in the Great Depression," *International Organization,* 38 (1984): 41–94; and Ferguson, T., "Industrial Structure and Party Competition in the New Deal," *Sociological Perspectives,* 34 (1991): 493–526.

4. For a discussion of religion in the 1950s, see, among many sources, Herberg, W., *Protestant, Catholic, Jew,* Revised edition (Garden City: Anchor, 1960).

5. For World War I, see among many sources, Goldstein, R. J., *Political Repression in Modern America* (Cambridge: Schenkman Books, 1978) and Meyers, G., *History of Bigotry in the United States,* edited and revised by Christman, H. (New York: Capricorn, 1960).
6. For the poll evidence from the 1940s, compare Page and Shapiro, *Rational Public,* pp. 68–69.
7. *Ibid.,* pp. 182–84 for the data on Germany; Page and Shapiro note that Germany, Italy, and Japan tended to be somewhat more unpopular at all points in the period, but that "isolationism" was widely espoused by the population in the middle of the decade. On the New Deal as a counterpoint to Nazism, see Weiss, "Ethnicity."
8. See, for example, Diggins, J. P., *Mussolini and Fascism: The View from America* (Princeton: Princeton University Press, 1972) for Il Duce; the case of Germany is too well known to require comment here.
9. The literature on the Jacksonian period is enormous. For a review of who appears really to have done what to whom, and the role of business and investor blocs, compare Ferguson, T., "Party Realignment and American Industrial Structure: The Investment Theory of Political Parties in Historical Perspective," in Zarembka, P., ed., *Research in Political Economy, Vol. VI* (Greenwich, CT: JAI Press, 1983), pp. 35–40. Like the New Deal essays, this essay started a variety of controversies; see my "Deduced and Abandoned: Expectations, The Investment Theory of Political Parties, and the Myth of the Median Voter," in Crotty, W., ed., *Political Parties in an Age of Change* (American Political Science Association, Political Organizations and Parties Section, forthcoming).

   Baltzell, E. D., *The Protestant Establishment* (New York: Random House, 1964), p. 73, has argued that anti-Catholicism was uncommon in America before the Civil War. I doubt that many historians would accept this, but in any event I believe that this claim cannot be defended: Arson directed at convents and a number of best-selling books purporting to reveal what "really" went on in convents or seminaries are powerful evidence of anti-Catholic sentiments.
10. On the temperance question and its connection to better off workers, as well as the critical role played by manufacturers in the controversy, see Johnson, P., *A Shopkeeper's Millennium* (New York: Hill & Wang, 1978). In 1864, the Republican Party platform explicitly endorsed immigration; the position was reaffirmed in 1868 and 1872. These planks, however, were scarcely expressions of affection for immigrants. They were part of a campaign by manufacturers—a core constituency of the new party—to lower the price of labor. In 1864 these efforts resulted in the passage of a law that authorized employers to finance passage in exchange for bind-

ing advance agreements for the immigrants' services. That law was repealed only four years later, after widespread criticism. See Bernard, W. S., "A History of U.S. Immigration Policy," in Easterlin, R., Ward, D., Bernard, W. S., Ueda, R., *Immigration* (Cambridge, MA: The Belknap Press of Harvard University Press, 1982), p. 85.

It should be noted that from the 1830s until 1875, when the Supreme Court voided state laws regulating immigration, the states were the active centers of immigration regulation. Thereafter the federal role became much stronger, with the West Coast an early center of agitation for restriction of immigration from Asia. Plenty of local controversies remained, however—notably, the long-running dispute over whether English should be the sole language of instruction in schools. This first great debate over bilingualism came to a sudden end during World War I.

11. Seigfried, A., *America Comes of Age* (New York: Harcourt, 1927), pp. 5–7. The last few lines of this passage, concerning the suspicion that continued to attach to second-generation children of immigrants, deserve careful attention. The literature on "Americanization" celebrates an alleged tendency for integration to be accomplished more or less completely with the children of immigrants. This is, to put the matter bluntly, more an expression of a hope or the ideals of the New Deal itself than a fact of American history. Consider, for example, a letter Fiorello La Guardia received after he criticized President Hoover in 1931: "It seems to me, a REPUBLICAN [like LaGuardia], that you are a little out of your class, in presuming to criticize the President. It strikes me as impudence. You should go back to where you belong and advise Mussolini on how to make good honest citizens in Italy. The Italians are preponderantly, our murderers and bootleggers . . . Like a lot of other foreign spawn, you do not appreciate the country which supports and tolerates you." Hirschman, "Melting Pot," p. 398, quotes this letter and, citing Baltzell, *Protestant Establishment*, p. 30, attributes it to Hoover himself. Hoover, however, did not write it, as Baltzell's own source, Mann, A., *La Guardia: A Fighter Against his Times* (Philadelphia: Lippincott, 1959), p. 298 and p. 368, is perfectly clear. But Seigfried is right that similar sentiments were widespread in the period.

12. Storey, M., *Politics as a Duty and as a Career* (New York: Putnam's, 1981), pp. 4–7. Storey's "liberalism" had distinct limits: he opposed the confirmation of Louis Brandeis to the Supreme Court.

13. On the strikes and their effect on suffrage sentiment, see Kolko, G., *Railroads and Regulation* (New York: Norton, 1970), p. 12.

14. Storey, M., *Politics*, pp. 4–7.

15. Yearly, C. K., *The Money Machines: The Breakdown And Reform of Governmental And Party Finance in the North: 1860–1920* (Albany: State University of New York Press, 1970), Chapter I. For Godkin, *ibid.,* p. 19.

16. Ibid., p. 20.

17. The table originally appeared in Ferguson, T., "Party Competition," pp. 52–53. For references and discussion of Rusk, Converse, et al., see Burnham, W. D., "Theory and Voting Research: Some Reflections on Converse's 'Change in the American Electorate,'" *American Political Science Review,* 68 (September 1974). See also the discussion of that controversy in my "Party Competition," pp. 50–53.

18. McCulloch, A. J., *Suffrage And Its Problems* (Baltimore: Warwick and York, 1929), pp. 151 and pages following.

19. Ibid.

20. For the turnout decline, see Burnham, W. D., "The Appearance and Disappearance of the American Voter: An Overview," in Ferguson, T., and Rogers, J., eds., *The Political Economy* (Armonk, New York: M. E. Sharpe, 1984), pp. 112–39.

21. See Witte, E. E., *The Government in Labor Disputes* (New York: McGraw Hill, 1932), p. 84.

22. Hacker, B. C., "The United States Army as a National Police Force: The Federal Policing of Labor Disputes, 1877–1898," *Military Affairs,* 33, 1 (April 1969): 259. For the regular army interventions, compare Weigley, R. F., *History of the United States Army* (New York: Macmillan, 1967): 281. See also the striking chronology and discussion in Wilson, F. T., *Federal Aid In Domestic Disturbances 1787–1903* (Sen. Doc. 209, 57th Cong., 2nd Sess., 1903). The latter instances involve a number of cases in which troops had to be called out to deal with riots involving (or against) Chinese workers in the West in the 1880s.

23. See the discussion in Blackman, J. L., *Presidential Seizure in Labor Disputes* (Cambridge, MA: Harvard University Press, 1967), particularly the appendices.

24. Cited in Bernstein, I., *The New Deal Collective Bargaining Policy* (Berkeley: University of California Press, 1950), p. 10. Andrew Mellon's famous "You can't run a coal mine without machine guns" sums up the whole situation. (What Mellon actually said was "You could not run without them.") Compare Koskoff, D., *Andrew Mellon* (New York: Crowell, 1978), p. 304.

25. A great deal more could be said about Prohibition and American industry than is now in the history books. Johnson's *Shopkeeper's Millennium* is an exception, but covers only the early 1800s. I have taken these facts from the manuscript of a chapter in my *Critical Realignment* (New York:

Oxford University Press, forthcoming). This draws almost entirely on contemporaneous letters and documents. Compare also my "Normalcy To New Deal," pp. 72–74 and following pages.

26. See my discussion of J. P. Morgan, Jr., and other financiers' quiet encouragement of Henry Ford's notorious ravings in my "Normalcy to New Deal," p. 70. The vehemently anti-Catholic American Protective Association and similar groups drew widely on business support—in the America of that period, no other sources of finance were available. Morgan, Jr., for example, was deeply suspicious of the Catholic Church.

27. Siegfried, *America*, pp. 121–22 is correct on this point, which many more recent sources gloss over. Note that Siegfried himself came from a textile-based French Protestant family.

On the growing opposition to immigration within the business community see Heald, M., "Business Attitudes Toward European Immigration, 1880–1900," *Journal of Economic History*, 13 (1953): 291–304. In 1917, the United States had passed a law providing for a literacy test for immigrants. Lieberson, *Pie,* pp. 204–214 has a very interesting discussion of how this law may have affected the subsequent fortunes of American immigrant groups, for it appears to have resulted in markedly increased skill levels of those who were admitted.

For a recent study of the passage of the literacy test, see Golden, C., "The Political Economy of Immigration Restriction in the United States, 1890–1921," National Bureau of Economic Research, Working Paper 4345, April 1, 1893. This interesting paper's tacit reliance on an modified "median voter" model of the political process produces a foreshortened picture of the political pressures for that bill. While careful to note the potential importance of business preferences, the paper does not incorporate them (through proxies, if nothing else) into its econometric estimates. I would, accordingly, be exceedingly cautious about its assessments of the role of the immigrant vote. Nor would I entirely accept the paper's suggestion that the preferences of business are necessarily so difficult to research. It was, after all, that ornament of the Boston Home Market Club and vigorous champion of a "navy second to none," Senator Henry Cabot Lodge, who introduced an early bill for a literacy test in 1896. And the Immigration Restriction League, which campaigned for years for the literacy test, was the 1894 brainchild of a group of Harvard-educated Brahmins. To make much progress in these matters, however, it is essential to have recourse to, for example, Lodge's papers at the Massachusetts Historical Society. The two or three miles that stretch between the Historical Society and the NBER, however, define a traverse in the scholarly world that is several times the distance between the earth and the moon.

Note also that as Daniels's *Coming* emphasizes, although the Chinese and Japanese were already barred from entering the United States, the restrictionist legislation of the 1920s did not seek to halt immigration from this hemisphere, so that substantial numbers of immigrants could still enter the United States via Canada.

28. The next few pages draw on my "Normalcy to New Deal" and "Industrial Structure and Party Competition" papers.

29. The Moley quotation is from an entry in his "Journal" for June 13, 1936, Raymond Moley Papers, Hoover Institution, Stanford, California and is quoted from my "Normalcy to New Deal," p. 68.

30. See the discussion in "Industrial Structure and Party Competition," passim.

31. Ibid. Note that this chapter's table 9.2 reports t-tests on the differences between large contributors to the Roosevelt and Landon (GOP) campaigns in regard to labor intensity and internationalism. (How these were measured is explained in the text.) The tests show wide differences for both dimensions between the two coalitions, just as my "Normalcy to New Deal" predicted.

The standard errors indicated in the table, however, are inconsequentially different from their most appropriate ("real") values. The t-tests reported there retained in the sample those who contributed to both candidates, instead of dropping them (the more common procedure in such cases). Because the number of cases is very large and the two groups differ widely on both dimensions, this procedure makes no practical difference to the results.

When I wrote the essay I was concerned—as immediately did occur—that the means between the two groups would be identified with "representative" industries (for example, steel vs. oil). I did not want to spend many years explaining how dropping contributors to both parties had shifted the apparent mean values of each coalition from what most people would regard as their "true" values. But I did not learn until I saw my essay in print that my note to this effect was not put into the text.

The t-tests reported in the version of this essay that appears in my *Golden Rule: The Investment Theory of Political Parties and the Logic of Money Driven Political Systems* (Chicago: University of Chicago Press, forthcoming) follow the more customary procedure of dropping joint contributors: this produces, of course, even more lopsided results in favor of my central hypotheses. The important point is that the results do not change, no matter how one does the tests.

32. On Ruml and the foundations, see for example, the discussion and references in Ferguson, T., "Normalcy to New Deal," p. 70. Ruml, incidentally, was particularly active on questions of race.

33. For the Cardinal and the Reciprocal Trade Act, see *ibid.*, p. 92; for his pioneering efforts to reduce the role of parishes organized by national or linguistic groups, see Cohen, L., *Making a New Deal* (New York: Cambridge University Press, 1990), pp. 83–94.

34. The banker was James Warburg, who knew firsthand what discrimination was, and who, because of his time in Germany, well understood what Nazism represented. There is, of course, no reason to idealize everything that either the AFL or the CIO did in regard to racial questions, especially the former. But as Freeman and Medoff, *What Do Unions Do?* (New York: Basic Books, 1984) observe, since the New Deal–organized labor has a considerable record of accomplishment in regard to civil rights. Because so many members of minorities are poor, minorities almost perforce benefit disproportionately from industrial unionism.

35. For the universities, see Schrecker, E., *No Ivory Tower* (New York: Oxford University Press, 1986), which mentions a number of cases in which would be economic historians became transformed into sociologists, or simply, historians. The case of Hollywood is too well known to require comment here. For the narrowing of wage differentials, see the paper by Goldin, C., and Margo, R. A., "The Great Compression: The Wage Structure in the United States At Mid-Century," National Bureau of Economic Research, Working Paper 3817 (August 1991). Though the precise links require more work, it is likely that this narrowing of wage differentials is a complex effect of a number of New Deal initiatives, including the (fitful—until the 1960s) efforts to stabilize demand; the rise in unionization; minimum wage legislation; and some of the New Deal regulatory initiatives for specific industries. These, of course, are all casualties of the late 1970s "right turn."

    The steady increase in schooling requirements and attainments is evident from the data in Lieberson, *Pie,* Chapters 6, 7, and 8. But it is striking that neither his or any other works known to me connect this with the New Deal; nor is the question treated by Goldin and Margo, "Compression." Yet surely, the remarkable rate of investment in people that marked this period was very important and merits much more emphases than it has so far received.

36. The literature on these events is vast—too vast to begin citing here. But on the transformation of "ethnicity" from the top down in a commercial and nationalist direction after the war, see Bodnar, J., *Remaking America* (Princeton: Princeton University, 1992), Chapter III, "The Construction

of Ethnic Memory." This chapter is best read in conjunction with Cohen's observations in *Making a New Deal*, passim, that the Depression greatly weakened the network of ethnic businesses and fraternal organizations by driving many into bankruptcy. It is quite clear that "ethnicity" was reconstructed during the later New Deal as a conservative response to the rise of organized labor, which itself often made use of ethnic appeals.

37. For labor in the postwar period, see, among many sources, Fraser, S., "The 'Labor Question,'" in Fraser, S., and Gerstle, G., eds., *The Rise and Fall of the New Deal Order* (Princeton: Princeton University Press, 1989), pp. 55–84. Given the importance of unionization to economically marginal minority groups, I would submit that they were the biggest losers in this deradicalization of the New Deal.

    Perhaps I should also note that the periodization of the New Deal offered here is directed to answering questions about the Great Assimilation. It is obvious that the New Deal underwent a metamorphosis in, for example, the late 1930s.

38. Note that George Meany, the one-time business agent of the plumbers union in the Bronx and (sole) designated signer for the Building Trades Unions of Greater New York of their celebrated agreement with Nelson Rockefeller for labor peace during the construction of Rockefeller Center, became head of the new AFL-CIO. See Collier, P., and Horowitz, D., *The Rockefellers* (New York: Holt, Rinehart & Winston, 1976), p. 205. For the loss of most Protestant workers to the mainline Protestant churches, see, for example, May, H. F., *Protestant Churches and Industrial America* (New York: Harper, 1949).

    Given the role the federal highway system played in wrecking (ethnically centered) city neighborhoods and opening up suburbs to quick transit, it merits a mention in a paper on assimilation.

39. Considering recent developments in that union, one is inclined to suggest that not only European stock markets, but European unions can profitably borrow another notion from the New Deal: stiffer standards for regulation of securities markets and insider trading.

    In regard to the constructive role unions could play in the Europe, one should not neglect an important lesson of the New Deal in regard to shorter hours. Though I lack the space to document or discuss the question in detail, it is a fact that the early moves of the New Deal to regulate and shorten working hours were *partially* motivated by considerations quite similar to those that are now leading the European labor movement, some businesses in Germany and France, and at least some high-ranking members of the European Commission, to recommend moves to a four-day week or other worksharing arrangements. Some contemporary critics of this movement contend that such moves would have deleterious effects on productivity. Here the example of the New Deal is quite interesting— in disjointed steps, policy during the New Deal years moved to embrace both shorter hours and massive investments in education. Worksharing, in other words, was accompanied by major social investments in people (along with major efforts to stimulate aggregate demand, or at least, buy weapons, after the late 1940s). This sort of combined policy had—and surely would again—quite different consequences for industrial productivity than simply warehousing people who, in the absence of effective demand, have no hope of ever finding employment.

40. On the role of unionization in achieving social equity, see Freeman and Medoff's *Unions,* and compare the discussion and data on the long-run development of American inequality in Williamson, J., and Lindert, P., *American Inequality* (New York: Academic Press, 1980).

41. Dr. Jan Singer-Carrel of the CNRS has pointed out to me that the French Law of March 21, 1884, allowed foreigners to be members of unions, but not to serve as officers. Article 10 of that law applied these provisions to Algeria and other parts of the empire, but forbade foreigners to join unions at all. An outgrowth of the 1968 explosion was a 1972 law that gave foreigners a right to vote in elections for factory committees. The law of March 11, 1975, finally allowed foreigners to become union officials. I know of no study of the rights of foreigners in unions in the rest of Europe, though the question is obviously of great interest.

In recent decades, U.S. unions have only occasionally interested themselves in enrolling foreigners—even the millions of migrant workers from Mexico. See Arturo Santamaria Gomez, "The Porous U.S.-Mexico Border," *The Nation,* October 25, 1993, p. 461.

The U.S. and contemporary European experiences with immigration might perhaps be differently affected by two other factors. First, radio became commercially available just as the United States moved to restrict immigration. By contrast, contemporary European immigration takes place in the midst of a communications revolution. To the extent that modern communications systems make it easier for external regimes to reach into other nation-states, one might wonder whether this difference might become important later in the decade, or even affect the pace of assimilation. On the other hand, foreign newspapers circulated all over the United States in the nineteenth century and an indigenous foreign-language press flourished. Today, a large Spanish-language press exists in the United States. Perhaps the differences are not so profound, after all.

A second question is closely related to this: the distance factor. Does it matter that proportionately more immigrants can potentially drive back to the home country for the weekend in Europe than in most parts of the United States?

42. See Ferguson, T., and Rogers, J., *Right Turn: The Decline of The Democrats and the Future of American Politics* (New York: Hill & Wang, 1986).

43. See Gomez, "U.S.-Mexico Border," pp. 460-61; his discussion of why the Mexican government concurs in this policy is very acute. For the early years of the Reagan-Bush record on labor and other issues, compare Ferguson, T., and Rogers, J., *Right Turn*, Chapters 3 and 4; for the later years, see Ferguson, T., "By Invitation Only: Party Competition and Industrial Structure in the 1988 Election," in Ferguson, T., *Golden Rule*, forthcoming.

44. On the differences and similarities between Clinton and the earlier Republican administrations, see Ferguson, T., " 'Organized Capitalism,' Fiscal Policy, and the 1992 Democratic Campaign," in Dodd, L. C., and Jillson, C., eds., *New Perspectives on American Politics* (Washington, D.C.: Congressional Quarterly Press, 1992), pp. 118–40. There has been considerable discussion in recent years of whether the progress made by various minorities in the 1960s and 1970s has stopped. See, for example, Amott and Mattei, *Race, Gender, and Work,* p. 179 and pages following, or Rosenbaum, E., "Race and Ethnicity in Housing: Turnover in New York City, 1978–87," *Demography,* 29, 3 (1992): 467–86.

For the stereotype, see "Images/Issues/Impact: The Media and Campaign 92," Research Report by The Center for the Study of Communication, University of Massachusetts, Amherst.

Several aspects of the current discussions of immigration in the United States merit additional comment. Senior congressional aides have described to me how in the 1980s, the CIA under William Casey repeatedly attempted to draw the attention of Congress to the question of immigration. The career of this question, however, suggests that the issue was really being raised as part of broader efforts to negotiate new arrangements with various countries, and not as part of a unique economic strategy.

Another question of considerable interest concerns the developing discussion of immigration within the business community. How firms rate access to masses of unskilled labor vis-à-vis the alleged costs of immigration (paid in the form of higher taxes for services) is of considerable interest. There is no reason why different firms should all view these the same way, any more than it is sensible to expect that different levels of the government will (the mismatch of tax revenues and immediate costs, for example, is far more likely to leave local governments short in recessions).

There has been a long, acrimonious discussion about whether the large numbers of immigrants into the United States affect the general level of wages. Certain aspects of this discussion, I think, are less than salutary: I have had conversations with noted econometricians in which they openly laughed at their own published conclusions that the level of wages was unaffected by immigration.

It seems patent that millions of immigrants, particularly in times of macroeconomic austerity, will affect wage levels. For analyses that the world is after all round, see, for example, the excellent discussion in Mishel, L., and Bernstein, J., *The State of Working America 1992–93* (Armonk, NY: M. E. Sharpe for the Economic Policy Institute, 1993), pp. 181–86, and Borjas, G. J., Freeman, R. B., and Katz, L., "On the Labor Market Effects of Immigration and Trade," National Bureau of Economic Research, Working Paper 3761, June 1991.

Note also that many multinational businesses are now cultivating American ethnic organizations, particularly from among minorities from countries on the Pacific rim. These organizations are in many cases obviously functioning as bridges between national business communities and nation-states. Other governments also play this game. Large American foundations and some globally oriented business figures have also thrown considerable organizational and financial support behind the cause of so-called multiculturalism. In some instances, these efforts have occasioned considerable controversy.

Whether or not countries dominated by multinational forms of business organization exhibit a long-run tendency toward the "denationalization" of many organizations and practices is an interesting question that, alas, cannot be pursued here for reasons of space. I believe there is some support for this proposition from British experiences.

ENDNOTES—COMMENTARY

1. See Pollard, S., *Peaceful Conquest* (Oxford: Oxford University Press, 1981).
2. Freeman, R., "Immigration from Poor to Wealthy Countries: Experience of the United States," *European Economic Review,* vol. 37, nos. 2–3 (April 1993): 443–51.

3. Freeman, R., 1993, op. cit. Burda, M. C., "The Determinants of East-West German Migration: Some First Results," *European Economic Review*; vol. 37, nos. 2–3 (April 1993): 452–61.

4. See, for example, Molle, W. T. M., and Zandvliet, C. T., "Migratie en Europese Integratic (Migration and the European Integration)" in Kramers, J. J. M., ed., *Inspelen op Europa* (Anticipating Europe) (Academic Service, Schoonhoven, 1993), pp. 277–93.

5. A number of studies show that especially the flexibility on the labor market in the United States is much higher than in Europe. See, for example, OECD, *High and Persistent Unemployment*, 1993. "Assessment of the Problem and Its Causes," Paris, 1993.

6. I have based my figures on M. van Rossum, "De kinderen van Malcolm X: De loden last van de Amerikaanse geschiedenis" (The Children of Malcolm X: The Heavy Burden of American History), *Intermediair*, vol. 29, no. 23 (June 11, 1993): 10–13.

IV

Pressures for Change:

The Future Roles of Markets and Governments

10

Pressures for Change: The Future Roles of Markets and Governments—An American Perspective

Robert D. Reischauer

Four aspects of the American experience have shaped American attitudes about what role market forces, as opposed to public sector forces, should play in the production and distribution of goods, services, and opportunities. These aspects are: a general distrust of strong central government; an emphasis on the individual rather than the community; a pragmatic, nonideological approach to public policy; and the existence of a strong and diverse nonprofit sector. All four have ensured that market forces and the private sector have been given the preeminent role. These aspects should continue to guide the basic allocation of responsibilities between the public and private sectors and will ensure that no radical shift occurs in the future.

Although cross-national comparisons tend to emphasize the degree to which the United States leaves things to market forces and the private sector, the reality is not as straightforward or simple as a public/private dichotomy. Virtually all private activity takes place in a domain in which government acts to shape and limit market forces. Moreover, the government's role in this domain has expanded steadily in the postwar period.

Demographic, technological, budgetary, and global economic pressures make it probable that this trend will continue. Some of this expansion will represent continued efforts by the government to make markets internalize negative externalities of private decisions. Much of the expansion of government, however, is less likely to represent an encroachment on the domain of private markets than it will the government expanding into areas and activities now largely left to private, nonmarket agents—namely, individuals, families, and nongovernmental communities.

Significant changes are also apt to occur in the ways in which the government acts to fulfill its responsibilities. The public sector will probably rely increasingly on market-type mechanisms and tools to fulfill its existing and expanded roles and rely less on traditional public-sector instruments such as rules, regulations, and restrictions. The government is also increasingly likely to use private-sector agents to fulfill public-sector objectives.

SHAPING ASPECTS OF THE AMERICAN EXPERIENCE

The American people have always been more comfortable with a small and decentralized government. These preferences have and will continue to shape the country's attitudes toward the appropriate domains of private markets and public action. The preference for small and decentralized government is rooted in the nation's origins, when many of its early citizens were fleeing the oppression of strong, autocratic governments and were understandably suspicious of powerful central governments. It was nourished by an abundance of land and natural resources, which meant that opportunity, wealth, and power were more likely to come from the exploitation of private resources than from the control of the instruments of government. It was reinforced by the new nation's geographic isolation and expanse, which gave the central government little reason to accrete power and authority in the name of national defense. Finally, this attitude is clearly reflected in the Constitution, which limits the powers of the central government, leaves state and local governments with considerable authority, and grants substantial rights to individuals.

The emphasis placed on the individual as opposed to the collective has also shaped American attitudes about the appropriate role of government versus private or market forces. No doubt this has its roots in the early settlers' desire to pursue religious and political freedom. Furthermore, the ethnic and racial diversity of the population and the diversity of conditions that inevitably exist in a continental nation reinforce such attitudes. America's extraordinary diversity has meant that government solutions, which tend to have a "one-size-fits-all" characteristic, may be unwanted or inappropriate in much of the nation.

Indeed, given the powerful emphasis on the individual, Americans are willing to tolerate considerable inequality of circumstances. Believing that opportunity is available to all and that competition is more or less free and fair, they are not as prone as those in nations with a stronger sense of community to view government intervention in the distribution of income or services as needed.

A third pervasive dimension of the American experience that colors American attitudes toward the proper domains of markets and government is a pragmatic, nonideological approach to public policy. By and large, political parties in American have not had a strong class or economic basis, nor have they been sharply divided in their views of the appropriate role of the government versus the private sector. No major political party has advocated that the central government own the means of production or that it directly provide major services— except for defense. In fact, throughout American history a good deal of energy has been expended ensuring that the federal government does not become an important supplier of education, public safety, health, and other services that are centrally controlled in many industrialized societies.

In the traditional view of most Americans, government should not compete with or substitute for the marketplace in providing goods and services. Rather, it should act to strengthen the private sector, cooperate with it, and aid in its growth. Nowhere is this more apparent than in the way the government has used its policies for transportation (canals, railroads, highways, and airways) and natural resources (hardrock minerals, petroleum, forests, hydroelectric power, and grazing areas) to enlist private interests to develop the nation's abundant resources.

At times, of course, when unconstrained markets have gotten out of hand, strong political movements have arisen against private interests. But these movements have generally rested on a belief that big businesses or large financial institutions were unfairly controlling and distorting free markets to the disadvantage of smaller players. The remedy, however, is telling: it was not to substitute big government for big business or large financial institutions, but rather to break the monopolistic power or corrupt practices of big business so that the market would work fairly for the smaller players.

In other instances, when private market forces have been unwilling or incapable of exploiting a resource or have failed to do so, Americans have pragmatically accepted some direct government action. The Tennessee Valley Authority and the several power marketing authorities in the West are only a couple of examples. CONRAIL, which was established to provide (temporarily) freight rail services in the Northeast, and AMTRAK, which was established to provide intercity rail passenger service for the nation, are others.

A strong, diverse nonprofit sector is the fourth aspect that has shaped American attitudes about the proper division of labor between markets and the public sector. The institutions that make up this sector play an important role in providing such services as health, education and training, social welfare, environmental protection, research, and income redistribution. They not only raise resources on their own but also obtain assistance from the private and public sectors.

As a result of this nonprofit sector, Americans have not had to decide whether the government or private market forces should produce or distribute a particular good or service: they have always had a third option—to allow the nonprofit sector to play an important role. As the size of the nonprofit sector has grown, it has acted to shield its domain from government encroachment. It has become an active agent arguing against direct government provision of goods and services.

From the government's perspective, nonprofit institutions represent a valuable mechanism through which public objectives can be pursued. They are not hobbled by the rules and regulations that bind public entities, nor are they open to the criticism and suspicion that profit-motivated agents must face when they provide government services on a contract basis.

To sum up, the aversion of Americans to strong central government, their glorification of the individual, their pragmatic and nonideological approach to public policy, and the existence of a strong and diverse nonprofit sector have circumscribed the role of government and left much to markets, the private sector, and individuals. The responsibilities of the central government have tended to expand slowly and only as a last resort when markets and private entities have failed or found themselves overwhelmed. These elements of the American experience will dominate future attitudes about the appropriate roles for market forces and public-sector mechanisms.

THE BLURRED DISTINCTION BETWEEN THE PUBLIC AND PRIVATE DOMAINS

Although political and economic discussion proceed as if a sharp dichotomy existed between the domain of private interests and market forces on the one hand and the domain of government on the other, reality, especially in the United States, is quite a different matter. In fact, the reality offers an important clue to how the roles of markets and governments might evolve in the future.

Except for national defense, no good or service is the exclusive province of government. Private or nonprofit institutions play important roles in producing and distributing education, health, income support, social services, mass transportation, policing, communications, electrical power, and other goods and services that in many advanced countries are almost exclusively the responsibility of the public sector. Even the regulatory role is shared between the central government, states and localities, and professional and business organizations.

Conversely, in no part of the economy or society are market forces allowed to operate in a completely unfettered manner. Rather, just as in other advanced nations, the government has established rules and regulations to bind and constrain market forces. For example, the national government sets rules governing wages and working hours, certain social insurance benefits (Social Security, Medicare, unemployment compensation, workers' compensation benefits, and so forth), fringe benefits (ERISA), working conditions (occupational health and safety), the production and disposal of environmentally damaging materials, and the like. State and local governments also set rules governing when, where, and under what conditions private markets can operate.

In addition, the American government's practice of contracting with private and nonprofit entities to carry out governmental functions further blurs the public/private distinction to an extent that is probably unique among advanced nations. For example, universities run the national research laboratories, private insurance carriers provide the administrative and payment services for the government's health insurance system for the aged, private companies generally run the nuclear weapons manufacturing and reprocessing facilities, and private firms provide the concessions in national parks and recreation areas. For the most part, these arrangements reflect the American aversion to big government and public sector bureaucracies. They also reflect a fundamental belief that private entities are inherently more efficient at providing services.

The American reluctance to apply government solutions to national problems has led us to develop complex mechanisms that encourage private agents to change their behavior in ways that help to achieve public purposes. For the most part these devices are found in the tax code. Health insurance offers the most visible example of this. Although the United States stands alone among advanced nations in its reluctance to provide a national system of health insurance for its population, the government encourages private employers to fill this role by allowing them to treat employer-provided health insurance as a business cost. At the same time, the government does not require employees to count this benefit as taxable compensation, which represents some $70 billion a year in tax expenditures. Similarly, the government provides tax credits or preferences for the construction of low-income housing, investments in worker training, expenditures on research and development, employment of low-skilled workers, the provision of private pensions, and a great many other things that the government might otherwise be under pressure to supply.

As pressures mount for greater involvement of government, the United States is not likely to expand direct government provision of goods and services. Rather, the government will probably increasingly contract with private-sector and nonprofit agents to fulfill its missions and will further structure private markets so as to reduce its need to take direct action.

PRESSURES FOR CHANGE

Demographic, technological, budgetary, and global economic pressures will heavily influence the relative roles that market forces and government will play in the next quarter of a century in the United States. Although these pressures should expand the role of the public sector, the mechanisms that the government will use to fulfill its growing responsibilities may more closely resemble market-sector instruments.

The expanded role of government is unlikely to significantly restrict or shrink the domain of private market forces. Instead, government is apt to continue to shape and regulate the environment in which market forces operate as it attempts to reduce the negative externalities of market competition and enlist private sector energies to solve societal problems.

Demographic Pressures

To a greater degree than citizens of other industrial societies, Americans have allowed market forces and patterns of personal saving to determine the distribution of income. Somewhat reluctantly, government has augmented the market incomes of vulnerable populations viewed by the public as worthy. The elderly and low-income single mothers with children are prime examples of the deserving. In the future, both groups will grow more rapidly than the overall population. Consequently, government will play an ever larger role in determining the distribution of income. This trend will be reinforced as the government increases its efforts to boost the incomes of low-skill workers who have experienced falling real incomes for the past two decades.

The fraction of the population over age 65 will change little during the decade of the 1990s—inching up from 12.3 percent in 1990 to 12.6 percent of the total by the year 2000. But during the first quarter of the next century, it will soar to 18.8 percent as the baby boom generation reaches retirement age.[1]

As is true elsewhere in the world, the aged in America depend highly on government transfers to maintain their living standards. Indeed, public-sector transfers provided over half of the total income (including health care and in-kind benefits) of the elderly in 1990. The oldest of the older population and those living singly depend even more on government transfers. As life expectancy lengthens and the cohorts with high divorce rates reach retirement age, the ranks of these most dependent of the aged will swell, thereby adding pressure on government to expand its redistributional role.

The government's role as an allocator of income has increased as the economic function of the family has continued to erode. Over half of first marriages occurring in the United States are projected to end in divorce.[2] Close to one-quarter of births take place out of wedlock and more than half of all children will spend some time before they reach maturity in a single- or no-parent household.[3] Although more than half of the mothers in single-parent households participate in the labor force, this group has low incomes and depends significantly on government transfers. Half of such families had pretransfer incomes below the poverty threshold in 1990; even after receiving public transfers, this group had a poverty rate of 45 percent. One-fifth of the total income received by such families consisted of cash and in-kind government transfers.

The assistance provided to this vulnerable population will probably increase in the future as the nation comes to realize that children raised in poverty can impose huge burdens on future taxpayers. But the increase is likely to take a slightly different form than simply augmenting traditional cash and in-kind assistance. Increased benefits are apt to be hinged on whether the recipient engages in some form of behavior that is expected to improve his or her long-run prospects for self-sufficiency. Pilot projects are already in place, providing increased benefits to teenage welfare mothers who do not drop out of school and older recipients who participate in job-training programs. The new administration has begun to debate the merits of limiting welfare benefits to set periods of time. Presumably, after a two- or three-year period, employment would replace welfare. If a private sector job were unavailable, public employment would be provided. Public sector jobs, however, are likely to be a good deal more expensive than traditional welfare.

Since the mid-1970s, disturbing gaps in earning have developed, which are likely to push the government toward expanding its redistributional role. Consider for example, what has happened to the growth in real earnings of full-time male workers between the ages of 25 and 34 according to their educational level. Between 1976 and 1990, the group without a high school degree experienced a 19.5 percent decline in real earnings, those with a high school degree saw their incomes fall by 14.7 percent, and those with a college degree enjoyed a 2.2 percent increase.[4] It is little wonder that the ranks of the working poor have grown as a result of these trends.

A provision of the U.S. tax code acts to offset this problem by providing earnings subsidies to families with children who have both low earnings and low total incomes. This Earned Income Tax Credit (EITC) has grown in generosity since its introduction in 1975. In 1994, under current law, it will provide a refundable tax credit to families with one child equal to 23 percent of earnings up to $7,990. Families with two or more children will have a credit equal to 25 percent of eligible earnings. The payment is reduced by 16.43 cents (17.86 cents for families with more than one child) for every dollar of income about $12,570.

The Clinton administration has proposed expanding this credit even more—to 34.4 percent of earnings up to $8,500 for a family with one child and 39.7 percent for a family with two or more children. More significantly, the administration has proposed extending the credit to childless couples and single workers at a 7.65 percent rate. In short, the EITC is evolving in the direction of a generalized wage subsidy that could significantly affect the distribution of income.

This device for redistributing income could become a bone of contention among nations if workers who receive the credit come to constitute a significant portion of the labor force producing a good or service that enters world trade. In such a situation, an argument might be made that the United States is unfairly subsidizing its producers. The chances of such a dispute occurring appear remote at this juncture for several reasons. First, most low-wage workers in the United States produce products and services that are not traded internationally— retail trade, personal services, health care, and the like. Second, the wages paid to these workers make up a small portion of the overall costs of the final goods and services.

Technological Pressures

In the areas of health and the environment, technological pressures are apt to lead to an expansion of the government's domain. This expansion, however, is not likely to lead the government into providing services directly; rather, it will increase regulation and control over private markets.

Over the course of the past few decades, medical care has become increasingly complex, sophisticated, and expensive everywhere. In the United States, where the market sector plays the dominant role in health care delivery and financing, costs have run amok. Health care costs have risen from 5.9 percent of GDP in 1965 to 14.6 percent of GDP in 1992 and are projected to increase to 18.9 percent of GDP by the turn of the century.[5]

A major reason for this startling growth is that there has been no effective brake on developing and using expensive new technologies. Citizens have not restrained their demands because third parties (insurers) pay much of the costs of health care—especially that involving expensive procedures. In fact, the fraction of care paid for out of pocket has declined from 45 percent in 1965 to 23 percent in 1983 to 19 percent in 1992, leaving the consumer less and less sensitive to price signals at the point of purchase. While insurance premiums have soared, workers have perceived, incorrectly, that their employers are bearing the escalating costs of their employment-related insurance.

Restraints are equally lacking for the 45 percent of care that government programs finance. Most publicly financed care is provided through open-ended entitlement programs that have no effective budget constraints. (The exception to this is the relatively small share of health care provided at military treatment facilities, veterans' hospitals, Indian health care clinics, and the Public Health Service.) When demands on the Medicare or Medicaid program grow, the budget deficit expands.

Efforts to control federal health care costs have taken the form of reduced reimbursement rates for providers. This approach, however, has not led to any reduction in the types or complexity of services offered to beneficiaries of public programs. Public policy has accepted the premise that Medicare and Medicaid beneficiaries should enjoy access to the same state-of-the-art care as those who are privately insured. Instead, the effects of reimbursement restraints have been to increase the volume of services provided and to encourage a good deal of cost-shifting onto private sector payers. The Prospective Payment Assessment Commission estimates that private insurers, on average, are required to reimburse hospitals at about 128 percent of costs in large part because the Medicaid and Medicare programs reimburse hospitals at only 82 percent and 89 percent of full costs, respectively. This cost-shifting undoubtedly is distorting the allocation of resources.

Providers also have little incentive to restrain costs or the use of fancy technology. Their professional training and ethical standards call on them to provide any care that might improve their patients' health, without regard to costs. Because the overwhelming majority of providers practice in a fee-for-service environment, a financial incentive reinforces the professional proclivity to provide more services. This incentive is compounded by the liability environment, which encourages tests and treatments to avoid malpractice suits.

Although competitive pressures are present in this marketplace, they do not reveal themselves in competition over prices or the cost-effectiveness of care. Rather, hospitals compete for physicians and patient referrals by providing unlimited access to the latest technology, a broad range of services, and amenities. Doctors compete for patients by promising ready access to care and amenities.

This system may feed on itself. As cost-increasing technology raises the cost of health care, it increases the demand for more extensive health insurance, which in turn encourages the development of more cost-increasing technology.[6]

The negative consequences of this unrestrained marketplace are several. First, the fraction of the workforce covered by employer-provided health insurance has fallen as insurance costs have risen. For example, the proportion of full-time workers with health insurance from their employer has fallen from 75 percent in 1980 to 62 percent in 1990. This trend has swelled the ranks of non-aged Americans who lack health insurance, a group that reached some 35 million in 1992.[7]

Second, soaring insurance costs have absorbed a significant portion of the real growth in worker compensation, thus holding down cash wages. Between 1973 and 1989, rising health insurance premiums swallowed up half of the increase in total compensation. That is certainly one reason why many workers believe that their living standards have stagnated.

Third, the health insurance situation is distorting American labor markets. Increasing numbers of workers are reluctant to change employers because they fear that they either will loose their health insurance coverage altogether or will be offered restricted coverage that does not cover some preexisting health problem.

Fourth and finally, the growing importance of provider cost shifting is distorting the efficient allocation of resources within the health care marketplace.

These and other consequences of the current system have helped to generate a consensus that the current method of providing and financing health care is unsustainable. Not only will costs continue to soar, but the number of uninsured will also grow (to an estimated 39 million by 2000) and the distortions in the labor market will cumulate. Both major political parties have responded to this by placing health care reform at the top of their policy agendas.

The precise form that a restructured American health care system will take will be debated over the next few years. Undoubtedly, the new form will involve a substantial increase in the government's role. At a minimum, the government will have to provide more resources to cover the uninsured. It will also have to establish regulations to restructure the insurance markets for small-group and individual policies to reduce the practices of medical underwriting and risk selection. Community-rated premiums—that is, premiums that do not vary with the risk associated with an individual or group—will once again become the norm. The medical liability system will probably also be reformed and the government will play an expanded role in establishing practice guidelines and measuring the efficacy of various diagnostic tests and treatments.

The government's role could expand even further if the health care system is reformed along the lines suggested by the managed competition approach. Moreover, the government could also impose caps on expenditures or price controls in an effort to hold down health care costs. Altogether, during the next decade, government policies are likely to alter significantly the marketplace in which doctors, hospitals, other medical providers, and insurance companies operate. Nevertheless, the primary actors in the American health care system are likely to remain private agents, but they will be required to practice in an increasingly regulated marketplace.

In addition, scientific and technological forces are likely to expand the government's role in the environmental area. Since the mid-1960s, knowledge about the possible harmful effect of the products, by-products, and waste products of the modern industrial and service economies has exploded. Scientists are now able to quantify the potential damage done by compounds and substances that were unidentified a decade or two ago. There is also a growing understanding of the fragility of the ecosystem and the possibility that irreversible damage can be done if limits are not placed on toxic discharges and the exploitation of some resources.

This knowledge has spawned political support for measures that protect the health and safety of workers and citizens and preserve the natural environment. The government has responded to these pressures by expanding its activity in three ways. First, it has filled a remedial role—that is, it has acted to clean up the damage done by an unfettered marketplace. Second, the government has enacted rules and regulations designed to limit or prohibit activity that harms the environment or the health and safety of its citizens. Finally, the government has attempted to create incentives that make markets compensate for the environmental damage done by private actions.

The emphasis of government activity has shifted over time. Until recently, most activity was confined to remedial and regulatory responses. Billions of dollars have been provided to state and local governments for the construction and rehabilitation of wastewater treatment plants. In addition, toxic waste sites are being cleaned up—albeit slowly—through the Superfund program, which requires private firms that generated the toxic waste in the past to pay for repairing the site. At the same time, regulations have severely restricted the types and volumes of materials that can be discharged into the nation's watersheds, sewer systems, and the air. Furthermore, regulations governing the storage, transportation, and disposal of toxic and dangerous materials have been strengthened, as have the regulations dealing with worker safety and health.

As a result of these efforts, air and water quality and workplace safety have improved modestly over the past two decades. At the same time, however, the true complexity of the environmental issue has become clearer to policymakers and politicians. Analysts have begun to recognize and calculate the costs, as well as the benefits, that environmental regulations impose on society and the economy. Furthermore, the nation has developed a growing appreciation of the fact that the ecosystem can handle a certain limited volume of pollutants without severe degradation. Regulatory strategies are being reassessed. Although uniform regulations appear to be equitable because they treat all polluters equally, policymakers are coming to recognize that they can be a terribly inefficient way to reduce pollution or improve health and safety.

As a result, policy has begun to turn toward the third approach—creating incentives that cause private-sector decision-makers to internalize the negative externalities of their activities. The Clean Air Act amendments of 1990 were a significant step in this direction. These amendments established sulfur dioxide limits for the nation and allocated emission allowances to the nation's utilities. Those utilities that bring their emissions down below their allowance can sell their unused balance to other utilities that might find it cheaper to buy these permits than to change their production processes in ways that reduce discharges. In all likelihood, the government will expand its use of market techniques like this in its effort to fill its expanding role in the environmental area.

Charges and taxes on pollutants and waste represent another mechanism through which the government can send signals to private markets that discourage harmful activity. Such taxes and charges are playing a small but growing role. Chemical feedstocks and petroleum products are taxes to support the cleanup of toxic waste sites (Superfund); gasoline and motor fuels are taxed to clean up leaking underground storage tanks and oil spills; coal is taxed to restore abandoned coal mines and care for miners with black lung disease; fees are charged on solid waste disposal for future site restoration; and ozone-depleting chemicals are taxed to reduce their production and use. Many other taxes are under consideration, including carbon charges, broad based energy taxes, and effluent charges on waterborne pollutants.

All such measures, however, have limited appeal in the United States, where interest groups and local interests play a strong role in shaping policy. Charges and marketable permits are often portrayed as "licenses to pollute." Those selling permits are disparaged as profiting by selling that which belongs to the public—namely, a clean environment. Those living near a facility that purchases additional permits or pays the charge instead of installing expensive scrubbers object and demand the equity inherent in regulations that treat all polluters equally. Despite this, the government's role in the environmental area will continue to expand, and the expansion will reflect a greater appreciation of the distortions and inefficiencies inherent in heavy-handed regulatory approaches.

Budget Pressures

The manner in which the American government provides goods and services to the private sector and individual citizens will change significantly because of the persistent budget pressures facing the government. In 1993, the federal government faced an imbalance of roughly $300 billion, or 5 percent of GDP, between its revenues and its expenditures. If policies are not adopted to raise taxes or cut expenditures, this gap will grow to more than $650 billion, or 6.8 percent of GDP, by the year 2003. Efforts to address this fiscal imbalance have and will continue to restrain any expansion of direct government activity and will also influence the manner in which the government fulfills its existing responsibilities. In particular, the government is likely to rely more heavily on market mechanisms that can reduce the net costs of its activities.

This development is nowhere more evident than in the area of natural resources, which historically has been an important concern of the American government because of its vast landholdings. The federal government owns 32 percent of the land area of the United States. Much of this is in the West, where more than 60 percent of the land area of Utah, Nevada, Idaho, and Alaska is federally owned. Even in the nation's most populated state, California, 45 percent of the land is in federal hands.

The federal government's traditional role has been to further regional economic development by encouraging private exploitation of natural resources on public lands. To this end, ranchers have been allowed to graze livestock on federal land at subsidized rates, logging companies have been able to harvest timber in federal forests after paying fees that do not even cover the government's costs of maintaining the forests, and mining concerns have been able to extract hardrock minerals on federal property after paying a token charge (a $2.50 per acre patent fee that has remained unchanged since 1872).

These activities compete with similar ones to exploit resources on private lands. Those fortunate enough to obtain access to public land reap rents. Furthermore, these policies increase the overall supply of timber, minerals, and livestock, thereby marginally reducing the prices received by all producers.

Budget pressures, reinforced by environmental concerns, are forcing a reconsideration of these policies. In the course of the 1990s, the level of resource exploitation on federal lands will probably decline, and the payments made for these rights will rise substantially. Suppliers who compete directly with those who operate on federal land will be aided, and the role of private market forces will expand.

Regulation has also created a set of scarce resources that the government has treated much like its natural resources—that is, it has given them away with the intention of encouraging economic development. These include the rights to use portions of the radio spectrum, geostationary orbits, fish harvest quotas for territorial waters, and landing slots at the nation's busiest airports. Facing excess demand, the government has allocated these resources by lottery or on the basis of past activity. But budgetary pressures have raised interest in using auctions or markets to allocate these rights. Already oil and natural gas leases on federal property entail this approach. The Clinton administration has proposed auctioning 200 megahertz of the radio spectrum for personal communication services and other uses, which has been estimated to bring in some $7.2 billion.

Budget pressures are also forcing the government to charge for its various regulatory activities. Currently, fees cover the full costs of the activities of the Nuclear Regulatory Commission and the Federal Energy Regulatory Commission. Fees partially covering costs are also charged for certain agricultural inspections, some of the supervision and regulation of financial institutions, and the testing of new pharmaceutical products. There is considerable potential to expand such practices in such areas as food (meat and poultry) inspections, workplace health and safety inspections, and the supervision of financial institutions.

In a similar vein, budget pressures will more than likely force the government to institute or increase charges for various services it provides to individuals and businesses. For example, charges are being raised for use of federal recreational facilities, some water distributed through federal projects, the use of federal grazing lands, and electricity generated by government hydroelectric dams. Policymakers have discussed charging fees for weather service information and for the retrieval of information from the Library of Congress.

The increased use of prices in allocating government goods and services has several implications. First, private-sector suppliers of services that heretofore have competed with government-supplied services will benefit, and overall resource allocation should be improved.

Second, charges are likely to give the government a clearer idea of the value citizens places on services. With such signals, the quality of services could improve. Third, the equity with which government services are distributed could be reduced.

Global Economic Pressures

In the postwar period, the public has come to hold government increasingly responsible for economic stabilization and growth. At the same time, national markets have become more integrated and interdependent, making these tasks ever more difficult to accomplish. Goods, services, and capital now move quickly and easily across national borders thanks to successive agreements to liberalize trade, financial deregulation, the communications revolution, and air transportation. As a result, the American economy is much more dependent on economic developments in Europe and the Far East than was true a decade or two ago.

Although these developments have undoubtedly increased living standards throughout the world, they have introduced a degree of external vulnerability that could affect future attitudes concerning the appropriate role of government intervention to control market forces. Increased pressure will be placed on the government to intervene to protect the domestic economy, from change that is perceived as too disruptive, and to ensure a level playing field in world trade.

When domestic markets are relatively open to producers throughout the world and exchange rates fluctuate freely, rather dramatic changes in production and trade can be telescoped into a few years. For example, over the course of two decades athletic shoe production can shift from the United States to Korea to China, and audio and video equipment manufacturing can move from the United States to Japan to Taiwan. Such rapid change can leave a trail of abandoned human and physical resources. In addition, world competition between producers can result in significant excess capacity, as has happened in steel, automobiles, petrochemical refining, shipbuilding, and other industries.

Rapid and disruptive change that results from international market forces can be widely perceived as unfair by the losers. Conversely, the competitive process is more likely to be regarded as fair when change results from domestic reallocations of supply and demand because new opportunities are created in expanding sectors. But when the expanding producers are several thousand miles away, the unutilized domestic resources have a difficult time finding alternative uses.

The pace of change also matters. When change took place at a slower rate, it was possible to withdraw both physical and human capital from shrinking industries in an orderly fashion that limited financial and personal suffering. Fewer workers had to face the prospect of changing jobs, industries, and location halfway through their working years.

In this new environment, Americans are likely to support policies that are ostensibly designed to protect specific industries from too rapid an assault from foreign market forces. These policies might take the form of public subsidies to help the affected industry develop a new comparative advantage; it could also take the form of interventions, such as gradually increasing import quotas, that would allow for the graceful demise of the industry. The past record of such forms of assistance for transition is not one that generates much confidence in their efficacy. Temporary assistance often becomes permanent, and one can only rarely teach old industrial dogs new tricks.

Attitudes concerning the appropriate role of government intervention in the marketplace are also likely to be shaped by a desire to level the playing field on which producers in various nations compete. As a result of Americans' desire to operate a complex economy and society with a minimal amount of direct government service provisions, numerous mandates and regulations have been placed on private producers. Some of these take the form of specific fees and charges. Others involve various types of health, safety, and environmental regulations.

There is a widespread belief in the United States that these regulations represent a burden on domestic producers that affects their world competitiveness. This conviction has not been shaken by economic arguments that suggest that many of these costs are shifted onto American labor and, therefore, do not affect the competitive position of the producer. Furthermore, Americans believe that the burdens placed on their industries are high relative to the regulatory burdens borne by producers elsewhere. Although this may be true with respect to producers in Latin American and much of Asia, Western European and Japanese regulations are probably even more onerous than those in the United States.

Unfortunately, the American government will be pressured to respond to these beliefs. Just what form of market intervention this response might take is difficult to know. One possible response is to pursue bilateral agreements with our trading partners that would govern minimal environmental and working conditions. This approach is being employed in the side agreements to the North American Free Trade pact with Mexico and Canada. It is hard to imagine why other countries would agree to such restraints or what options would be available to the United States under the GATT to enforce its wishes. Nevertheless, Americans are likely to put pressure on their government to intervene in markets to level what they regard to be a tilted playing field.

CONCLUSION

Barring war or major economic upheaval, Americans are not likely to change what they regard to be the appropriate role of the public sector versus the domain best left to market forces. The private and nonprofit sectors should continue to dominate the distribution of goods and services. The public sector will confine its activities largely to defense, redistributing income, and regulating private markets to protect the health and safety of citizens, the environment, and the financial infrastructure of the economy.

The government's role in infrastructure will continue to be circumscribed compared with that of other advanced nations. The transportation, communications, and utility industries will continue to be left in the hands of private companies and state and local governments. As has been the case in the past, government regulation of these areas, where natural monopolies might exist, will ebb and flow. The period extending from the mid–1970s through the late 1980s witnessed significant deregulation of transportation (airlines and trucking), communications (the breakup of AT&T, cable television, and so forth), and the financial services industry. A new phase of regulation could be beginning in response to the financial difficulties of the airlines and the overcapacity and reckless behavior of the financial services industry.

In all likelihood, Americans will continue thinking that the more extensive role played by governments elsewhere places American producers at a significant disadvantage. They will continue to believe that American firms do not get their fair share of foreign government procurement, that American producers are burdened by excessive costs that are picked up directly by governments elsewhere, and that government participation in some industries abroad represents subsidies for foreign producers. As long as the American economy is not performing up to expectations and large trade deficits persist, the public will pressure the government to take action to redress these perceived imbalances.

ENDNOTES

1. U.S. Bureau of the Census, *Statistical Abstract of the United States, 1994,* 114 edition, (Washington, D.C.: Government Printing Office, 1994), Table 23.
2. Bumpass, L. L. and Sweet, J. A. "Children's Experience in Single-parent Families: Implications of Cohabitation and Marital Transition." *Family Planning Perspectives,* 21 (1989): 256–60; Hofferth, S. L., "Updating Children's Life Course," *Journal of Marriage and the Family,* 47 (1985): 93–116.
3. Martin, T. C. and Bumpass, L. L., "Recent Trends in Marital Disruption" *Demography,* 26 (1989): 37–51.
4. U.S. Bureau of the Census, Current Population Reports, "Money Income in 1976 of Families and Persons in the United States," Vol. P–60, no. 114, pp. 203–204, and "Money Income of Households, Families, and Persons in the U.S.," 1990 Vol. P–60, no. 174, pp. 157, 159 (Washington, D.C.: The United States Government Printing Office).
5. Congressional Budget Office, *Trends in Health Spending: An Update,* (Washington, D.C.: Government Printing Office. June 1993) Congressional Budget Office, *Projections of National Health Expenditures: 1993 Update,* (Washington, D.C.: Government Printing Office, October 1993).
6. See Weisbrod, B., "The Health Care Quadrilemma: An Essay on Technological Change, Insurance, Quality of Care and Cost Containment," *Journal of Economic Literature,* vol. 23 (1991): 523–52.
7. Congressional Budget Office tabulations from the Current Population Surveys of 1980, 1990 and 1992.

REFERENCES

Cochrane, W. W. *The Development of American Agriculture.* Minneapolis, MN: University of Minnesota Press, 1979.

Committee on Ways and Means. *Overview of Entitlement Programs, 1993 Greenbook.* Washington, D.C.: Government Printing Office, 1993.

Congressional Budget Office. *Economic Implications of Rising Heath Care Cost.* Washington, D.C.: Government Printing Office, 1993.

Ellwood, David T. *Poor Support*. New York: Basic Books, 1988, p. 67.

Final Report of the National Commission on Children. *Beyond Rhetoric: A New American Agenda for Children and Families*. Washington, D.C.: Government Printing Office, 1991.

Garfinkel, Irwin and McLananhan, Sara. *Single Mothers and Their Children*. Washington, D.C.: The Urban Institute, 1986.

Pechman, Joseph A. *Federal Tax Policy*. 5th edition. Washington, D.C.: The Brookings Institution, 1987.

Portney, Paul. *Public Policies for Environmental Protection*. Washington, D.C.: The Resources for the Future, 1990.

Probst, Katherine, Fullerman, Don, Lita, Robert and Portney, Paul. *Footing the Bill for Superfund Cleanup: Who Pays and How?* Washington, D.C. Brookings Institution and Resources for the Future, 1995.

Reisner, Marc. *Cadillac Desert, The American West and Its Disappearing Water*. New York: Viking, 1986.

Salamon, Lester M. *America Nonprofit Sector: A Primer*. New York: Foundation Center, 1992.

Schmalensee, Richard and Willig, Robert, eds. *Handbook of Industrial Organization*. Part 5, "Government Intervention in the Marketplace." The Netherlands: Elsevier Science Publishers, 1989.

The Constitution of the United States. Washington, D.C.: Government Printing Office, 1987.

Tietenberg, Tom, ed. *Innovation in Environmental Policy*. Brookfield, VT: Ashgate Publication, 1992.

Tocqueville, Alexis de. *Democracy in America*. New York: Vintage Books, 1990.

U.S. House of Representatives. Subcommittee on Oversight and Investigations of the Committee on Natural Resources. *Taking From the Taxplayer: Public Subsidies for Natural Resource Development*. Washington, D.C.: Government Printing Office, 1994.

Weidenbaum, Murray. *Business and Government in the Global Market Place*. Englewood Cliffs, NJ: Prentice Hall, 1995, p. 485, Ill. 24.

Wilkinson, C.F. *Crossing the Next Meridian: Land, Water and the Future of the West*. Washington, D.C.: Island Press, 1992.

11

Pressures For Change:
The Future Role of Markets and Government—
A European Perspective

Theo Peeters

INTRODUCTION

The vision about the future development of the world's leading socioeconomic systems put forward half a century ago by the great Austrian-born Harvard professor of economics, Joseph Schumpeter, has definitely been proven wrong. In his book *Capitalism, Socialism and Democracy* (1942), he developed the thesis that capitalism would inevitably lead to socialism. Today his prediction has been turned upside down: socialism has inexorably given way to capitalism. In the future, socioeconomic rivalry will focus on the rivalry between various forms of capitalism. This shift in focus is the subject of a book by Michel Albert, *Capitalism against Capitalism* (1991). In this book the author discusses the advantages and the drawbacks of the Anglo-Saxon capitalist model against what he calls the "Rhineland" capitalist model of Germany and continental Europe.

Capitalism is indeed far from a homogeneous socioeconomic system. The role markets and governments play differs across countries notwithstanding the fact that they adhere to the basic characteristics of capitalist societies. Not only is there diversity across countries, the role of markets and governments also varies over time. The spatial as well as the time dynamics of societal development should, however, not obscure some stylized common facts that will be analyzed from a European perspective in the following pages.

LESS GOVERNMENT, MORE MARKET IN ECONOMIC DECISIONMAKING

The superiority in economic life of decentralized decisionmaking through markets has been greatly reinforced by the growing complexity and requirements of postindustrialization. Indeed, capitalism has proven to be far more flexible and adaptable to the new economic conditions created by technological change and the new information society than socialism.

But the same pressures that have forced socialism to give way to capitalism are also changing the nature of capitalism itself. The changing nature of capitalism directly affects the importance of the role of governments and of markets in economic decisionmaking processes. Less government and more market is today a universal trend dictated by the growing complexities of societies. The increased role of markets over government is also heavily influenced by the changing perception and shift in the underlying theoretical justification for government intervention in economic activity.

The post–World War II paradigm of government intervention, which existed until the Thatcher-Reagan era, was based on interfering in the economy with market mechanisms to correct for market failures. The fact that markets fail justified without great criticism government action as a substitute for the invisible hand of free market forces. The growth of the welfare state particularly in Europe was based on this paradigm. The basic flaw in this logic, however, was the acceptance without serious challenge of the underlying assumption that governments offer cures to societal problems, particularly in the cases where markets fail.

Experience has taught us in the meantime that this is far from being true. On the contrary, governments do fail. Moreover, substituting market failure with government failure can result in outcomes that are worse than those occurring in freely functioning markets. Consequently, the pendulum is swinging back to more market and less government. Deregulation, which stood high on the agenda of governments during the 1980s, particularly in the Anglo-Saxon world, is a typical illustration of this shift. There is general agreement today that the efficiency of markets has been underestimated and the power of governments to correct market failures has been overestimated.

This does not mean that the socioeconomic functions and responsibilities of the government have moved completely backstage. But it does mean that the role of governments in socioeconomic life needs to be fulfilled particularly in Europe in a different way than the "former" conventional approach. In Europe there is a shift away from discretionary and interventionist government action in the economy and toward rules and government behavior that conform with market principles. This shift is evident across a large spectrum of government actions, which dictate various government responsibilities vis-à-vis the economy.

RULES VERSUS DISCRETION IN MACROECONOMIC POLICY FORMULATION

The core of the heated debate among academics and practitioners over the role and efficiency of macroeconomic stabilization policy is based on "rules which conform to market principles" versus "discretionary intervention." In the neo-Keynesian tradition, activist macroeconomic policies are designed to fine-tune the tradeoff between inflation and growth. Disenchantment with activist discretionary monetary and budgetary policies resulted from the stagflation experience of the 1970s and early 1980s. High inflation and slow growth prevailed notwithstanding activist expansionary monetary and budgetary policies.

Fine-tuning aggregate demand has since lost much of its appeal as the basis for sound macroeconomic policies. Emphasis has shifted toward structural adjustment, supply-oriented policies, and demand-management policies that stress stability and predictability of the policy framework. This is true for both monetary and budgetary policies.

Monetary policy focuses on stability-oriented targets, in particular price stability. In the European Union inflation has resulted from the Maastricht Treaty's almost exclusive focus on targeting monetary policy. The future European Central Bank, modeled after the Bundesbank, will be sufficiently independent from government pressures and the political election cycles. This is in strong contrast with a longstanding tradition in many European countries to adjust interest rates as an anticyclical tool to control unemployment and stimulate growth.

The rules vs. discretion debate is also key for designing budgetary policies in Europe. The budgetary convergence criterion of the Maastricht Treaty again reduces the scope of fine-tuning. Fiscal retrenchment rather than fiscal stimulation remains the name of the game at a time when Europe is in one of its severest postwar recessions.

Underlying this shift in policy is the belief that activist macroeconomic government policies have more often been a factor of pro- rather than anticyclical behavior. Against the same background it can be understood why the turbulence inside the European exchange rate mechanism (ERM) in the early autumn of 1992 and the summer of 1993 has strengthened, rather than weakened, the determination to move toward monetary union in Europe before the end of the decade. The shockwaves that went through the ERM have highlighted the danger of competitive devaluations as an alternative to activist macroeconomic anti-unemployment policies. European monetary union and a single European currency are intended to deter this kind of policy divergence and to foster monetary discipline.

The creation and maintenance of a stable and supportive macroeconomic environment, which supports market forces (rather than constraining them as has often happened in the recent past), is an essential element of the European Union's strategy for growth and employment.[1]. Commission President Delors's White Paper has summed it up as follows:

> The main task facing macroeconomic policy-makers is to eliminate the conflicts among policy objectives which have plagued the Community over the last 20 years and, more acutely, over recent years. Eliminating these conflicts will make growth, employment and real convergence compatible again with price stability and nominal convergence and will ensure that progress towards EMU will go hand in hand with stronger employment creation. . . .
>
> At the macroeconomic level, the first medium-term objective will be to maintain the stability of monetary policy. Monetary authorities have, over recent years, behaved in a way which is consistent with an inflation target of between 2 and 3%. It is necessary that budgetary policy and wage behavior adapt to this objective as soon as possible and remain compatible with it. . . .
>
> Budgetary policy will have to contribute to the medium-term goal of more growth and employment essentially in two ways: i) achieving debt sustainability and ii) contributing to the necessary increase in national saving. The first goal is necessary to reduce the burden that unbalanced

budgetary policies exert on monetary policies and on fiscal flexibility.
. . . In a longer-term perspective, budgetary policy will have to contribute
to increased national saving. This will require increasing substantially
public saving and will imply budget deficits significantly below the 3%
reference value indicated in the Maastricht Treaty (between zero and one
percentage point). . . .

There is a widespread consensus on the need for continued wage
moderation and on the positive results it could produce. . . .

There is evidence of inconsistency between the stability objectives of
the central banks and past and current wage behavior which bears part
of the responsibility for the continuing high level of short-term interest
rates. . . .

The elimination of this conflict is a necessary condition for the
return to growth in the present situation, but once the Community's
economy is again on a sustained growth path, it will be important to
ensure that wages continue to increase in line with the stability objective and the need to allow for an increase in investment profitability
and competitiveness."[2]

THE GROWING IMPORTANCE OF STRUCTURAL
ADJUSTMENT POLICIES

A stable macroeconomic framework as a basis for sustainable job-
creating growth does not suffice. The scale of present difficulties results
from insufficient adaptation of the structures of the European Union's
economy to the changing technological, social, and international
environment. Moreover, there are strong interactions between macroeconomic and structural policies. Structural policies increase the
effectiveness of macroeconomic policies through the removal of constraints that limit their use. A sound macroeconomic environment,
conducive to growth, is necessary to achieve positive effects from
structural policies. At the same time, structural adjustment policies are
easier to implement in a growth-oriented context.

The White Paper of the European Commission has focused on three
main areas of necessary structural measures. All three measures emphasize market flexibility instead of interventionist rigidities.

There is a general plea for greater flexibility in the economy as a
whole. There is a call for determined actions aimed at increasing the
competitiveness of European industry and at removing the rigidities

that curb dynamism and prevent reaping full benefit from the single market. In particular, the regulatory framework must be made more enterprise-friendly and an adequate framework for the development of new market opportunities is needed.

Special emphasis is currently on strategies that create labor markets, which respond to new competitive situations. Structural changes in regulations limiting the expansion of certain sectors (notably the service sector) should make it easier to employ people. This should also help increase the employment content of growth, an area in which the European Union has consistently not performed well over the past decades.

The international environment must also remain open. Protectionism would be suicidal for the European Union. The globalization of the European economy, especially in relation to its eastern and southern neighbors, is unavoidable. As the world's largest trading power, the European Union's full participation is recognized as critical in the expansion of those areas of the world where not only the biggest potential of unsatisfied demand exists but also where the highest rates of growth over the next decade are most likely to occur.

The priority of the European Union to transform GATT into a fully fledged World Trade Organization is, therefore, another illustration of the EU's preference for open markets and a shift toward rules rather than discretion.

The following quote from the White Paper highlights the EU's belief that open markets are the best guarantee for a sustainable and harmonious development: "The strengthening of the multilateral trading system, its effective application and the transparency of its rules are, for the Community, the best guarantee of success with its own effort to adjust."[3]

THREE EXAMPLES OF REAPPRAISING THE ROLE OF THE STATE AND ITS MARKETS

The ongoing reappraisal of the role of governments and markets in the European economies is evident in three specific areas: the Single Market project, the common agricultural policy, and the steel industry.

The opening up of markets in Europe, provided countries manage to pursue reasonable policies of adjustment and modernization, has been and is instrumental in unleashing growth potential. For the European Union the successful conclusion of the Uruguay Round is not the only recent step in this direction. The Single Market project (Objective 92) demonstrates that each of the major bursts of growth in the European economies has started with a qualitative leap in international trade. Thus, part of the reasoning behind the Single Market project was a strengthened confidence in decentralized decisionmaking coordinated through market mechanisms. The aim of the Single Market was not only to achieve economies of scale but also to foster the dynamism and creativity inherent in competition.[4]

Decentralization of decisionmaking power explains more than just a greater reliance on market mechanisms in the economic domain; subsidiarity has also become a key issue in the political domain. Decentralization reflects a radical change in the organization of our societies. Confronted with the growing complexity of both economic and social life and the legislative and regulatory environment, the importance of the local level at which all the ingredients of political action blend together most successfully is growing.

The success of the Single Market program is the result of a major shift in policy following the Cockfield report in 1985. Up until 1985 efforts toward a single market to complement the customs union failed because the focus was to harmonize national policies by attempting to melt them together into a centralized common European policy. The Cockfield report replaced this centralized policy harmonization with three complementary principles: (1) agreement on a minimum common framework of rules and standards; (2) mutual recognition of national rules and standards to the extent that they are compatible with the minimum common norms; and (3) home country control. This approach implies that national policies in the member states must be brought in line with overall principles of commonly agreed on regulations. However it does not imply that the rules should be uniform across countries or imposed by the Parliament in Brussels. Once national regulations conform to the common standards, mutual recognition of these standards and control by the home countries assure that free circulation throughout the European Union can be achieved without further restrictions by other member states.

The Common Agricultural Policy (CAP) is a second example of a shift in Europe from an interventionist market-distorting policy toward a more open, market-oriented approach. Indeed, the foundations of the CAP resulted from the Rome Treaty and are based on three principles: (1) uniform market organization, which results in uniform agricultural prices throughout the European Union despite productivity differentials; (2) preference for European Union producers, which implies strict control mechanisms for external European Union agricultural trade;

and (3) financial solidarity among the member states to shoulder the burden.

These principles were implemented through an elaborate market organization and pricing policy supported by the European Agricultural Guidance and Guarantee Fund. The established preference to European Union products combined with the objective of market stabilization resulted in an upward pressure on common agricultural prices. As a result, food supplies were in excess at prices well above world markets. The high food prices were not only a direct burden for the consumer, but they also imposed a heavy budgetary cost on governments coping with the excess supplies through market intervention. Price support and market intervention, in turn, distorted the normal functioning of the market mechanism and prices were not able to signal an optimal allocation of resources.

The structural surpluses, the growing financial burden of shouldering an inefficient and interventionist market approach, and the intensified conflicts over agricultural trade forced the European Union to slowly shift toward a less-interventionist CAP. The Mac Sharry reform of CAP includes the abandonment of unlimited price support.

From now on price support for key products, such as grain and dairy products, is conditional upon production controls, which guarantee a better balance between market supply and demand. Price supports, as instruments of market regulation, are also supplemented by direct income support measures. This combination of measures has twofold benefits. First, direct income support for farmers lowers prices and thus shifts part of the burden from the consumer to the taxpayer. This improves the transparency of the agricultural support mechanisms, which may also lead to greater democratic accountability and control. Second, the role of prices as the prime regulator of market equilibrium is gradually restored.

Reform of the CAP with a more market-oriented approach also opened the way for agreement on agricultural trade in the Uruguay Round, following the Blair House agreement.

There is also a marked contrast in the way the current crisis in the steel sector is being handled compared to how the previous crisis was handled in the early 1980s. The steel sector, together with the coal mines, was brought under European rule as early as 1951 when the European Coal and Steel Community (ECSC) was founded. This was a time in Europe when government intervention in economic activity was accepted almost unquestioned. The ECSC Treaty was a rather dirigist agreement that included subsidies and industry levies to ease the pain of closing many steel mills, which has resulted in a loss of approximately 500,000 jobs in the past 20 years. State aid has only kept the uneconomic plants in operation and produced an overcapacity of 30 million metric tons a year, despite umpteen attempts to restructure the industry in the 1980s.

Clearest proof of the dirigist character of the ECSC Treaty is in the authority it conveyed to the European Commission through declaring a "manifest crisis'" and ushering in an official cartel with production quotas and price-fixing arrangements. This solution was implemented in the early 1980s under the Davignon plan but it failed. Capacity cuts were insufficient and state aid was not eliminated.

Today steelmakers, sitting together in their industry club Eurofer, are again putting pressure on the European Commission to declare a state of "manifest crisis," which would again allow an officially sponsored cartel supported by massive state aid. The European Union, however, is not only resisting these pressures, but on February 16, 1994, it fined 16 firms a total of 104 million ecus ($117 million) for running an illegal cartel in the late 1980s.

This change in attitude is symptomatic and important because it indicates to firms in other sectors the determination of the European Union to resist the call for crisis cartels. Given past failures, the choice of the European Union is to let the market sort the problem out. Eventually, steel firms will have to cut capacity or die. This option has a certain brutal charm. But there remains one major snag. Even if crisis cartels are resisted, state aid is not automatically cut, or at least not by not enough. The result, therefore, could be that the wrong firms perish first. Inefficient subsidized mills could drive out self-sufficient firms or force them to claim subsidies. The challenge for the European Commission, therefore, is to make sure as a condition sine qua non that state aid must be linked explicitly to privatization and/or capacity cuts; in addition future state aid should be banned.

In summary, the clearest symptom of the reappraisal of the role of governments and markets in the economy is found in the waves of privatization in Europe today. Budgetary needs also undoubtedly underlie this process; the pressures for improved management and efficiency in certain public utilities, notably telecom, are also driving forces in this process of reappraisal.

CONCLUDING REMARKS

A reappraisal of principles inherited from an age when socioeconomic rivalry, particularly in Europe, focused on antagonism between capitalism and socialism is well under way. Broad guidelines are being set which are predominantly market-oriented and economically based. These guidelines cannot be dissociated from current major trends toward a healthy, open, decentralized, competitive economy based on solidarity. The latter feature, of solidarity, is characteristic of the European blend of capitalism.

In Europe, more so than in the United States, it is recognized that markets underestimate what is at stake in the long term, affect different social categories unequally, and spontaneously promote concentration, which results inequality between regions. Awareness of these insufficiencies in the marketplace has led European countries to develop collective solidarity mechanisms in varying degrees. The burden of these solidarity mechanisms and the subsequent costs primarily in terms of economic inefficiency has often been underestimated. The social welfare system in many member states needs to reduce costs through greater individual responsibility. More reliance on price signals and market-oriented mechanisms needs to be built into the welfare system. The essence of collective solidarity mechanisms, however, is not questioned. The welfare state needs to be leaner and fitter. Economic and social cohesion still remain essential pillars of the European variant of the capitalist model.

ENDNOTES

1. See Commission of the European Communities, "Growth, Competitiveness and Employment: The Challenges and Ways Forward into the 21st Century" (White Paper), *Bulletin of The European Communities,* supplement (June 1993): 47.
2. Op. cit., pp. 50–51.
3. Op. cit., p. 13.
4. Op. cit., p. 13.

Conclusion:
Adjustments to Change—Speculations from the
American and European Experiences

Bert A. Rockman

CAPITALIST DYNAMICS

A basic, if not very novel, assumption behind the speculations outlined in this book is that the responses of states and supranational regimes in the long term are governed by a *need to adapt* to economic dynamics. Ultimately, this is what is meant by the dynamics of market capitalism.

In general, there are differences across states in traditions of economic organization, in the power of labor unions and agricultural producers, and in the influence of distributors and others who might benefit from economic inefficiencies. Similarly, there also are differences in political coalitions, and the preferences they hold. Certainly, there are differences in the methods governments might seek to circumvent the constraints that markets impose upon their policy discretion. Therefore, in the short run, all of these differences make for variable responses to underlying capitalist dynamics. In the longer run, however, adjustments to those dynamics must be made—all the more so as the international economic system is both clearly market-oriented and no longer exogenous to national or regional systems.

As a result of these dynamics, two types of convergence between systems may come into existence: (1) a common discourse dictated by a common sensitivity to universal stimuli—long-term interest rates, inflation, budget deficits, and currency stability as well as international and regional regulatory regimes, and (2) common responses to these stimuli to prevent massive outward capital flows.

The latter type of convergence limits, of course, the autonomy of politics and of policy. Convergence of this nature—to the extent it occurs—does not mean there will be convergence of interest between national or regional actors, because like major investors in securities markets, economically powerful states are often in a position to manipulate the currency markets of other states in the short run. The international economy makes all national actors vulnerable and makes financial hostage-taking a part of the process of bargaining and mutual adjustment.

The open nature of the international economy makes for competition on the part of the players as each tries to penetrate the markets of others. National leaders, however, still will not readily accept penetration of their domestic markets they think it will endanger national interests or, more cynically, if the penetration will cost them vital or demonstrative political constituencies. But ultimately, when wages have increased over and above productivity gains and prices of goods are in excess of a competitive market outcome, investments go abroad. For example, when the U.S. labor market had little slack and its wages were the highest in the world, American-based multinationals invested abroad. Currently, investments from higher wage countries come to the United States and take advantage of a skilled but relatively lower wage labor market. The simple point, of course, is that in an open liberal, international economy labor is vulnerable and capital is robust.

ECONOMIC AND SOCIAL ORGANIZATION

Several trends appear to be at work in altering the character of economic and thus social organization. First, new industries are capital-intensive rather than labor-intensive. Such industries—software design, robotics, and others employing relatively high levels of technological specialization—tend to be small and capital-intensive. In some ways, the classic postindustrial firm is more like the preindustrial one, being modeled more along the lines of a shop than a factory.

Because the firms in these industries are small, capital-intensive, and dependent upon highly skilled labor, such industries tend to fragment labor markets. As a consequence, they weaken trade unions. Industrywide labor agreements are of no use when the industries are composed of many rather than a few producers and each producer has a few rather than many workers.

A second trend is that producers are similarly more fragmented in these industries. By no means is the gargantuan enterprise extinct, nor should we expect to see its demise anytime soon, if ever. However, the apogee of the conglomerate probably lies in the past. Even among current conglomerates, downsizing has become the current buzzword. Downsizing involves reducing the labor force but also, to some extent, it involves diversification, bringing a the variety of enterprises within a single corporate empire.

These trends, however, are not presently the dominant conditions. But the tendencies toward smallness, capital-intensiveness, and fragmented labor markets and producer communities, as well as the shift from manufacturing to service producers, all have important consequences, among other things, for social organization and the prospects for governmental mediation between producers and labor organizations.

One thing that is clear is that if these trends become increasingly prominent, the present theories of governance based on centralized and aggregate organizational forms will be less notable. For example, corporatism, or similar ideas which are based on the social contract, depends on centralized governmental mediation, which incorporates producer and worker interests. When these interests become fragmented, the premise of inclusiveness behind such cooperative arrangements is likely to be fatally compromised. Thus, the capacity to bargain is commensurably diminished because too many players and recipients will be left out. As a result, practices of centralized collaboration between large social organizations and the state will be harder and harder to achieve and may vanish altogether. In that admittedly speculative event, the process of political influence will increasingly resemble a marketplace rather than an oligopoly of big producers, big labor organizations, and the state. Influence will be more fragmented and the process of pursuing it more frenetic than has been the postwar norm of most European politics. Everything, in other words, is likely to be less ordered through political discourse and more ordered (if that is the right word) through economic dynamics. As states recede, markets gain.

Another factor that contributes to the overall trend for the reduction of corporatist and other social contractual practices in Europe, and probably Japan as well, is the end of the social surplus. Deep pockets are increasingly harder to find. High unemployment, budget deficits, the decline of state-subsidized industries, and the economic squeeze on firms in various combinations have plagued much of Europe and the United States. The end of the social surplus, or at least a declining amount of it, may well create labor unrest, which was unimaginable in the 1960s, because it will be understandable for labor leaders to ask why demands should be disciplined if there is no pot of gold at the end of the rainbow.

REGULATORY REGIMES AND MARKETS

In contrast to Europe, where regulation is often done by negotiation between the regulating authority and the industries to be regulated, the history of regulation in the United States typically has been adversarial in nature. There are exceptions to this, for instance, regulation involving transportation and a situation in which a regulatory regime is imposed essentially to manage burdens and prices on the part of the producers. Whether the issues be air pollution or worker safety and health matters, the patterns on the two sides of the Atlantic are very different. Traditionally, regulatory definitions are imposed in the United States so that they are defensible in litigation proceedings if necessary. There is also a tendency in the United States for the regulator and the regulated to sharpen their positions before they cut deals. This probably is influenced by the role of politics in these proceedings, which is often posed in the form of public goods vs. jobs, the role of advocacy groups, and the short half-life of regulatory issues as politically mobilizing ones. The narrower window for policy action in the United States works to maximize position-taking early, even if these stances must later be retreated from later. The U.S. legal system and culture, being heavily influenced by adversarial procedures, also ensures that regulators will seek ironclad standards that cannot later be exploited as ambiguities in the law.

While clearly leaving an enormous amount of regulation to its states, especially in areas of professional standards, licenses, and so on, the American national government over time has brought increased regulation in the national sphere. Simultaneously there has been a growing rationalization of regulation in the United States. The communal rationalization of regulation, of course, also is one of the outcomes of the Maastricht Treaty for the European Union. As in the United States, many matters continue to be left within the jurisdiction of the member states, although more and more regulation clearly is being centralized and, for the most part, the regulatory regimes are being rationalized. One issue this raises is whether the process of rationalizing regulation will make business and the state (or in this case, the EU bureaucracy) into adversaries as they generally have been in the United States? Another question that also remains to be answered is whether the regulatory regimes at the EU level will come into conflict with those of the member states. Presumably, these matters already have been negotiated, but it would be unwise to expect that the present settlements will remain stable. In the United States, federal regulations, for example, often impose mandates on state governments, which forces onto them the direct costs of regulation (adding to expenditures by new enforcement requirements) and indirect costs (cutting into revenues by increasing business costs).

On the American side of the Atlantic there has been an intense debate about the wisdom of regulation through legal mandates versus regulation through economic incentives. Partly because many more American politicians are lawyers rather than economists, the outcome of this debate should surprise no one. Overall, the legal mandate conception has been the clear winner. This has happened partly because politicians, advocates, and even the bureaucrats themselves can point to seemingly tangible standards expressed in law as a sign of achievement (or defense). Nevertheless, there have been some victories by the advocates of using economic incentives and markets for regulating negative externalities. Most notably, amendments to the Clean Air Act of 1990 set up a regulatory regime based on the trading of allowable pollution credits between firms based on the air quality of their sites. In such a system, there is obviously an incentive to locate where air quality already is good. The expectations are that overall median air quality should improve, but air quality in polluted areas should significantly improve while air quality in clean areas may moderately deteriorate.

Another use of quasi-market mechanisms in regulation is reflected in the oxymoron "managed competition." This idea has recently entered the vocabulary of American public policy, particularly the Clinton program for a national health care system. The idea of managed competition is to bring large providers of health care into competition with each other so that people will choose the most efficient of these. Just in case the competition does not work to hold prices down, however, the Clinton plan proposes a seven-member board to regulate prices. Because the market has become a mantra for policymakers' and government programs' forbidden language, the market metaphor reigns supreme, even when it conceals direct regulation.

No doubt the market will hold more allure as a metaphor in the United States than in Europe. No doubt too, Americans will continue to ignore pleas for more state direction of economic investment, commonly known as industrial policy. Similarly, the fragmented political system of the United States will be unable to generate a labor market policy that is both focused on human capital development and connected to entitlement programs. The Clinton administration talked some about both issues when it was merely the Clinton candidacy. But talk has turned out to be both braver and cheaper than policy.

Certainly, there will continue to be significant differences between European and American regulatory and sectoral policy norms and practices. As well, European experiences (those of Northern Europe) will continue to be a beacon for some American thinkers. But the general drift is likely to follow the North Atlantic current eastward from the American shores to European ones. Despite paying a great deal more attention to the social contract than American firms, European firms and state enterprises are in the process of cutting back and eliminating employees. If, in the 1980s, the phrase "made in Japan" meant high quality, then in the 1990s, "made in America" is likely to mean high efficiency. This is certainly a reason why restructuring in the United States will be, for better or worse, a model for Europeans.

THE WELFARE STATE

By European standards, the United States has been a welfare laggard. For the most part, the United States came later than most European states to the development of welfare programs, with less universality to them, and under conditions of greater controversy. While Europeans have long enjoyed the benefits of universal health coverage, this is only now being debated in the United States. American style federalism has produced enormous variability in welfare standards across the country. Some states have had quite expansive programs; others have been threadbare. Until New York City's fiscal crisis of the mid-1970s, it was, for all practical purposes, a virtual socialist city-state.

As a general matter, the last two decades have not been flush times for the welfare state. Governments are paying more (and sometimes citizens too) while benefits are declining. Ironically, while the health care bill is debated in the United States, cutbacks on the margins of health programs are appearing in Europe.

Changing demographics, the appearance of large and often dependent immigrant or marginalized populations, the breakdown of inhibitions in seeking benefits, and the uncertainty of labor markets all have contributed to the rising cost of maintaining the welfare state. High rates of unemployment throughout contemporary Europe have raised the costs of unemployment insurance. Older populations mean more health care and pension costs. A higher proportion of marginalized populations means more maintenance costs. In the United States, the Aid to Families with Dependent Children (AFDC) program (a part of the original Cosical Security legislation from the 1930s) has had soaring costs while delivering actually less money to its recipients. Obviously a massive growth in illegitimate children born into financially dependent households has caused the great growth in costs while paradoxically generating less supplementary income per household.

Conventional wisdom has it that entitlements are where the big money is for budget-cutters looking to save a buck, a mark, or a franc. And that is true. Conventional wisdom also has it that at least those entitlements that are universalized are thus made politically invulnerable to cutbacks. In general, it is certainly fair to say that they are less vulnerable to the budget-cutter's ax, but certainly no longer invulnerable. Governments have begun to place more of the burden of health care on recipients or, in the U.S. case, also on suppliers and ultimately insurers and their clients. Cutting the dole is no longer an unmentionable; it has begun to happen in some places.

The basis of universalizing is itself coming under attack because even though universalizing is politically efficient, it is financially inefficient. Universalizing ensures the same standard of care or support to all. By so doing, universalizing also creates a massive constituency in support of whatever good is being universalized. (In the United States, programs for the elderly normally have been highly popular because we all grow old and because the elderly are among the most single-focused, politically mobilized groups in society.) At the same time, a service or revenue stream is going to individuals regardless of their need for it. In the United States, where the struggle for universalizing always has been most challenged, the means test has now affected, if in subtle ways, such sacred cows as social security pension benefits. The tactic here has been to increase the percentage of tax liability for social security income.

Because budgetary slack has worn away and the costs of the social welfare state have massively increased, the social welfare state is no longer impregnable. The costs of the social welfare state will not shrivel, but their rate of growth is under fierce pressure to be brought under control. Otherwise, governments will drown in red ink. Thus, more means testing is likely to come about.

If, as I have already suggested, economic restructuring weakens labor unions and creates pressures for a more competitive economic environment, pressures for budget restraint and lower taxes will rise as the sources of organized support for the welfare state, labor unions chief among them, decline. The social contract, which helped sustain the welfare state and regulated labor markets in return for labor peace, is clearly fraying at the edges and has the potential to collapse. In other words, neither in the United States nor in Europe will the welfare state be immune from cutbacks.

Of course, some similarities in response are a function of having similarly disposed governments in power. Politics, in other words, may account for some of these responses. For nearly all of the 1980s and much of the first half of the 1990s, conservative leadership has dominated in the United States, the United Kingdom, and Germany. Moreover, conservatives have come to power in Denmark and Sweden, among other places. Is it possible that similar responses are not the product of seemingly ineluctable economic and social conditions, but rather a function of like-minded regimes sharing similar predispositions and dipping into similar ideas in an increasingly rich international market of policy ideas? However, party dogmas and constituencies *in the short run* influence the nature of adaptations to economic dynamics. There is no doubt that parties differ in what they would like to do and, above all, what may be demanded of them by their constituencies. Parties are able to give freest expression to those preferences and interests if the preferences and interests are in opposition or coincide with adopting a program of austerity. But parties in power are another matter. For example, it did not take the then newly elected Socialist government in France long to discover that it could not control capital outflows in an open international economy unless it altered its course. The ideology of governments and its role in influencing both policy and economic change is both much debated and much researched. The research findings strike me as unequivocal. Namely, parties exert much sound and fury in policy debates that, in the end, signify nothing. In the big scheme of things, the impact of the ideology of governments in open economic systems is imperceptible.

THE FEDERAL EXPERIENCE AND PUBLIC INVESTMENT

For the most part, the fact that the United States is a federal state gives it a different history than nearly all of the states (Germany being the obvious exception, Belgium and Spain possibly being others) within the European Union. Federalism makes for an important difference in countries' histories and in the nature of fiscal dependencies. In a federal system, the relevant actors often are the states rather than the state. Despite the growing role of the federal government in the United States, it is difficult to think about American economic development without considering the role of federalism in it.

At least in its American form, federalism needs to be viewed as a set of structures through which fiscal bargaining takes place. The nature of the bargains depends upon the character of the federal system. In Germany, the nature of the federal system can best be described as a form of "cooperative federalism," whereas in the United States, the federal system tends toward "competitive federalism." In the American case, the strategy of state and local governments and paragovernments (authorities) is to evade a web of federal regulations that limit the ability of the federal government. The inducements that state and local authorities use to generate investment capital in private bond markets represent a form of tax expenditure (revenues given up through tax exemptions). Thus, the strategy of the federal government is to limit the tax expenditures used by state and local governments to entice investors into public and, especially, quasi-public capital investments. The federal government in the United States seeks, therefore, to limit access to the financial marketplace (of tax-exempt bonds), whereas the subnational governments seek to explore new worlds of tax expenditures to allow them or, more precisely, investors to gain access to markets for public projects. Inherent to this game of cat and mouse is the definition of what is a public investment. In this game, the federal government seeks as narrow a definition as possible, whereas the subnational governments seek as broad a definition as possible.

On the whole, in the American case state and local governments have an incentive to foster cooperative relations with business. Such an incentive fosters cooperative relations with business. Such an incentive is less powerful for the federal government. Subnational governments in the United States have a great dependency on the issuance of securities to finance capital investment projects because they need these investments to induce business investment. They need business investment in order to provide a stable tax base. Among the variety of incentives that subnational governments seek to offer business investors are tax incentives, infrastructural development and public amenities, financial market access, and, in some cases, even labor market regulation, such as restrictions on union organization and right to work laws.

Unlike the European states, even the federal ones, the American subnational governments have a unique dependency on financial markets for raising capital for public investment. It is possible, therefore, that this dependence on markets for public goods rather than federalism itself is what is peculiar about the American developmental experience. From that perspective, it may well be that as Europeans develop a quasi-federal union, the American experience still will have been *sui generis,* characterized by its dependency on the private capital market even more than the national state for large-scale public investments.

The role of the public sector in Europe, I suspect, will continue to remain more autonomous from the vagaries of the private capital market than is the case in the United States. However, strange things are happening. In the pages of the Sunday edition of *The Times,* for example, advertisements for a position entirely new in the experience of British universities (all public, of course) have begun to appear. The position is called a development officer. The task is to seek external, private support. Is this an omen?

LESSONS FROM THE AMERICAN EXPERIENCE

The federal experience in the United States and its dependence on market criteria induce marketlike responses even from state and local governments. Welfare costs are a financial drag and so there is an effort to reduce them regardless of the implications for the beneficiaries especially the lower-class ones. Creating an environment for investment, however, generates revenue, especially if that environment can be created by shifting the costs to the national level of government. A suitable climate for business activity is a paramount need because economic growth produces the revenues needed to balance governmental budgets. Public investments, which normally compete in a different bond market than private ones, are essential to creating a favorable atmosphere for business location.

The American experience—or at least the ideology of that experience—extols liberal economy and, thus, economic rationality. The U.S. experience does not include social contracts, for example, or other devices to manage labor markets politically. As I have noted, by the experience of operating in a less restricted market setting or at least by the prevailing mythology that they have, American firms seem to be in a better position to respond to longer term changes in the world economy. Unencumbered by strong labor unions or a commitment to high wages or job security, American companies have streamlined themselves extraordinarily and enjoy a very high rate of productivity. To the extent that this model of economic rationality is found attractive on the European side of the Atlantic, it will force greater competitiveness and more adaptability to dynamic economic processes. To the same extent, economic responsiveness to market forces will become more powerful than political (state) forces. We should not, therefore, be very surprised to see shops in Germany, for example, open in the evenings or all day on Saturdays in the quite foreseeable future as working women compete with labor unions to influence issues vital to their convenience as well as their opportunity to compete in the labor market.

In a brave new world of economic rationality, no one will be strategically positioned to call the shots. Labor will be weaker, business will be weaker, and probably, central governments will be weaker. Interests will become increasingly fragmented and splintered. My guess is that we will soon learn (perhaps again) about both the virtues and vices of more competitive markets and, thus, the virtues and vices of economic rationality. We will, I imagine, see greater aggregate progress and also more political grumbling. Above all, if these predictions are correct, we will see not only the weakened leverage of labor unions but also a labor force that is increasingly squeezed between the threat of lower wages and massive, perhaps permanent, layoffs in societies less able to afford the generous levels of social insurance to which their workers have become accustomed. Change and adaptation are part of the logic of the dynamics of capitalism. But the price of that can be steep.

N A

APPENDIX

Participants in Markets and Society Conference, June 16–18, 1993, RAND European-American Center, Delft, the Netherlands

Dr. Roger Benjamin
RAND
1700 Main Street
Santa Monica, CA 90210
USA

Professor Nikos Christodoulakis
Athens University of Economics
and Business
76 Patission St.
Athens 14034
GREECE

Professor Dr. E. O. Czempiel
Abteilung Internationale
Beziehungen
Johann Wolfgang Goethe-
Universität
Robert-Mayer-Strasse 5
Postfach 111932
D-6000 Frankfurt AM Main 11
GERMANY

Dr. Thomas Ferguson
Political Science Dept.
University of Massachusetts
Boston, MA 02125
USA

Mr. K. P. Goudswaard
Center for Research in Public
Economics
Leiden University
Hugo de Grootstraat 27
2311 XK Leiden
THE NETHERLANDS

Mr. A. Grejebine
Centre Détudes et de Recherches
Internationales
4, Rue de Chevreuse
75006 Paris
FRANCE

Prof. drs. V. Halberstadt
Center for Research in Public
Economics
Leiden University
Hugo de Grootstraat 27
2311 XK Leiden
THE NETHERLANDS

Dr. John Ikenberry
Department of Political Science
University of Pennsylvania
Philadelphia, PA 19104
USA

Drs. Hans van de Kar
Center for Research in Public
Economics
Leiden University
Hugo de Grootstraat 27
2311 XK Leiden
THE NETHERLANDS

Mr. J. Ketelsen
Directorate-General External
Relations
Unit for Relations with the USA
Commission of the European
Communities
Rue de la Loi 200
B-1049 Brussels
BELGIUM

Henk Kloosterhuis
RAND European-American Center
Landbergstraat 6
2628 CE Delft
THE NETHERLANDS

Professor Robert T. Kudrle
Hubert Humphry Institute of Public
    Affairs
University of Minnesota
301 19th Avenue South
Minneapolis, MN 55455
USA

Mr. H. H. J. Labohm
Clingendael
Postbus 93080
2509 AB Den Haag
THE NETHERLANDS

Mark Nelson
Carnegie Endowment for Peace
2400 N Street, N.W.
Washington, DC 20037
USA

Dr. C. R. Neu
RAND
1700 Main Street
Santa Monica, CA 90407
USA

Dr. William Niskanen
The Cato Institute
224 Second Street, S.E.
Washington, DC 20003
USA

Denise D. Quigley
RAND/RGS
1700 Main Street
Santa Monica, CA 90407
USA

Dr. John Van Oudenaren
Director
RAND European-American Center
Landbergstraat 6
2628 CE Delft
THE NETHERLANDS

Professor Pier Carlo Padoan
Istituto Affari Internazionali
Via Angelo Brunetti 9
Palazzo Rondinini
Rome 00186
ITALY

Professor Theo Peeters
Jagersdreef 3
B-3210 Linden
BELGIUM

Dr. Robert Reischauer
Director
U.S. Congressional Budget Office
402 Ford House office Building
Washington, DC 20515
USA

Professor Bert Rockman
The University of Pittsburgh and
The Brookings Institution
Government Studies Program
1775 Massachusetts Ave., NW
Washington, DC 20036-2188
USA

Dr. Jarig van Sinderen
Ministry of Economic Affairs
Dept. AEP
P.O. Box 20101
2500 EC Den Haag
THE NETHERLANDS

Mr. Christian Stoffaes
Chief of the Planning Division
Electricité De France
2, Rue Louis Murat
75384 Paris Cedex 08
FRANCE

Professor Susan Strange
Buckingshire
Weedon Hill House
Aylesbury
Bucks HP 22-4DP
UNITED KINGDOM

Professor Jacques Vandamme
Chairman
Trans European Policy Studies
  Association
Faculty of Economic Law
Egmontstraat 11
1050 Brussels
BELGIUM

Mr. Paul Vandoren
Deputy Head of Unit for Relations
  with the USA
Commission of the European
  Communities
Directorate-General I External
  Relations
Rue de la Loi 200
B-1049 Brussels
BELGIUM

Dr. Georges Vernez
RAND
1700 Main Street
Santa Monica, CA 90407
USA

INDEX